THE WORM
AT THE CORE

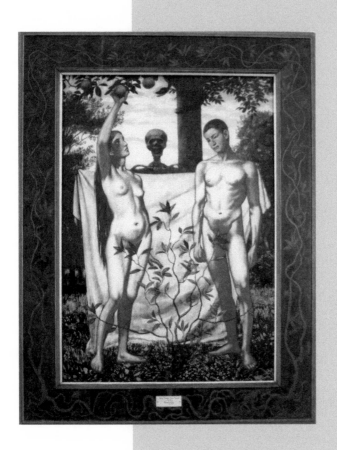

RANDOM HOUSE

NEW YORK

THE
WORM
AT THE
CORE

On the
Role of
Death
in Life

———

SHELDON SOLOMON,
JEFF GREENBERG,
and TOM PYSZCZYNSKI

Copyright © 2015 by Sheldon Solomon, Jeff Greenberg, and Tom Pyszczynski

Published in the United States by Random House,
an imprint and division of Penguin Random House LLC, New York.

RANDOM HOUSE and the HOUSE colophon are
registered trademarks of Penguin Random House LLC.

Grateful acknowledgment is made to the following for permission to reprint
previously published material:

Freer Gallery of Art, Smithsonian Institution: Painting entitled "Dreaming of Immortality
in a Thatched Cottage" by T'ang Yin. Courtesy Freer Gallery of Art, Smithsonian
Institution, Washington, D.C.: Purchase, F1939.60.

Random House, an imprint and division of Penguin Random House: "The Cultural
Presupposition" from *W. H. Auden: The Collected Poems* by W. H. Auden, copyright
© 1945 by W. H. Auden and copyright renewed 1973 by The Estate of W. H. Auden.
Reprinted by permission of Random House, an imprint and division of Penguin
Random House LLC. All rights reserved.

LIBRARY OF CONGRESS CATALOGING-IN-PUBLICATION DATA
Solomon, Sheldon.
The worm at the core : on the role of death in life / Sheldon Solomon,
Jeff Greenberg and Tom Pyszczynski.
pages cm
Includes bibliographical references and index.
ISBN 978-1-4000-6747-3
eBook ISBN 978-0-679-60488-4
1. Death—Psychological aspects. 2. Fear of death.
3. Terror. I. Greenberg, Jeff, 1954– II. Pyszczynski, Thomas A. III. Title.
BF789.D4S66 2015
155.9'37—dc23 2014033937

Printed in the United States of America on acid-free paper

www.atrandom.com

9 8 7 6 5 4 3 2 1

FIRST EDITION

*Frontispiece: Hans Thoma, Adam and Eve (1897).
Hermitage Museum, St. Petersburg, Russia.*

Book design by Barbara M. Bachman

Contents

Introduction

———

Back of everything is the great spectre of universal death, the all-encompassing blackness.... We need a life not correlated with death ... a kind of good that will not perish, a good in fact that flies beyond the Goods of nature.... And so with most of us: ... a little irritable weakness ... will bring the worm at the core of all our usual springs of delight into full view, and turn us into melancholy metaphysicians.

—WILLIAM JAMES,
*The Varieties of
Religious Experience*

ON A RAINY, GRAY DAY IN DECEMBER 1973, PHILOSOPHER SAM KEEN, WRITing for *Psychology Today,* trundled down the halls of a hospital in Burnaby, British Columbia, to interview a terminally ill cancer patient who doctors said had just days to live. When Keen entered the room, the dying man told him, with a touch of mortal irony: "You are catching me *in extremis.* This is a test of everything I've written about death. And I've got a chance to show how one dies ... how one accepts his death."

The man in the hospital bed was cultural anthropologist Ernest Becker. Becker had devoted his academic career to writing books synthesizing insights from anthropology, sociology, psychology, philosophy, religion, literature, and popular culture to get to the bottom of the ancient question "What makes people act the way they do?"

In his latest book, *The Denial of Death,* which he described as his "first mature work," Becker concluded that human activity is driven largely by unconscious efforts to deny and transcend death. "We build character and culture," he told Sam Keen, "in order to shield ourselves from the devastating awareness of our underlying helplessness and the terror of our inevitable death." Now, lying on his deathbed, Becker explained that his life's work had been about coming to terms with the grinning skull looking back at him.

Ernest Becker died on March 6, 1974, at the age of forty-nine. Like many visionaries, Becker died too young. Two months later, *The Denial of Death* was awarded the Pulitzer Prize.

Back in the late 1960s, Becker was an intellectual insurgent. He was immensely popular with students, who flocked to hear his lectures. However, colleagues and university administrators were not particularly enamored with an interdisciplinary thinker who drew together ideas from all corners of the academy, public discourse, and popular culture, and who challenged their academic and political orthodoxy.

Becker thus became a kind of academic vagabond, drifting from Syracuse University (1960–1963) to the University of California, Berkeley (1965), where students offered to pay his salary after the anthropology department declined to renew his contract. After a stint at San Francisco State (1967–1969), he found an academic home at Simon Fraser University in Vancouver, British Columbia (1969–1974), where he wrote the second edition of *The Birth and Death of Meaning, The Denial of Death,* and his posthumously published *Escape from Evil.*

A few years later, in the late 1970s, the three authors of this book met after enrolling in the doctoral program in experimental social psychology at the University of Kansas. We quickly discovered a shared interest in understanding the fundamental motivations that direct human behavior. Our studies and discussions led us to focus on two very basic human proclivities. First, we human beings are driven to protect our self-esteem. Second, we humans strongly desire to assert the superiority of our own group over other groups.

But we had no idea what underlies these prides and prejudices until we stumbled upon Becker's books as young professors in the early 1980s. Like the Rosetta Stone, they were to us a revelation. Mixing deep philosophical prose and straightforward layman's language, Becker explained how the fear of death guides human behavior. He illuminated many of the key social-psychological phenomena that we had for years been studying and teaching but without fully grasping. Suddenly, we had a way to understand *why* we so desperately crave self-esteem, and *why* we fear, loathe, and sometimes seek to obliterate people who are different from ourselves.

Brimming with youthful enthusiasm, we were excited to share Becker's ideas with fellow social psychologists at the 1984 meeting of the Society of Experimental Social Psychology. There we introduced what we dubbed *terror management theory* in order to build on Becker's claim that people strive for meaningful and significant lives largely to manage the fear of death. The audience started drifting away as soon as we mentioned that our theory was influenced by sociology, anthropology, existential philosophy, and psychoanalysis. When we got to the ideas of Marx, Kierkegaard, Freud, and Becker, renowned psychologists were storming the conference room exits.

Bemused but undaunted, we prepared a paper for the American Psychological Association's flagship journal, *American Psychologist*. Feedback arrived a few months later. "I have no doubt that this paper would be of no interest to any psychologist, living or dead," read one rather pithy single-line review. But we kept at the editor, repeatedly asking him to explain why our ideas were unworthy. Our queries outlasted the original editor's tenure, and finally a second, more sympathetic (or perhaps more beleaguered) editor gave us something we could work with: "Although your ideas may have some validity," he told us, "they won't be taken seriously unless you can provide evidence for them." That's when it dawned on us that our graduate training in experimental social psychology had prepared us to do just that.

We've spent the last quarter century investigating the influence of the fear of death on human affairs. At first, we conducted the research with our own students. Later, as our theory gained traction, we were joined by colleagues around the globe. Today, terror management theory is widely studied by psychological scientists and scholars in other disciplines as well, yielding an array of findings that go well beyond what Becker could ever have envisioned.

There is now compelling evidence that, as William James suggested a century ago, death is indeed the worm at the core of the human condition. The awareness that we humans will die has a profound and pervasive effect on our thoughts, feelings, and behaviors in almost every domain of human life—whether we are conscious of it or not.

Over the course of human history, the terror of death has guided the development of art, religion, language, economics, and science. It raised the pyramids in Egypt and razed the Twin Towers in Manhattan. It contributes to conflicts around the globe. At a more personal level, recognition of our mortality leads us to love fancy cars, tan ourselves to an unhealthy crisp, max out our credit cards, drive like lunatics, itch for a fight with a perceived enemy, and crave fame, however ephemeral, even if we have to drink yak urine on *Survivor* to get it. Death makes us uncomfortable with our bodies and ambivalent about sex. Awareness of the inevitability of death could easily contribute to our own extinction if we don't change how we deal with it.

The fear of death is one of the primary driving forces of human action. In the course of this book, we will show how this fear contributes to human behavior far more than most of us realize. In fact, it drives us so much that any effort to address the question "What makes people act the way they do?" is profoundly inadequate if it doesn't include the awareness of death as a central factor.

In these pages, we present terror management theory and research in conjunction with relevant findings from other fields such as anthropology and archaeology. We also illustrate points with historical and contemporary examples. When describing the research, we've tried to avoid academic jargon and minimize cumbersome technical details. We also tried to enliven the accounts of some of the key experiments by describing them from the perspective of individual participants, whose names have been changed.

In part 1, we introduce the basic tenets of terror management theory and the two pillars of terror management: cultural worldviews and self-esteem. In part 2, we delve into ancient history in an effort to address the questions "How did the problem of death arise for our ancestors?" and "What did they do about it?" In part 3, we consider the impact of intimations of mortality on a wide range of personal and interpersonal endeavors. In the last chapter, we offer some thoughts about the implications of our work for understanding the modern world and coping with the reality of death.

Continuing Becker's intellectual journey, our overarching goals are to reveal the many ways the knowledge that we are mortal underlies both the noblest and the most unsavory of human pursuits, and to consider how these insights can lead to personal growth and social progress.

PART
ONE

TERROR
MANAGEMENT

CHAPTER 1

Managing the
Terror of Death

———

The cradle rocks above an abyss, and common sense
tells us that our existence is but a brief crack of light
between two eternities of darkness.

—VLADIMIR NABOKOV,
Speak, Memory: A Memoir

ON CHRISTMAS EVE 1971, SEVENTEEN-YEAR-OLD JULIANE KOEPCKE AND
her mother, Maria, a German ornithologist, were flying from Lima, Peru, in
a plane with ninety other passengers over the Amazon jungle. They were
on their way to celebrate Christmas with Juliane's father, the brilliant zo-
ologist Hans-Wilhelm Koepcke, in the city of Pucallpa. Suddenly, a bolt of
lightning hit the airliner's fuel tank. The entire plane broke apart in smoke,
fuselage, and cinders, two miles above the gigantic, sparsely inhabited rain
forest.

Swept from the plane, Juliane found herself flying into the open sky. All
was silent. Strapped into her seat, she felt herself tumbling through the air
and saw the jungle canopy spinning toward her as she hurtled earthward
toward what seemed like her certain death. Her fall was broken by the thick
foliage. She fainted.

When she came to, she unbuckled herself from the still attached seat
and felt around. One shoe was missing, as were her glasses. She felt her

collarbone; it was broken. She discovered a deep gash in her leg and a wound in her arm. One of her nearsighted eyes had been swollen shut; the other was just a slit. She was dizzy from a bad concussion. But because she was in shock, she felt no pain. She called, and called, and called for her mother. No response. She found that she could walk. And so she walked.

For eleven days, Juliane stumbled through the Amazon jungle—home to caimans, tarantulas, poisonous frogs, electric eels, and freshwater sting-rays. She endured torrential downpours, sucking mud, brutal heat, and the constant onslaughts of swarming, stinging insects. Eventually, she found a small creek. Remembering what her father had taught her—that most people tend to live near waterways—she followed the stream to a larger river. She waded into the piranha- and stingray-infested water and began slowly swimming and floating downstream.

Her state of shock saved her. She wasn't really hungry, and felt as if she'd been psychologically "muffled in cotton." But the clouds of biting, stinging insects tortured her. She tried to rest under the trees, but sleep was nearly impossible. Maggots took up residence in her wounds. Her insect bites became badly infected. She got so sunburned from floating on the river under the Amazonian sun that she bled. But she pressed numbly on.

Finally, she came upon a motorboat. She had the presence of mind to pour gasoline from a small tank on the maggots, killing many of them. After a few days, the owners of the boat found her near their small hut and took her to the nearest town, seven hours away.

She was the only survivor of the crash.

WE'VE ALL HEARD AMAZING TALES of people who defy death against all odds: the survivors of the Donner Party and the *Titanic*, those who lived through the bombings of Dresden, Hiroshima, and Nagasaki. Such stories reflect the fact that all living beings are born with biological systems ori-ented toward self-preservation. Over billions of years, a vast array of com-plex life-forms have evolved, each distinctively adapted to survive long enough to reproduce and pass their genes on to future generations. Fish have gills; rosebushes have thorns; squirrels bury acorns and retrieve them months later; termites eat wood. There seems to be no limit to the marvelous variety of ways creatures of all species adhere to the fundamental biological imperative: staying alive.

If you discover a bat flittering around in your closet and you enter the dark space with a tennis racket to kill it, you'll be in for a battle royal, because that creature will fight to survive. Even earthworms strenuously avoid death, as anyone who's tried to bait a hook can attest. You split them in two; they persist. You try to get them on the hook; they struggle mightily. Once impaled, they defecate on your hand.

Unlike bats and worms, however, we humans know that no matter what we do, sooner or later we will lose the battle against death. This is a profoundly unnerving thought. We may think we are afraid to die because our bodies will rot, stink, and turn to dust, because we will leave our loved ones behind, because we've left important things unaccomplished, or because we have the sneaking suspicion that no loving God awaits us, ready to enfold us in his arms. But underlying all these concerns is that fundamental biological imperative. As Juliane Koepcke and other survivors have discovered, we will do just about anything to stay alive. Yet we live with the knowledge that this desire will inevitably be thwarted.

How did we get into this predicament? Although we humans inherited the basic imperative to survive, we are different from all other forms of life in several crucial ways. We are not terribly impressive from a purely physical perspective. We are not especially large, nor are our senses particularly keen. We move more slowly than cheetahs, wolves, and horses. Our claws are no more than fragile, dull fingernails; our teeth aren't constructed for tearing into anything much tougher than an overdone steak.

But the small band of African hominids from which we all descended were highly social, and, thanks to the evolution of their progeny's cerebral cortices, our species eventually became extremely intelligent. These developments fostered cooperation and the division of labor, and they ultimately led our forebears to invent tools, agriculture, cooking, houses, and a host of other useful things. We, their progeny, multiplied and thrived; our civilizations took root around the world.

The evolution of the human brain led to two particularly important human intellectual capacities: a high degree of self-awareness, and the capacity to think in terms of past, present, and future. Only we humans are, as far as anyone knows, *aware of ourselves* as existing in a particular time and place. This is an important distinction. Unlike geese, monkeys, and wombats, we can carefully consider our current situation, together with both the past and the future, before choosing a course of action.

This awareness of our own existence gives us a high degree of behavioral flexibility that helps us stay alive. Simpler life-forms respond immediately and invariably to their surroundings. Moths, for example, invariably fly toward light. Although the moth's behavior is generally useful for navigation and avoiding predators, it can be deadly when the source of illumination is a candle or campfire. Unlike moths, we humans can shift attention away from the ongoing flow of our sensory experience. We aren't inexorably sucked toward the flame; we can choose to act in a number of different ways, depending not only on our instincts, but on our capacity to learn and think as well. We can ponder alternative responses to situations and their potential consequences and imagine new possibilities.

Self-awareness has generally served us well. It has increased our ability to survive, reproduce, and pass our genes on to future generations. It also feels good. We can reflect on the fact that each of us is, in Otto Rank's lovely words, a "temporal representative of the cosmic primal force." We are all directly descended from, and consequently related to, the first living organism, as well as to every earth-dwelling creature that has ever been alive or will live in the future. What a joy it is for us to be alive, and at the same moment know it!

However, because we humans are aware that we exist, we also know that someday we will no longer exist. Death can come at any time, which we can neither predict nor control. This is decidedly unwelcome news. Even if we are lucky enough to dodge attacks by poisonous insects or biting beasts, knives, bullets, plane crashes, car accidents, cancer, or earthquakes, we understand that we can't go on forever.

This awareness of death is the downside of human intellect. If you think about this for a moment, death awareness presents each of us with an appalling predicament; it even feels like a cosmic joke. On one hand, we share the intense desire for continued existence common to all living things; on the other, we are smart enough to recognize the ultimate futility of this fundamental quest. We pay a heavy price for being self-conscious.

Terror is the natural and generally adaptive response to the imminent threat of death. All mammals, including humans, experience terror. When an impala sees a lion about to pounce on her, the amygdala in her brain passes signals to her limbic system, triggering a fight, flight, or freezing response. A similar process happens with us. Whenever we feel mortally threatened—by a car spinning out of control, a knife-wielding mugger, a tightening in the chest, a suspicious lump, extreme turbulence on an airplane, a suicide bomber exploding in a crowd—the feeling of terror consumes us; we are driven to fight, flee, or freeze. Panic ensues.

And here's the really tragic part of our condition: only we humans, due to our enlarged and sophisticated neocortex, can experience this terror in the *absence* of looming danger. Our death "waits like an old roué," as the great Belgian songwriter Jacques Brel noted, lurking in the psychological shadows. This realization threatens to put us in a persistent state of existential fear.

The poet W. H. Auden eloquently captured this uniquely human conundrum:

> *Happy the hare at morning, for she cannot read*
> *The Hunter's waking thoughts, lucky the leaf*
> *Unable to predict the fall, lucky indeed*
> *The rampant suffering suffocating jelly*
> *Burgeoning in pools, lapping the grits of the desert,*
> *But what shall man do, who can whistle tunes by heart,*
> *Knows to the bar when death shall cut him short like the*
> *cry of the shearwater,*
> *What can he do but defend himself from his knowledge?*

This ever-present potential for incapacitating terror is the "worm at the core" of the human condition. To manage this terror of death, we must defend ourselves.

HOW WE MANAGE TERROR

Fortunately, we humans are an ingenious species. Once our intelligence had evolved to the point that this ultimate existential crisis dawned on us, we used that same intelligence to devise the means to keep that potentially devastating existential terror at bay. Our shared *cultural worldviews*—the beliefs we create to explain the nature of reality to ourselves—give us a sense of meaning, an account for the origin of the universe, a blueprint for valued conduct on earth, and the promise of immortality.

Since the dawn of humankind, cultural worldviews have offered immense comfort to death-fearing humans. Throughout the ages and around the globe, the vast majority of people, past and present, have been led by their religions to believe that their existence literally continues in some form beyond the point of physical death. Some of us believe that our souls fly up to heaven, where we will meet our departed loved ones and bask in the loving glow of our creator. Others "know" that at the moment of death, our souls migrate into a new, reincarnated form. Still others are convinced that our souls simply pass to another, unknown plane of existence. In all these cases, we believe that we are, one way or another, literally immortal.

Our cultures also offer hope of symbolic immortality, the sense that we are part of something greater than ourselves that will continue long after we die. This is why we strive to be part of meaningful groups and have a lasting impact on the world—whether through our creative works of art or science, through the buildings and people named after us, through the possessions and genes we pass on to our children, or through the memories others hold of us. Just as we remember those we loved and admired who died before us, we feel the same will be done for us. We "live on" symbolically through our work, through the people we have known, through the memorials marking our graves, and through our progeny.

These cultural modes of transcending death allow us to feel that we are significant contributors to a permanent world. They protect us from the notion that we are merely purposeless animals that no longer exist upon death. Our beliefs in literal and symbolic immortality help us manage the potential for terror that comes from knowing that our physical death is inevitable.

This brings us to the central tenets of terror management theory. We humans all manage the problem of knowing we are mortal by calling on two basic psychological resources. First, we need to sustain faith in our cultural worldview, which imbues our sense of reality with order, meaning, and permanence. Although we typically take our cultural worldview for granted, it is actually a fragile human construction that people spend great energy creating, maintaining, and defending. Since we're constantly on the brink of realizing that our existence is precarious, we cling to our culture's governmental, educational, and religious institutions and rituals to buttress our view of human life as uniquely significant and eternal.

But we don't just need to view life in general this way; we need to view *our own* life this way. The paths to literal and symbolic immortality laid out by our worldviews require us to feel that we are valuable members of our cultures. Hence, the second vital resource for managing terror is a feeling of personal significance, commonly known as *self-esteem*. Just as cultural worldviews vary, so do the ways we attain and maintain self-esteem. For the Dinka of Sudan, the man who owns the largest herd of long-horned cattle is the most highly regarded. In the Trobriand Islands, a man's worth is measured by the size of the pyramid of yams he builds in front of his sister's house and leaves to rot. For many Canadians, the man who best uses his stick to slap rubber pucks into nets guarded by masked opponents is considered a national hero.

The desire for self-esteem drives us all, and drives us hard. Self-esteem shields us against the rumblings of dread that lie beneath the surface of our everyday experience. Self-esteem enables each of us to believe we are enduring, significant beings rather than material creatures destined to be obliterated. The twin motives of affirming the correctness of our worldviews and demonstrating our personal worth combine to protect us from the uniquely human fear of inevitable death. And these same impulses have driven much of what humans have achieved over the course of our history.

THE IDEA THAT KNOWLEDGE of our mortality plays a pivotal role in human affairs is ancient. It can be found in the Bible, the Torah, the Qur'an, and ancient Buddhist texts. Twenty-five hundred years ago the Greek historian Thucydides, in *The History of the Peloponnesian War,* saw the problem of death as the primary cause of protracted violent conflict. Socrates defined the task of philosophy as "learning how to die." For Hegel, history was a record of "what man does with death." Over the last two centuries, these ideas have been taken up by philosophers (such as Søren Kierkegaard and Friedrich Nietzsche), theologians (for instance, Paul Tillich and Martin Buber), psychoanalytic and existential psychologists (from Sigmund Freud to Otto Rank to Robert Jay Lifton), not to mention enduring works of literature by everyone from Sophocles to Shakespeare to Philip Roth.

But in the realm of scientific psychology, the problem of death has never garnered much attention. Even today, many psychologists remain surprisingly indifferent. If you scour the influential contemporary social science tomes that attempt to shed light on matters such as human nature, the mind, culture, religion, war, history, and consciousness, you might conclude that death is not only unimportant, it scarcely exists.

This is probably due to the widespread belief that the effects of our relationship to death could not be understood or tested in a rigorous scientific manner. In the post-Freudian era in which psychology was still struggling to be taken seriously as a legitimate science, psychologists were wary of big, sweeping ideas, especially those involving the impact of unconscious thoughts and emotions on everyday behavior.

As experimental social psychologists, we wondered about this. Why *couldn't* these ideas be framed scientifically and then put to the test? Perhaps the scientific method could be deployed to explain exactly how people cope with subconscious existential fears.

We began conducting studies in which one (experimental) group of participants was reminded of their mortality, and another (control) group was not. We wanted to see whether, when reminded of death, people in the experimental groups would intensify their efforts to uphold their culturally acquired beliefs. We started back in 1987 by testing this idea with twenty-two municipal court judges in Tucson, Arizona. That's when things started getting interesting.

Enter Judge Michael Garner, who helped us out in our first scientific experiment.

JUDGING A HOOKER

Reviewing the prostitute's case and setting her bail was all part of the day's work for Judge Garner. He came into work in the morning and sat down in his chambers to look over the files recording the usual misbehavior committed during the previous night: drunk driving, shoplifting, disorderly conduct. Then he opened the file containing the prosecutor's notes for the case of one Carol Ann Dennis.

The police citation and the prosecutor's report noted that the twenty-five-year-old woman had been arrested a little after 9:30 P.M. on a stretch of the Miracle Mile. Dennis, dressed in short shorts, high heels, and a halter top, had stood on the street corner soliciting johns. A man in his thirties had driven up in a pickup truck and pulled over, rolling down the window. Neither of them saw the unmarked police car lurking down the street.

According to the report, Dennis was handcuffed and helped into the back of the police car. She was then carted off to the city jail and charged with soliciting for acts of prostitution. Because she couldn't verify a permanent address, she was waiting to be released on bond.

Judge Garner closed the file and sighed. He'd seen cases like this before; the typical bail for this type of infraction at that time was $50. Then he turned to another folder, which contained some personality questionnaires that a fellow judge had asked him to fill out for his girlfriend, who was helping her professor with an academic study on "personality, attitudes and bond decisions."

One of the questionnaires was a two-question "Morality Attitudes

Personality Survey." First, we asked the judge to "please briefly describe the emotions that the thought of your own death arouses in you."

"I don't think about it much, but I guess I would feel very sad for my family, who would miss me," he wrote.

Next we asked the judge to "jot down, as specifically as you can, what you think will happen to you as you physically die, and once you are physically dead."

He wrote: "I feel that I will enter a tunnel of pain and then release into the light. I will notice that my body will be buried and eventually decay under the earth, but my soul will rise up to heaven where I will meet my Savior."

After completing a few more questions, the judge chatted with his clerk for a few minutes, then returned to his chambers to resume his work.

HOW DID JUDGE GARNER and the other judges who'd thought about their own mortality before setting Carol Ann Dennis's bond respond? The judges in the control group who did not complete the survey imposed the average bond of $50. However, the judges reminded of their death hammered Carol Ann (who, by the way, was not a real person) with a far more punitive bond—on average, $455, more than nine times the typical tab. The scales of justice were tipped, if not toppled, by the judges who had pondered their demise.

Judges are supposed to be supremely rational experts who gauge cases based on the facts. And indeed, the judges insisted that answering some questions about death could not possibly have had any effect on their legal pronouncements. How, then, could a brief reminder of death so radically—and without their knowing it—alter their decisions?

When we set up the experiment, we figured that judges, generally speaking, were people who had pretty strong views of right and wrong to begin with, and we thought that Carol Ann Dennis's behavior would offend their moral sensibilities. The results showed that the judges who thought about their own mortality reacted by trying to do the right thing as prescribed by their culture. Accordingly, they upheld the law more vigorously than their colleagues who were not reminded of death. By setting an extremely high bond for the alleged prostitute, they ensured that she would show up for trial to receive not just a mere slap on the wrist, but also the punishment she "deserved" for her moral transgression.

Reminders of death don't just provoke more negative reactions to those who fail to live up to our values. They also spawn more positive responses to people who uphold them. In one study, death reminders tripled the monetary reward people recommended for someone who reported a dangerous criminal to the police. And the effects of death reminders aren't limited to those we judge to be immoral or noble. They also increase our general desire to fortify our faith in the correctness of our beliefs and the goodness of our culture. So after being reminded of death, we react generously to anyone or anything that reinforces our cherished beliefs, and reject anyone or anything that calls those beliefs into question.

In another study we conducted shortly after our research with the judges, we had a group of American students come to our lab. We asked those in the control group to simply describe something neutral— specifically, the emotions that the thought of food and the act of eating aroused in them. Those in the experimental group answered the same unsavory, death-related questions we'd asked Judge Garner.

A few minutes later, we asked each group to read two interviews that we (falsely) told them had come from *Political Science Quarterly:* one with a professor who was staunchly in favor of America's political system and another with a professor who railed against it. In his interview, the pro-U.S. professor conceded the United States had its difficulties. Economic inequality was a problem, he noted, and the government had made foreign policy mistakes. But in general, he concluded, "In this country, the people and not the government will be the final judges of the value of what I have to say. That is what makes this country a great place to live freely."

The anti-U.S. professor, on the other hand, acknowledged some of America's many virtues but went on to emphasize the malignant influence of the power elite and the "economically motivated and amoral behavior of the United States abroad." He concluded that "morality has absolutely nothing to do with our foreign policy. That's why the idea that the U.S. is a promoter of world democracy and freedom is a total sham." He even suggested that a violent overthrow of the present government was in order.

All the students in our study liked what the pro-U.S. professor had to say. They found him to be more knowledgeable and truthful than the anti-U.S. professor. But the people who had first thought about their eventual death rated the pro-American much more positively, and the anti-U.S. interviewee far more negatively, than those in the control group.

Since we embarked on this path, more than five hundred studies and counting have demonstrated the many ways that cultural worldviews protect us from the terror that the knowledge of the inevitability of death might otherwise arouse. When confronted with reminders of death, we react by criticizing and punishing those who oppose or violate our beliefs, and praising and rewarding those who support or uphold our beliefs. Participants have been reminded of death in many different ways. Aside from answering questions about death, they might see gory accident footage, write one sentence about death, or just be standing near a funeral parlor or cemetery. Fascinatingly, their belief-supporting responses are *uniquely* correlated with reminders of death. This is important, because reminders of other negative events, such as social rejection, failing an exam, intense pain, or losing a limb in a car accident, do not produce the same effects as being reminded of one's own mortality.

Throughout this book, we will show how efforts to manage existential terror affect virtually all human affairs. In fact, concerns about mortality influence everything from the mundane to the momentous—what you eat for lunch, how much sunscreen you put on at the beach, whom you voted for in the last election, your attitudes about shopping, your mental health and physical well-being, whom you love and whom you hate.

But we're not born with this terror. As infants, we are too young to focus on anything beyond being fed and kept warm. Why and how, then, does each human child become embedded in, and a defender of, a symbolic world of meaning and self-worth? And when and how does death enter the psychological picture?

CHAPTER 2

The Scheme of Things

———

The scheme of things is a system of order.... It is self-evidently true, is accepted so naturally and automatically that one is not aware of an act of acceptance having taken place.... We seek the largest possible scheme of things, not in a reaching out for truth, but because the more comprehensive the scheme the greater its promise of banishing dread. If we can make our lives mean something in a cosmic scheme we will live in the certainty of immortality.

—ALLEN WHEELIS,
The Scheme of Things

WE BEGIN LIFE AS DIAPER-DRENCHING, PACIFIER-SUCKING CREATURES, but we don't remember that time. We know our names but do not recall having received them. Yet we have fairly solid recollections of our lives after the age of five, give or take a year or two: favorite pets, toys, teachers, friends, unwelcome hugs by overzealous aunts, scoring a goal, summer camp, Halloween trick-or-treating. Eventually, we each become aware of ourselves, not just as individuals but as part of a broader social context: we become Brazilian, Nigerian, Mexican, Italian, Lebanese, Chinese, Dutch, Mexican, Japanese, or American, in a wider world of meanings and symbols.

"From the child of five to myself is but a step," Leo Tolstoy observed, "but from the new-born baby to the child of five is an appalling distance." How do we transform from crying, cooing neonates to adults with names and nationalities, seeking significance in our respective cultures? And how does this transition allow us to function securely in the world? Let's consider how this appalling distance is traversed, how concerns about death influence the course of the journey, and what happens thereafter.

THE NEED FOR
PSYCHOLOGICAL SECURITY

Our early years are very important for establishing psychological security. If they don't go well, the journey toward adulthood can be incredibly harrowing.

Consider the case of Cyprian, a healthy and cute baby boy born in Carpenis, Romania, in April 1990. The baby's birth mother, Alin, really didn't want to bring him into the world. He was her fourth child. The government of Romania, under the dictatorship of Nicolae Ceaușescu, had outlawed both contraception and abortion, and Alin and her family barely survived on the chickens they raised on their tiny farm and the few vegetables from their scrappy yard. Desperately poor, she and her husband decided they could not afford to keep their new son. So right after he was born, they dropped him off at a state orphanage and went back to the grim work of keeping themselves and their remaining children alive.

Cyprian was one of about 170,000 Romanian babies crammed into orphanages that were like terrible zoos. The babies were barely fed and only occasionally changed. They were never taken outside into the fresh air. The rooms they were housed in reeked of urine and body odor. With a ratio of dozens of children to one or two caregivers, the abandoned babies were never cuddled. They had no toys to play with. Because they were often tied to their filthy cribs, they didn't learn to crawl or walk. Instead of learning to talk, they banged their heads on the metal bars of their cribs. By the time Cyprian's adoptive parents picked him up in Bucharest in the summer of 1992, he was "failing to thrive," meaning that he'd stopped growing and developing. Physically, he was a shrunken, malnourished two-year-old; mentally he was far worse off.

Cyprian was one of the few lucky ones. His new parents renamed him Cameron and brought him to America. His new family showered love and care on him. He was coddled and fed; he learned to walk and grew to a normal weight for his age. For a while, he seemed to be normal and healthy. But at around the age of four, he began behaving strangely. "He was terrified of walking on the grass," recalls his father, Daniel. "He developed an obsession for patent leather shoes. He stuffed food into his cheeks like a squirrel. He often fell into violent, screaming fits. He broke things. He didn't pick up on social cues. We had no idea what was wrong with him."

Only when Cameron entered therapy at the age of five did Daniel and his wife begin to understand what afflicted their beautiful son. Cameron suffered from a severe psychological condition called "reactive attachment disorder," which shows up in traumatized children who don't have an opportunity to bond with their very first caregivers—usually their mothers. Cameron's disorder was due to his desperate but unmet need, as an infant, for psychological security.

THESE FEELINGS OF SECURITY are every bit as critical to a baby as milk and warmth. But such feelings don't come easy to little humans. Guppies are born swimming, eating, and dodging predators. Puppies and kittens are fully weaned and completely independent in two months. In contrast, human newborns are the most immature and helpless of all living creatures. Fresh out of the womb, we can't even lift our heads or turn over without assistance. Forming strong emotional bonds to parents assures that children get what they need to survive and thrive. How does this happen?

For most of the twentieth century, psychologists believed that babies love their parents for one reason only: their parents feed them. According to Sigmund Freud, milk produces pleasure, which causes the baby to form an attachment to its mother and to develop affection for her. Basically, Freud thought that as infants, we love those who make us feel this pleasure. Later on, behavioral psychologist B. F. Skinner theorized that bonding in infancy was all about reinforcement: whoever shows up with milk, over and over, receives the baby's attachment and affection because she or he is reliably associated with getting fed.

Freud's disciple Otto Rank disputed this view of why infants form attachments. He and other psychoanalytic thinkers, such as Harry Stack Sullivan and Melanie Klein, argued that emotional bonds are forged by feelings of being loved and protected. However, this alternative view of attachment wasn't widely accepted until the late 1950s, when Harry Harlow conducted a set of famous experiments. Harlow separated rhesus monkeys from their biological mothers at birth and raised them in cages with two inanimate "mothers," one made of bare wire mesh and the other covered with soft terry cloth. The monkeys spent most of their time clinging to the terry cloth mother, even when nourished by a bottle mounted on the bare wire mother.

In another study, the monkeys were separated; one group was fed by wire mothers while another group was fed by the terry cloth mothers. Although both groups of monkeys drank equal amounts of milk and grew at the same rate, they responded very differently in novel and frightening situations. When wandering around their cages and unexpectedly exposed to a mechanical teddy bear beating a drum, the monkeys with the soft terry cloth mother scampered to her and clung to her tenaciously. Seemingly comforted, they then ventured forth and explored their surroundings. Interestingly, the other monkeys, rather than making their way back to "Mother Metallica," hurled themselves on the ground, rocked back and forth, or groped themselves and screamed in obvious distress—very much as the neglected children in the Romanian orphanages behaved.

The baby monkeys, Harlow argued, used their terry cloth mothers as a secure base. Once their initial fright was quelled by comforting contact with the soft mother, they regained their confidence. We don't love our parents because they feed us, he concluded; we love them because physical contact with our parents provides comforting security.

While Harlow was conducting his experiments, psychiatrist John Bowlby was developing a companion idea he called "attachment theory."

The theory was based on Bowlby's psychoanalytic training, his knowledge of primate evolution and ethology, and his studies of young children who had been separated from their parents during World War II. Bowlby proposed that if an infant is to survive, he or she needs to be emotionally attached to a responsive caregiver. Because of their helplessness and vulnerability, fledgling humans are especially prone to anxiety, and separation from attachment figures, literally or figuratively, is the ultimate threat to them. Hence, he observed, it was vitally important for infants to develop "basic trust," the sense that they are safe and sound, in the first year of life. And they could do this only through the seemingly omnipresent and omnipotent help of people who cared about them.

TRUST AND TRIBULATION

Today, thanks to the work of Rank, Harlow, Bowlby, and others, we understand that the primary source of psychological security in early infancy is parental love and protection. When we cuddle and coo over our babies, they feel secure and emboldened to explore. They crawl around on the floor and happily investigate every nook and cranny they can reach, which is why soon-to-be parents often "childproof" their homes.

If you are lucky enough to be born into a loving family, it's pretty cool to be a new baby. You snuggle into your mother's warm breast, where you receive sweet nourishment. You are swaddled, cuddled, fed, and entertained. When you pee or poop, the wetness disappears into soft dryness. In your early days, simply existing is sufficient for you to be showered with love and comfort from all those wonderful people who look at you with their shining, admiring eyes. When you successfully grasp a toy and get more food into your mouth than on the floor, it's a blissful occasion for your parents. Later, a first step, a gurgling approximation of "Mommy" or "Daddy," or bouncing a tennis ball off the dog's head evokes effusive displays of pride and affection from your adult fans.

As you become a toddler, it takes a bit more work for you to elicit these sorts of pleasurable parental reactions, especially when you do things that Mom or Dad doesn't like. You might put dirt into your mouth. You might pee in the fishbowl instead of the toilet. You might chase a runaway ball into the street. And when you are corrected, it's not pleasant. If Mom pulls your grabbing hands away from the candy counter or stops you from pulling the dog's tail, you become decidedly unhappy; you scream and wail.

To stay in their parents' good graces, children must learn to do things they do not want to do, and not to do things they do want to do. Sometimes the stakes are literally life and death. Tumbling off the diving board of the family swimming pool can make for a hasty departure from the family gene pool. Long before youngsters are mature enough to be persuaded by reason to abstain from risky, unpleasant, or socially unacceptable behaviors, parents use approval to promote preferred actions and disapproval to deter undesirable ones. When our children do what we want them to do, we praise and reward them; our approval keeps our kids feeling safe and secure. But when they behave inappropriately, as they inevitably do, we parents respond with rebukes, time-outs, physical punishment, or the stark absence of approval. Confronted by these disturbingly stern adult behaviors, little boys and girls feel upset, anxious, and sometimes terrified.

In his exquisite rendering of a growing self-image in *A Portrait of the Artist as a Young Man,* James Joyce's little-boy protagonist Stephen fearfully hides under the table. Why? Because the boy has declared that "when they were grown up he was going to marry Eileen." Eileen, as it turns out, is the neighboring child of a Protestant family—anathema to Stephen's strictly Catholic one. And if the child doesn't apologize for wanting to marry a Protestant, warns his aunt Dante, "the eagles will come and pull out his eyes." The petrified youngster repeats this threat in his head like a chant:

> *Apologise,*
> *Pull out his eyes,*
> *Pull out his eyes,*
> *Apologise.*

What could be worse than being attacked or abandoned by your security base? Even at this early age, Stephen learns that if he doesn't behave the way his family expects him to, he won't be rewarded with warmth and approval; instead, he will be brutally attacked.

In this fashion, over time, being a "good" girl or boy becomes associated with protection and well-being, while being a "bad" girl or boy becomes associated with anxiety and vulnerability. This is why we all need self-esteem—to feel that we are good and valued—and why self-esteem is essential for managing our terror of death.

SOAKING UP THE SCHEME OF THINGS

As they become attached and socialized, children are also absorbing the cultural scheme of things. Most children are thoroughly ensconced in their worldviews by age five, although it was a little tougher for Cameron because he missed out on that first experience of basic trust. Cameron was, however, still a lucky little boy. He was able to catch up in the immersion process with the help of psychological counseling and some special schools where wonderful teachers taught him to read and write, add and subtract, and manage his many difficult mood swings.

Meanwhile, he enjoyed the usual benefits of growing up in a loving home. Cameron's parents were politically moderate, middle-class people who believed in hard work, community involvement, and helping others who were less fortunate than they. His parents sang to him and read him *Goodnight Moon* and *The Velveteen Rabbit*. Cameron learned the names of his relatives, his teachers, the people at church, and his friends, as well as the names of plants, animals, and inanimate objects. He reached out to explore his world. He watched Disney movies and enjoyed the rides at Disney World; he slid down the twisty slides at the park and played tag with the waves at the beach. When his parents discovered that he was happiest when dancing and singing, they paid for lessons.

Cameron learned to say the Pledge of Allegiance and to sing "The Star-Spangled Banner." In his Cub Scout troop, he learned the proper way to fold the American flag. On Sundays, his parents took him to church, where he attended Sunday school and the teacher taught him about the stories of

Moses and Jesus. At Easter, Cameron went hunting for candy eggs before going to church. He took part in the annual Christmas pageant and had his picture taken with Santa, who miraculously listened to his wishes and showered him with the toys he wanted most on Christmas morning. He learned that weddings are about people celebrating love; funerals are about saying goodbye to people who die; graduations are for people who are finishing school. His birthdays were for celebrating the passage of time, which he came to perceive in the way his American culture diced it up, into an orderly succession of recurring seconds, minutes, hours, days, and months in an ongoing progression of years.

Every time Cameron's parents took him to the school, church, or psychiatrist, every time he watched a movie or overheard his parents talking, Cameron received signals about what was good and what was bad. The world was easily divided into black and white. Cinderella and Batman were good; Cruella de Vil and the Wicked Witch of the West were bad. Exercise was good; smoking was bad. Counting to ten was good; screaming and throwing tantrums when you lost patience was bad. His relatives were good; terrorists were bad. Once Cameron began to sort out good from bad, right from wrong, he began to feel more relaxed. Secure in his knowledge, he felt increasingly in command of himself, for his social world reinforced what his parents had tried to teach him.

Gradually, often deliberately, and sometimes unconsciously, Cameron's parents conveyed the scheme of things, as they understood it, to their young charge as he grew. They passed on their own worldview and their understanding of right and wrong to him. Their worldview dictated just about everything Cameron learned about reality, and he began to internalize what he was learning.

And everywhere he looked, Cameron's understanding of his culture's worldview was buttressed by emblems, banners, pictures of presidents, and other images and physical objects that represented the commonly held values of American society. He noticed that people saluted flags and visited monuments erected to historical figures and events. The names of good citizens were inscribed on everything from street signs and freeways to the ornate government buildings, all attesting to an overarching political scheme of things. He saw that skyscrapers, parks, schools, streets, and public buildings were named after wealthy benefactors who verified and affirmed the public scheme of things. He saw crosses on churches and stars of David on synagogues that attested to the religious scheme of things. All these confirmed Cameron's sense of reality.

In short, Cameron's parents, and everyone and everything else around him, conferred on him a certain description of reality, one that Cameron, like all children, didn't just passively accept but ardently embraced. When children learn to be good and feel valued as prescribed by their culture, the same psychological benefits that were originally afforded by their parents' love and protection are extended and expanded. At every age, we humans need that sense of security to survive and flourish, because the terrors are legion.

HOW CHILDREN DISCOVER DEATH

Even before children are fully aware of what they are frightened of, their faith in a worldview that provides order, purpose, and significance helps them manage their fear. This has everything to do with the problem of death.

Thrust from the comfortable, warm wash of the womb, babies are frequently plagued by pains, hunger pangs, chills, rashes, and a panoply of other problems. Although infants and toddlers don't know what they are afraid of or why, they react with distress to many potential threats to their survival. As children become aware of themselves, typically between eighteen and twenty-four months, their budding grasp of their smallness and vulnerability makes them increasingly terrified by even more real and imagined dangers. They are scared of the dark, strangers, big dogs, monsters, and ghosts. From their point of view, all are real threats to survival.

By around age three, the grim handmaiden of self-consciousness—death awareness—begins to make her appearance. Rocks seem to last forever, but living things are impermanent and can disappear in death. Children may encounter a maggot-ridden squirrel on a path. They may see Grandma covered with a sheet and being carted out of the house. A first goldfish or the beloved dog dies. Maybe Mom and Dad bury Fido, with all the appropriate funeral rites, in the backyard.

Soon after children become aware of death, it dawns on them that they could die, too. As they ponder their own existence, they begin to realize that they also could not exist. They become little Hamlets as, over time, specific childhood fears coalesce into a general fear of no longer existing.

Most of us can remember having nightmares as young children. Nightmares and night terrors are vivid manifestations of a child's emerging knowledge of vulnerability and death. One of us recalls having the following recurring nightmare around the age of five:

> A gory purple creature with one huge bloodshot eye emerges from under my bed. I leap up and slam into my bedroom door; somehow I escape into the hallway with the slobbering Cyclops in hot pursuit. I cut across the living room, hurdle the couch, and scramble into the kitchen. The enraged monster is roaring and spewing green slime as it lumbers ever closer. I think to get a knife, but there's no time. In a panic, I hide in the broom closet holding my breath. Suddenly the closet door bursts open—

Each time he dreamed this, he awoke up terrified, in a cold sweat. But he was quickly comforted, either by his dad leaning over him saying "Everything is okay, it was just a bad dream, you're a good boy, I'll never let anything happen to you," or by simply realizing that Mom and Dad were sleeping in the next room, as if they would always be there. In childhood, we all awoke from such nightmares with great relief. The monster was no longer chasing you. You were safe, Mom and Dad loved you, and everything was all right.

In nightmares, the feeling that someone or something is hiding under the bed, breaking in through a window, or suddenly materializing out of nowhere is common. Such terrors reflect a dawning awareness of the precariousness and fragility of life. Although most people remember some fearful moments from childhood, few of us recall being haunted by feelings of smallness and vulnerability, the threat of annihilation, the realization that death is inevitable, and the ensuing dread. Still, evidence suggests that children as young as three are aware of and uncomfortable about death, and that they begin to employ rudimentary versions of some of the terror management strategies they will come to rely on as adults.

IN THE LATE 1960S and early 1970s, British educational psychologist Sylvia Anthony worked with mothers to conduct interviews with their own children. She found that even very young children are concerned about death. When three-year-old Jane asked if dead people "came back again in the spring like flowers," her mother, who had no orthodox religious beliefs, answered that they did not return the same, but possibly came back as babies. Jane was worried by this answer, because she hated change and didn't like the fact her grandmother, "Nan," was getting old.

"Will Nan die?" the little girl asked.

"Yes," said her mother.

Jane broke into heartbreaking tears, repeating over and over, "But I don't want to die, I don't want to die."

As children mature cognitively, their understanding of death deepens and the ways they manage their terror become more elaborate. At bath time, according to the mother of five-year-old Richard, as "he swam up and down in his bath he played with the possibility of never dying: 'I don't want to be dead, ever; I don't want to die.'"

Here's an exchange Anthony recorded between five-year-old Theodor and his mother:

THEODOR: "Do animals come to an end, too?"

MOTHER: "Yes, animals come to an end, too. Everything that lives comes to an end."

THEODOR: "I don't want to come to an end. I should like to live longer than anybody on earth."

In another study, researchers interviewed children between the ages of eight and twelve, asking them what they were typically afraid of and worried about. The researchers also interviewed the children's mothers. Although mothers typically said that their children were more afraid of snakes and poor grades than getting sick or dying, the children themselves said that they were more afraid of illness and death than serpents and bad report cards. It turns out that children are much more troubled about death, and at a much earlier age, than most of us realize.

DODGING DEATH

According to the great developmental psychologist Jean Piaget, children's conceptions of death typically vary with their stage of cognitive development. Young children often initially view death as a sleeplike suspended animation. They think, "I go to sleep at night, but I will wake up in the morning," or "Grandma may be old and nap a lot in her old recliner, but she always wakes up." Everyone wakes up from naps and nightly slumbers and sooner or later returns from even the lengthiest ones. Accordingly, children sometimes expect the dead to be reborn at a seasonably auspicious moment. They might pour water on deceased creatures in an effort to bring them back to life.

Children also use all kinds of mental tricks to dodge death, starting by simply declining to think about it. Three-year-old Jane, in her budding awareness of death, worriedly asked her mother whether dead people opened their eyes again, whether they spoke, ate, and wore clothes. "Suddenly, in the middle of all these questions and tears," her mother reported, "she said, 'Now I will go on with my tea.'" Similarly, after his mother told five-year-old Richard that he wouldn't die for a long time, the little boy smiled and said, "That's all right. I've been worried, and now I can get happy." Then he said he would like to dream about "going shopping and buying things."

These diversionary tactics are strikingly similar to what happens when adults think about themselves dying. They react by trying to stop thinking about death and distracting themselves with mundane concerns. Research finds that after a reminder of death, adults also search for "don't worry, be happy" thoughts. And it is quite common for adults to react to thoughts of death by turning to comfort foods and luxury goods: "Let's do lunch and go shopping!"

Children also plan to stay young forever. They tell themselves, "Only old people die. I'm not old. Therefore, as long as I stay young I won't die." Peter Pan, the boy who never grew up, is a classic example of this gambit from children's literature. The late entertainer Michael Jackson, the boy who never grew up at his Neverland estate, is a haunting illustration of this ploy from real life.

In many children's stories, death is personified in bad characters. Wicked witches, goblins, trolls, ogres, and the like put shapes and faces on mortal terror; they make the idea of death—something abstract and difficult to imagine—concrete and manageable. Giving death a human form makes it easier to circumvent. If death were a person, he or she could be reasoned with, bargained with, tricked, or overwhelmed by one's own superior wit or strength or that of a magical intercessor. Between the ages of five and nine, children think of death as avoidable if you are swift or smart enough to avoid getting caught.

Indeed, in many fairy tales, child heroes often evade death in clever ways. Think of the Brothers Grimm and Hans Christian Andersen's compendium, overflowing with mortal threats, which children rarely succumb to; or *The Wizard of Oz*, in which Dorothy escapes certain death at the hands of the wicked witch. Pinocchio transforms from a wooden puppet into a real human boy, while Harry Potter's clever wizardry saves him from the attacks of his mortal enemy, Lord Voldemort (whose very name recalls the French phrase *vol de mort*, meaning "flee from death").

A complementary death-denying strategy is the belief in a personal and personified savior. From a child's perspective, parents are gigantic and seemingly all-powerful beings with a knack for showing up whenever bodily or emotional needs arise. It's natural, therefore, for a young mind to also believe in stories about omnipotent beings interceding in matters of life and death. Neither Snow White nor Sleeping Beauty is really dead; they are just waiting to be saved through the affection of a protective, rescuing, paternal caregiver. Though Jesus suffered terribly on the cross, he didn't really die; God interceded to take Him up to heaven. In so doing He saves you, Mom and Dad, Grandma and Grandpa, and all those you love from eternal death, and after all of you die, you will meet again in heaven.

Given comfort from parents and encouragement from the stories in their culture, children can become expressly confident in their personal inviolability. It's not uncommon to hear young children suddenly exclaim that they will never die. At age six, one of our own kids was not so certain, but was nonetheless hopeful: "My three wishes," he declared, "would be to never die, be the richest person in the world, and have all the video games."

TOO DEEP FOR TEARS

As children mature, they eventually become savvy enough to realize that death is inevitable and irrevocable. One day, they realize that the stomped-upon worm on the sidewalk will wiggle no more. Grandpa isn't napping in his underground box as he did in his chair in the living room. The dog that had cancer and had to be "put to sleep" will not be waking up anytime soon.

Suddenly, you grasp the horrible truth: Death is not just an unfortunate accident that occasionally befalls the aged, the hapless, and the wicked. Sooner or later, you realize, death will happen to everyone, including you; the curtain will surely fall while you are strutting across the earthly stage, and your ultimate fate will be the same as that of the disemboweled squirrel splattered on a roadside, or that skeleton you so fear.

This realization is momentous. "Nothing was more difficult for me in childhood than to admit the notion of death as a state applicable to my own being," wrote the poet William Wordsworth. Such thoughts "often lie too deep for tears." In this instant, you became fully human.

Once children understand that they, as well as their mothers and fathers, are perpetually vulnerable and ultimately finite, they shift from their parents to their culture as their primary source of psychological equanimity. Deities and social authorities and institutions now appear to be more stable and enduring than our all-too-mortal and therefore all-too-vulnerable parents, grandparents, and pets.

Research conducted by our Israeli colleagues (the late) Victor Florian and Mario Mikulincer support this account of how children's burgeoning awareness of death instigates a shift from their parents to their culture. The researchers surveyed two groups of Israeli children, ages seven and eleven. Half of each group of children was asked twenty-six open-ended questions related to death. The questions included queries such as "Does a dead man know what is happening to him?" and "Will every man die at some time?"

Next, all of the children looked at pictures of other children who were the same age and gender. Each picture was accompanied by the child's name and his or her birthplace. Some of the pictures were of Israeli-born children; others were of Russian immigrant children (in Israel, Russian immigrants are stereotyped as cultural outsiders). For each picture, the children rated how willing they would be to play with the child and be his or her best friend.

The results of this study showed that the seven-year-olds had not yet transferred their psychological eggs to their cultural basket. After being asked about death, the younger children reacted more negatively to pictures of both Israeli and Russian children. They were afraid of death, but they had not yet deployed their culture to manage their fear.

It was a different story for the eleven-year-olds, however. After being asked about death, these older children were more eager to befriend fellow Israeli children and rejected the idea of befriending the Russians. In short, the eleven-year-olds reacted to reminders of their mortality in the same way that adults do. Having realized that death is inevitable and irreversible, they pledged permanent psychological allegiance to their culture.

RALLY ROUND THE FLAG

The pattern observed in the eleven-year-old Israeli children has been found consistently in adults from many nations. As we have already seen in chapter 1, Americans reminded of death had more positive reactions to those who praised the United States and more negative reactions to those who criticized it. Similarly, Italians reminded of death viewed Italy more favorably and felt a stronger bond with fellow Italians. Moreover, although Germans interviewed in front of a retail shop showed no particular preference for things German, those interviewed in front of a cemetery preferred German food, German cars, and German vacation spots to foreign alternatives.

LET'S IMAGINE STEVE, a fully acculturated young American adult. If we visited his Facebook page, we might learn that Steve was many things: a rock guitarist in a band; a good son, nephew, brother, and grandson; a high school graduate; an independent voter who believes in equal rights for all; a college student; a man with a plan to become a teacher; and so on. Like most young adults, Steve has transferred his loyalty from his parents to the surrounding culture, cementing his belief systems and bolstering them with new devotions to groups to which he wants to belong. And in so doing, Steve is fortifying the psychological armor against existential terror that he's been developing since childhood.

Now imagine that you are Steve and you're studying psychology at a major American university. As part of one course, you're asked to participate in some research. When you show up to the lab at the appointed time, the researcher tells you the experiment is about the link between personality and creativity. "A lot of personality research has been done on members of the armed forces," she says. "During military exercises in the California desert, military personnel were observed using common military objects in a creative way, for tasks such as filtering sand from abrasive fluids and creating innovative construction tools. Preliminary findings from the military population show connections between personality and creativity, and we are now interested in generating data on the general population.

"Here you go," she continues, handing you a packet. "Please take some time to complete these questionnaires. When you're finished, come out into the hallway."

You're in the experimental condition. You fill out a little questionnaire about personality, and then you're confronted with the same nasty questions the judges we described in chapter 1 answered: "Please describe the emotions the thought of death arouses in you" and "Jot down what you think will happen to you as you physically die and once you are physically dead."

When you're through with the questionnaires, the experimenter takes you into another room, where you see a lot of objects sitting on a table: a package of hot chocolate mix, two plastic tubes, a thin rope, a paper clip, a compass watch, a rubber band, netting, a glass jar, a cup filled with black dye, a nail, a cup filled with sand, a small flag, and a sturdy crucifix.

The experimenter pours the black dye into the sand. Then she tells you your tasks: to figure out a way to separate the sand from black dye, because "soldiers had used ordinary objects to separate out sand from noxious substances," and to hang the crucifix on the wall, because fastening things to walls "is a common task in the service, but hammers aren't always available."

You think about the tasks for a minute. You then realize that you can use the flag to strain the dye from the sand and the crucifix to bang the nail into the wall. But this thought makes you decidedly reluctant and tense. After all, you've been taught to revere these symbolic objects from the time you were a little boy. It feels like desecration to use them in this way. But you realize you really don't have any other choice; none of the other objects will serve. Slowly, you pick up the flag, put it over the top of the glass jar, and pour the black-dyed sand over it, filtering the ink into the jar. Time elapsed: six minutes.

When this is finished, you turn to the next task. You slowly take up the crucifix and the nail and walk to the wall. You hesitate for several seconds, thinking about how you are using this sacred object for such a mundane task. "This is sacrilege," you think, and let out a deep sigh. Then you slowly begin hammering. Time elapsed: six minutes.

There were three other versions of the experiment that served as control conditions. In one, the students were asked innocuous questions about watching television rather than ones about death. In two others, students were asked about either death or television, but then on the table, instead of a flag, there was a plain white cloth, and in addition to the crucifix, a solid wood block. In these latter two conditions, the students could solve the problems without using the cultural symbols inappropriately.

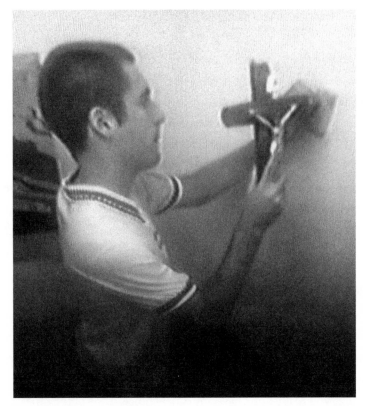

Participant hammering with the crucifix

As expected, the white cloths and wood blocks made for quick, easy, and stress-free solutions to the problems of filtering and nailing. Even students in the group who'd been asked to think about death beforehand had no problem with that. And those who answered innocuous questions and had to use the flag and crucifix did fine, too. In the control conditions, it took three minutes on average to get each job done. But those like Steve, who had thought about death and had to violate culturally sacred objects, took more than twice as long. They also said that they found the problems very difficult and felt considerable tension in trying to solve them.

The findings of this study establish that cultural icons help keep mortal terror at bay. Indeed, cultural beliefs would be fleeting and unsustainable without visible symbols and tangible icons that are imbued with extraordinary significance.

William Carney served with the 54th Massachusetts Volunteer Infantry in the July 18, 1863, assault on Fort Wagner in Charleston, South Carolina, where he was wounded. Later on, Carney received a medal for the simple act of holding the American flag up off the ground while the Union troops charged. Afterward, Carney modestly said, "Boys, I only did my duty; the old flag never touched the ground!"

ROUSING THE WORM AT THE CORE

If the cultural scheme of things helps to banish the dread of death, what happens when cherished beliefs are called into question? Do thoughts of death creep closer to consciousness?

LET'S SAY YOU'RE STROLLING down the street on a sunny summer's day to meet a friend for lunch. As you walk, you are enjoying the sights and sounds of the neighborhood. You pass a women's clothing boutique with a sale rack outside, a bookshop announcing an author's reading, a drugstore, an insurance company, and a Starbucks coffee shop. Passing the Starbucks, you briefly note the delicious smell of coffee, but you quickly forget it.

A few moments later, you see a woman holding a baby, and the baby makes you smile.

As you walk on, you see two people talking, one holding a clipboard. "Oh, not someone else asking me to sign a petition," you think. As you pass, you hear a snippet of their conversation.

"Just fill in these word stems with the first word that pops into your mind," says the woman holding the clipboard. She passes it to the fellow listening to her, who is smiling.

Intrigued, you stop and watch for a minute as he jots down his answers, then passes the clipboard back to her. "Thanks!" she says.

You're curious. "What are you up to?" you ask casually.

"I'm a graduate student helping to conduct a study of associative thinking," she says cheerfully. "We're asking people to fill in the following words. Would you like to help out?"

"Sure," you say.

Here are some of the words:

COFF _ _

SK _ _ L

GR _ _ _

At any given moment, some thoughts pop into consciousness more easily than others. Recent—even subconscious—experiences make thoughts related to them more accessible. Highly accessible thoughts come to mind quite readily. They are, as it were, close to consciousness. Since you happened to walk by a Starbucks, you might complete the word stems as

COFFEE

SKILL

GRIND

But let's say you passed a funeral parlor instead of a Starbucks on your way down the street. In that case, you would more likely complete the word stems as

COFFIN

SKULL

GRAVE

WE CONSTRUCTED A LIST of twenty word stems, six of which could be completed with either death-related words or non-death-related words. We figured that the more death-related completions people produced, the more death thoughts were hovering on the fringes of their consciousness. To see if this technique worked, we had people fill in the stem words a few minutes after they responded to our usual essay questions about death. Sure enough, the folks who wrote about themselves dying produced more death-related words than those in the control condition.

But would threatening people's cherished beliefs also bring thoughts of death closer to consciousness? To find out, Jeff Schimel and his colleagues at the University of Alberta brought groups with two very different belief systems—Canadian creationists and evolutionists—into their lab. All the study participants read a passage from an article by evolutionary biologist Stephen Jay Gould.

In the text, Gould cited evidence from the fossil record that directly contradicts the creationist view. Specifically, he wrote about the "walking whale," *Ambulocetus,* which lived 50 million years ago. This creature could walk as well as swim, proving that whales evolved from land- to sea-based mammals. "If you had given me both a blank sheet of paper and a blank check," Gould wrote, "I could not have drawn you a theoretical intermediate any better or more convincing than *Ambulocetus.* Those dogmatists who can make white black, and black white, by verbal trickery will never be convinced by anything, but *Ambulocetus* is the very animal that creationists proclaimed impossible in theory."

The passage undercut a central creationist claim: that evolution must be wrong because there are no transitional forms or missing links connecting various species. Then everyone completed the word-stem exercise. Creationists confronted with evidence in stark opposition to their core principles produced higher numbers of death-related words.

This finding is not confined to religious beliefs. In another study, Canadians read essays that belittled either common Canadian or Australian values. The anti-Canada essay was titled "Down with Canada" and opened with the statement "Everyone hates Canada, here are a few of the reasons I do." The tirade went on to mock Canadian food, health care, and sports. "In the U.S.," the writer noted, "hockey receives about as much attention and commands about the same fan-base as Monster Trucking.... ONLY Canadians care about hockey. Does the U.S. have hockey teams? Yeah. We also have professional bowlers, billiard players, sport fishermen, and poker players. We have loads of professional athletes playing insignificant sports ... LIKE HOCKEY."

Then came the word-stem task. Sure enough, Canadians pelted with condemnations of their country generated more death-related responses than those who read the comparably nasty assault on Australians. For creationists and Canadians, inducing doubt about a central tenet of their worldviews brought the worm at the core closer to consciousness.

THE APPALLING DISTANCE

We have now seen how human infants embark on the long journey from birth to acculturated individuals in a wider world of meanings and symbols. And it is no surprise that children perceive the world much as their elders describe it, given the enormous efforts people undertake to modify their surroundings to fit their culture's version of reality. Indeed, cultural beliefs, values, and ideals would be hard to sustain unless they were physically reinforced by signs and symbols everywhere, from crucifixes and flags on public buildings to movies in which masked heroes vanquish planet-threatening bad guys.

The scheme of things is so deeply ingrained that virtually everything we think, feel, and do is shaped by it. It not only provides each of us with our knowledge and explanations of the world, it also supplies the fundamental structure of our conscious experience. Right now, your current author and professor of psychology is writing this important book on Friday, October 10, 2014, at 1:55 P.M. sitting in his office in the United States of America. What could be more meaningful than that? But if he peers in from outside his cultural worldview and the meanings it provides, he sees just a warm-blooded animal pecking at a piece of plastic in the midst of an undifferentiated flow of experiences that will, sooner or later, inevitably be interrupted by a heart attack, cancer, car accident, or the ravages of old age. What time is it now for you, the reader? What does it mean that it's some day of the week, some month, some year? Isn't that all an illusory structuring of your conscious experiences provided for you by your culture to help you impose order and permanence on something chaotic and fleeting? If this is a Thursday, how comforting an illusion it is that there will be another Thursday, and another one after that.

All of which raises the issue of why you are now reading this book. Maybe we should stop writing, and you should stop reading. But we won't stop, and we hope you won't, either, because we'd rather slip back into the cultural drama in which we, American psychologists in the fall of 2014, are explaining how people cope with their existential predicament; and you, intelligent knowledge seekers that you are, are engaged in the meaningful pursuit of insight into the human condition and how it drives human behavior.

Take all the cultural trappings away and we are all just generic creatures barraged by a continuous stream of sensations, emotions, and events, buffeted by occasional waves of existential dread, until those experiences abruptly end. But in a world infused with meaning, we are so much more than that. Still, it is not enough to be equipped with our scheme of things. We humans feel fully secure only if we consider ourselves valuable contributors to that world we believe in.

To this vital striving for self-esteem we now turn.

CHAPTER 3

Self-esteem:
The Foundation
of Fortitude

———

The seemingly trite words "self-esteem" are at *the very core of human adaptation*. They do not represent an extra self-indulgence, or a mere vanity, but a matter of life and death. The qualitative feeling of self-value is the basic predicate for human action. . . . Unlike the baboon who gluts himself only on food, man nourishes himself mostly on self-esteem.

—ERNEST BECKER,
The Birth and Death of Meaning

FRANCISCO VELAZQUEZ, A FRESHMAN AT BALBOA HIGH SCHOOL IN SAN Francisco, was a pretty cool-looking guy, with spiky hair and sunglasses. He also had a gnawingly empty stomach by lunchtime. The smell of oregano-tinged, cheesy, pepperoni-laced pizza and salty, oily French fries in the cafeteria drove him crazy, but he couldn't afford to pay for those tasty items. He did, however, qualify for the free government-financed meal, which included an entrée of chicken teriyaki. Despite this, he and most of his friends decided not to eat at all during lunch period.

As it turns out, Francisco was not alone, as only 37 percent of eligible students were eating free lunches in San Francisco schools. Why?

Federal law requires subsidized meals to have nutritional value, so junk foods like pizza, French fries, soda, and candy are sold in a different part of the cafeteria. Students eating the free lunches are well nourished, but they are also easily recognized and stigmatized by their more affluent peers. As Lewis Geist, the student body president at Balboa High, explained, accepting government assistance "lowers your status" because lunch "is the best time to impress your peers.... Kids who wear nice shoes and nice clothes don't want to be associated with food that says 'I'm not able to provide for myself.'"

For Francisco and his friends, nourishing their self-image was more important than nourishing their own body. But why would they go hungry to preserve their self-worth? We have to delve into the nature of self-esteem to find out.

WHAT IS SELF-ESTEEM?

Self-esteem is a concept most people grasp only superficially. It means feeling good about yourself and believing that you are a worthy individual. But what does that actually mean? You might say to yourself, "I feel good about myself because I am a highly regarded member of my profession, a loyal and devoted partner and parent, and I generally try to do the right things." However, these sources of self-esteem do not spring fully formed from some deep inner self. Rather, they are a reflection of the roles and values provided by your culture's scheme of things. Your understanding of what the "right" things to do are, what social roles are of value, and how to properly fulfill your own role depends on your worldview. Accordingly, self-esteem is the feeling that one is a valuable participant in a meaningful universe. This feeling of personal significance is what keeps our deepest fears at bay.

Since cultures vary in what they value, the very same attributes and behaviors that provide self-esteem in one time and place may diminish it in another. In the United States, thirteen-year-old Jewish boys often mark the transition to adulthood with a bar mitzvah, involving a rather elaborate ceremony that includes singing a passage from the ancient Torah, followed by a celebration of dancing to hip-hop music and gorging on dessert. Sambian boys in Papua New Guinea mark the same transition by participating in the Flute Ceremony, which includes playing ritual flutes and performing fellatio on older boys and elders of their tribe. Imagine if the Sambian and American Jewish boy suddenly changed places. We'd witness how a momentous source of pride to members of one culture could be a totally meaningless or humiliating experience to members of another, because the behaviors and achievements that confer self-esteem do so only to the extent that we embrace a cultural worldview that deems them worthy.

People perceive what's "right" and "correct" as obvious truths, because those perceptions are shared. If everyone around you believes in the importance of the Flute Ceremony, there is little doubt that this is the way things are meant to be. How others react to our behavior tells us how well we are meeting the standards of our culture and, ultimately, whether we really are the valued people we want to be.

As we saw in the previous chapter, the seeds of the link between self-esteem and psychological security are sown in early childhood. Being good and doing good become associated with parental love and protection, while being bad and doing bad become associated with anxiety and insecurity due to the prospect of losing that love and protection. Cultures then reinforce these associations throughout our lives by promising great rewards to those who do good, and punishments to those who do bad, both here in this plane of earthly existence and usually in one or more subsequent ones.

Living up to cultural roles and values—whether we are called "doctor," "lawyer," "architect," "artist," or "beloved mother"—embeds us safely in a symbolic reality in which our identity helps us transcend the limits of our fleeting biological existence. Self-esteem is thus the foundation of psychological fortitude for us all.

HOW SELF-ESTEEM BUFFERS ANXIETY

Hundreds of studies have found that people with durable, high self-esteem enjoy better physical and mental health than those who don't have a stable sense of self-worth. People who lack self-esteem struggle with anxiety as well as a host of physical, psychological, and interpersonal difficulties. This large body of evidence certainly squares with the idea that self-esteem affords psychological security, but when measured variables—like self-esteem and anxiety—are associated with each other, we can't be sure which way the causal arrow runs. Does low self-esteem cause anxiety, or does anxiety cause low self-esteem?

In the 1970s, social psychologists began trying to sort out this conundrum by looking at what happens when self-esteem is undermined. In some studies, people were told that they did poorly on an intelligence test. Sure enough, this unwelcome news reduced their self-esteem and increased their anxiety, defensiveness, and hostility. Of course this is hardly surprising. But is the converse true? Does raising people's self-esteem shield them from anxiety?

To find out, we recruited participants for an experiment billed as "a study of the relationship between personality and reactions to emotionally laden stimuli." Everyone received a seemingly personalized psychological profile, supposedly based on their responses to questionnaires completed a few weeks earlier. These profiles were constructed to seem applicable to virtually anyone, but they were designed to convey either a very positive or a neutral evaluation of the recipient's personality. The neutral evaluation included statements such as "While you have some personality weaknesses, you are generally able to compensate for them" and "Some of your aspirations may be a bit unrealistic." The positive evaluation, designed to momentarily increase self-esteem, included statements such as "While you may feel that you have some personality weaknesses, your personality is fundamentally strong" and "Most of your aspirations tend to be pretty realistic."

To arouse some anxiety in half of the participants, we had them watch a short clip from a grisly documentary called *Faces of Death*. Banned in more than forty countries, the film shows shocking footage of napalm bombings in Vietnam, battle scenes from World War II, an autopsy, and a death row electrocution. The other participants watched a benign, death-free film clip of nature scenes.

Afterward, everyone completed questionnaires that measured anxiety and self-esteem. Not surprisingly, participants who received the positive personality assessment reported higher self-esteem than those who received the neutral assessment. And as you might imagine, those who received neutral evaluations reported more anxiety if they watched the clip from *Faces of Death* than if they watched the benign clip. But those who had their self-esteem momentarily boosted reported no more anxiety after viewing the graphic depictions of death than did those who had looked at the nature footage.

This experiment showed that self-esteem buffers anxiety, at least when people tell us how they are feeling. But talk is cheap. Maybe high self-esteem leads people to claim they are calm when really they're not. If self-esteem really blocks anxiety, does it also reduce the *physiological* reactions that accompany anxiety?

"THANKS FOR COMING IN TODAY, GEORGE," said our experimenter, Mark, convincingly costumed in a white lab coat. "This is a study of the relationship between mood, cognitive and physical stimulation, and physiological responses. You will soon be exposed to cognitive and physical stimulation while we measure your physiological responses."

Mark motioned toward a physiograph, a small machine that measures physiological arousal, and placed two small electrodes on George's fingers and a larger metal plate on his wrist. Mark then left the lab after giving George a questionnaire booklet and telling him that he would receive recorded instructions for the experiment.

"This is Sheldon Solomon of the Psychology Department speaking," the recording said. "The cognitive stimulation in this study will be provided by the Thorndike Anagram Test, a reliable and valid measure of verbal intelligence. Recent data have shown that scores on the Thorndike predict future career success. The Thorndike consists of twenty anagrams. You will have five minutes to solve as many anagrams as you can."

The first few anagrams were pretty easy. "LELB can be BELL, and

FIRTU is FRUIT," George thought. "I'm not sure about BLTAE or NORGA, but KASTE is STEAK for sure."

Five minutes later, the recording came back on: "Stop. The experimenter will now come back in to prepare for the rest of the study."

Mark entered the lab and tallied George's responses. "You did very well, George. Eighteen correct. No one in the study has gotten more than sixteen right so far. This puts you in the ninetieth percentile."

"Not too shabby for a psych major!" George mused as the experimenter went back to the control room for the next part of the study.

The recorded instructions continued: "After I am finished giving you these instructions, there will be a ninety-second waiting period during which the yellow light mounted in front of you will come on so we can measure your physiological responses in the absence of physical stimulation. The waiting period will be followed by an experimental period during which the red light mounted in front of you will come on. The stimulation that we will be studying during the experimental period will be provided by electrical shocks administered through the plate on your wrist. The shocks may be quite painful, but will cause no permanent tissue damage."

"Maybe I should have been an English major," George thought apprehensively. "Then I wouldn't have to be in these damn studies."

"You will receive between one and six electric shocks delivered at random intervals by a shock generator," the recording continued. "Because the shocks are generated randomly, they may come at any time in the experimental period. They may all come at the beginning of the period, or they may come at the end of the period, or they may be spaced evenly throughout the period. The wait period will begin now."

George noticed that his hands were beginning to sweat a bit as the yellow light went on. Anticipating the shocks, he recalled that the informed consent statement he'd signed said he could leave whenever he wanted and still get credit for being in the study. "I can take it," he thought. Then the red light went on, and it stayed on for ninety seconds.

That minute and a half seemed like an eternity. George was then relieved, and a bit surprised, when the red light went off and the recording announced that the experiment was over, although he never received any shocks. "Maybe the shock machine broke," he thought. "Or maybe Mark got shocked in the control room instead of me. That would be sweet."

Mark came back to the lab, disconnected the electrodes, and told George that the study was designed to determine the effects of elevated self-esteem on physiological indicators of anxiety in response to threat. "Generally, the more anxious a person is, the more the person perspires," Mark explained. "The electrodes on your fingers measure how quickly a small electric current moves across your skin. Because perspiration speeds the conduction of electricity, the more you were perspiring, the faster the current moved across your skin."

The backstory was this: Half of the participants in the experiment did not get any feedback about their performance on the Thorndike Anagram Test (which we concocted for the study), so their self-esteem didn't change. The remaining participants, including George, received feedback that they did especially well on the test of verbal intelligence. George really did get 18 anagrams right, but so did just about everyone else; the average score was between 16 and 18. It wasn't true that a score of 18 was the highest in the study, or that George placed in the 90th percentile. That embellishment was added to momentarily boost George's self-esteem.

Mark then went on to explain that half of the participants learned that the physical stimulation for the second part of the experiment would come from the light waves from the red bulb. The others, like George, expected to receive electrical shocks. "We figured that watching colored lightbulbs is pretty innocuous, but anticipating electrical shocks would cause considerable anxiety, except for study participants like you who were told they did really well on the test," Mark continued. "But no one was actually shocked, because previous studies had shown that expecting shocks is just as threatening as actually receiving them. Anyway, thank you so much for helping us today," Mark said, escorting George from the lab. "You're welcome," George replied. "This was a cool study, even though I didn't like the thought of being shocked. I wonder what you'll find."

The findings were, in fact, astonishing. Participants who received no feedback on the anagram task perspired considerably more if they expected to receive shocks than if they expected to see colored lights; no surprise there. However, participants like George who received the self-esteem boost perspired substantially less while anticipating the shocks, and were no sweatier than participants who watched the colored lights.

This is strong evidence that self-esteem keeps the physiological arousal associated with anxiety in check. Self-esteem is more than a mere mental abstraction: it is felt deeply in our bodies. Other studies have since shown that feelings of self-worth also diminish defensive reactions to thoughts of death. As you recall from chapter 1, people who are reminded of death typically defend their worldviews by becoming especially harsh toward critics of their culture. But when Americans who are naturally high in self-esteem or who are given a self-esteem boost are reminded of their own death, they don't react negatively toward those who express anti-American sentiments. Self-esteem takes the edge off our hostile reactions to people and ideas that conflict with our beliefs and values. With it, we face things that would otherwise upset us with far more equanimity.

Moreover, when self-esteem is undermined, death thoughts come more readily to mind. Recall that Christian fundamentalists generated more death-related word completions when confronted with evidence in support of evolution, and Canadians generated more death-related word completions when someone belittled their country. Threats to self-esteem have the same effect. Participants asked to describe themselves at their worst produced more death-related words than those asked to describe themselves at their best. In other studies, people produced more death-related words after receiving low scores on a supposed IQ test or being told that they had unrealistic career goals. Taken together, these studies demonstrate that self-esteem protects us from deeply rooted physical and existential fears.

DEATH AND SELF-ESTEEM STRIVING

Senator Edward (Ted) Kennedy hadn't excelled as his older brothers did. He was seen as the least promising of the four. His brothers all died as heroes and martyrs. Joseph Jr., a naval aviator, was killed in action over

Europe on August 12, 1944, at the age of twenty-nine. John, Ted's mentor and president of the United States, was assassinated in Dallas on November 22, 1963, at the age of forty-six. And Robert, the insurgent candidate for the Democratic presidential nomination, was assassinated in Los Angeles on June 6, 1968, at the age of forty-two.

A year after Robert's death, in the early hours of July 19, 1969, Ted took a wrong turn and drove his car off a bridge and into an ocean channel off Chappaquiddick Island, Massachusetts. His passenger, Mary Jo Kopechne, drowned, and Kennedy pleaded guilty to leaving the scene of the accident.

He had come to know a lot about death.

In 1979, Ted Kennedy decided to run for the presidency as an insurgent Democratic candidate against his own party's president, Jimmy Carter. He had outlived his brothers and felt ready to take on their mantle. But the scandal of Chappaquiddick effectively crushed his chances of winning the nomination.

Kennedy, nearly fifty, was a man with several counts against him. But he set out to carve his own niche, championing the causes of the underprivileged. The "lion of the Senate" fought tirelessly for the poor, the uninsured, the old, the disabled, the children, immigrants, refugees, and all the other "untouchables" of American society. He roared and clawed until the end of his life for their causes, and in so doing, he arguably achieved far more for them in his life than any of his older brothers did.

In May 2008, Kennedy was diagnosed with a lethal form of brain cancer. From then until his death in August 2009, he devoted himself to health care reform. "This is the cause of my life," he told the Democratic National Convention in 2008, saying that "I've got to get this right for history." And sure enough, Senator Kennedy intensified his efforts in the last fifteen months of his life to help push Congress toward ensuring that all Americans could have access to affordable health care. Ted Kennedy was a prime example of a central principle of human life: we combat mortality by striving for significance.

Research has borne out the fact that we strive for higher self-esteem in the face of mortality. After thinking about their death, Israeli soldiers whose self-esteem was strongly tied to their driving ability drove faster on a simulator. Elsewhere, those who based their self-worth on physical strength generated a stronger handgrip after they thought about death; those who based their self-worth on physical fitness reported increased intentions to exercise; and those who based their self-worth on beauty reported greater concern about their appearance.

Of course, when people are working out at the gym, or fixing their hair in front of the mirror, they don't necessarily think of themselves as pursuing a sense of personal value. They think about the exercise machine, or their hairstyle. But the need for self-esteem is constantly at work, prodding us on beneath the surface of awareness to maintain our protective shield against terror.

Like bats and worms, we fight like hell when faced with physical death. But we humans go much further. Even the slightest intimation of our mortality prods us to work harder to leave our mark on the world. We fight to prove our worth, even in the smallest of ways. Approval from our boss, a compliment from a friend, even an approving nod from a passing stranger can bolster our feelings of worthiness, while disapproval, criticism, and being ignored can send us reeling with a rush of anxiety. This unrelenting struggle to prove our value is one of the many ways we, in the words of poet Dylan Thomas, "rage against the dying of the light."

THE SCOURGE OF LOW SELF-ESTEEM

"If there were any doubt that self-esteem is the dominant [human] motive... there would be one sure way to dispel it," Ernest Becker wrote, "and that would be by showing that when people do not have self-esteem they cannot act, they break down." What makes it difficult to acquire and maintain self-esteem? And what happens when self-esteem is lacking?

There are two main ways self-esteem can break down. First, individuals, or groups of people, can lose faith in their cultural worldviews. Such disillusionment can be precipitated by economic upheaval, technological and scientific innovations, environmental catastrophes, wars, plagues, or unwelcome intrusions by other cultures. For example, before the arrival of the first Europeans, the Yup'ik people of Alaska belonged to a thriving culture ruled by deep customs, traditions, and spiritual beliefs. Their tribal and individual codes of conduct were defined by what they called the Yuuyaraq ("the way of being a human being"), which told each member how to behave in any situation. When the Europeans—carrying guns, germs, and steel that killed a majority of the population—imposed their Christian worldviews on the Yup'ik, the aboriginal people lost their identity. The medicine men grew ill and died, and with them the ancient spirit of the Eskimo and the code of Yuuyaraq. Everything the Yup'ik had believed in failed, and their whole world collapsed.

Such catastrophes occurred all over the world where indigenous cultures were subject to colonization. But other circumstances can erode faith in a cultural belief system as well. Even the United States may be in the midst of such erosion in the wake of economic uncertainty, church and sports scandals, and political polarization. As of this writing, seven in ten Americans believe that the country is on the wrong track; eight in ten don't agree with the way the nation is being governed. Church attendance, even in as strongly religious a country as the United States, has steadily declined. Public schools, particularly in urban areas, are in disarray. "We have lost our gods," Laura Hansen, a sociologist at Western New England University, told reporters for *The Atlantic*. "We lost [faith] in the media: Remember Walter Cronkite? We lost it in our culture: You can't point to a movie star who might inspire us, because we know too much about them. We lost it in politics, because we know too much about politicians' lives. We've lost it—that basic sense of trust and confidence—in everything."

When people lose confidence in their core beliefs, they become literally "dis-illusioned" because they lack a functional blueprint of reality. Without such a map, there is no basis for determining what behaviors are appropriate or desirable, leaving no way to plot a course to self-esteem.

And even when faith in the cultural scheme of things is intact, one still has to feel a valued part of it. Falling short, whether due to your ascribed place in society, your own failings, or unrealistic cultural expectations, is the second cause of struggles with self-worth. According to Hindu beliefs originating at least fifteen hundred years ago, the "touchable" castes emerged from distinct parts of a primordial being. Brahmans, the priests and teachers, came from the mouth. Kshatriyas, the rulers and soldiers, came from the arms. Vaisyas, or merchants and traders, came from the thighs. Sudras, or laborers, came from the feet. The Achutas, or "Untouchables," were repudiated by the primordial being, deemed dirty and impure, and consigned to tasks requiring physical contact with "impure" things such as blood, excrement, dead animals, and dirt.

Untouchables were beaten if their shadows came in contact with someone from a higher caste. They carried buckets to spit in to avoid contaminating the ground. They wore bells to signal their approach. Although discrimination against Untouchables is now technically illegal, prejudice and ill treatment against them abounds. In 2003, after trying to exercise his legal right to use the village well, Girdharilal Maurya's farm was looted, his house burned to the ground, and his wife and daughter beaten. "People treat animals better than us," Maurya observed. "This is not natural.... Why did the gods let me be born in such a country?"

Self-esteem is hard to come by when people inhabit social roles that others in the cultural mainstream view negatively. The Untouchables are perhaps the most famous example of this, but here in the United States, we also have plenty of stigmatized groups. Many white Americans still consider African Americans to be criminal and lazy. Many men think of women as little more than hyperemotional sex objects. People in "red" and "blue" states denigrate each other. It seems that every culture has social roles reserved for designated inferiors. And while having a socially sanctioned group of people to disparage is psychologically uplifting for those granted higher social status, there is little doubt that the people who are belittled often struggle to feel good about themselves.

Finally, self-esteem plummets when cultures embrace standards of value that are unattainable for the average citizen. For example, think of the many occupational roles in contemporary American society that aren't highly regarded. If you are a baker at Safeway, you know that you are not a famed dessert chef on the Food Network, that there are thousands of other Safeway bakers around the country, all wearing the same uniform and using the same recipes as you do. If you were a village baker in seventeenth-century Europe, people who depended on you for their daily bread appreciated your skill. If you were particularly good at producing a sweetly scented loaf or a tray of delicious buttery rolls, your reputation as the best baker in town would spread, perhaps among the surrounding villages, and you would feel a sense of ownership and pride. But today, the average baker at Safeway doesn't have much room for craftsmanship or creativity. Fellow Americans generally don't show much appreciation of their cake-decorating accomplishments; customers treat expert bakers like servants. Their paycheck doesn't express much appreciation either.

American society, in particular, puts great value on attributes and achievements that are unreachable for most individuals. The cultural value of wealth, and the humiliation of not having it, is a source of anxiety for millions, thanks to a glut of wealth-celebrating commercialism.

Consider the message in a 1990s-era American Express television ad. The ad portrayed a wealthy businessman trying to get home on a miserable, rainy evening to see his daughter perform in her school play. When his flight was canceled, he booked a first-class seat on another flight with the American Express card, while hordes of other disconcerted travelers resigned themselves to being stranded at the airport. After landing, the businessman grabbed a wad of cash from an ATM and dashed past a clump of dejected voyagers pelted by torrential rain at a bus stop; he hopped into a limousine that arrived at the school just as the play began. The commercial ended by reminding viewers that "membership has its privileges." The message was simple: You can be a person of unique value if you have enough disposable income to buy transportation luxuries that will get you where you need to go when other people can't. And to achieve that, you must have an American Express card.

The playwright Arthur Miller showed us the sad underbelly of this kind of cultural mirror in 1949, in his play *Death of a Salesman*. His protagonist, Willy Loman, has been striving all his life to be a successful traveling salesman. But as age and infirmity set in, his identity begins to slip away. The son of the man who first hired him hands him a pink slip. He's pinned his hopes on his athletic but underachieving son Biff, but Biff, too, is a failure. Desperate to bolster his own self-esteem, Willy imagines that both his self-worth and net worth to his family will increase if he commits suicide and Biff becomes the beneficiary of his $20,000 life insurance policy.

"Can you imagine that magnificence with twenty thousand dollars in his pocket?" Willy dreams happily. His tragic end is consummated in a self-inflicted car crash.

FOR AMERICAN WOMEN, YOUTHFUL beauty remains a primary determinant of self-esteem. Young girls compare themselves to Barbie dolls and the skinny and bosomy young women they watch cavorting in music videos and magazines. "They're so beautiful and everything," noted one young female high school student in a recent study of media and self-concept. "They have these really great bodies and they have the perfect hair, the perfect boyfriend, the perfect life, and they're rich and everything." In reality, the average female model these days weighs about 23 percent less than the typical woman, a weight that is up to 20 percent below what is healthy for her age and height. Models' pictures are routinely retouched to enlarge eyes, shrink ears, embellish hairlines, straighten and whiten teeth, and modify necks, waists, and legs—to produce images of inhuman proportions. When impossibility is the standard, most women are bound to fall short and disparage themselves accordingly.

Very few women are model-thin; none stay young. Very few men have the vast resources of Donald Trump or Bill Gates. And very few men, women, or children become famous authors, movie stars, musicians, and athletes. Given such unrealistic standards of value, it's no wonder that shaky self-esteem is the norm in the United States. And it is hardly surprising that one in ten Americans is clinically depressed and that so many suffer from anxiety, eating disorders, and substance abuse. These problems are, at least in part, a direct consequence of a culture that promotes rarely achievable standards for feeling worthy.

———

BECAUSE SELF-ESTEEM PROTECTS PEOPLE from their deepest fears, they will do just about anything to get it. The pursuit of self-esteem is a driving force behind just about everything that people want in life. As William James put it,

> A man's Self is the sum total of all that he *can* call his, not only his body and his psychic powers, but his clothes and his house, his wife and children, his ancestors and friends, his reputation and works, his lands and horses, and yacht and bank-account. All these things give him the same emotions. If they wax and prosper, he feels triumphant; if they dwindle and die away, he feels cast down.

Unfortunately, things don't always go as we would like. We all experience various failures, criticisms, rejections, and embarrassments that poke holes in the protective veneer of our positive self-concept. And we shield ourselves from the anxiety that our shortcomings would otherwise produce by telling ourselves little white lies to salvage our dignity: the low grade on the test was due to the deviously deceptive questions the professor asked; the spurned romantic advance reflects the superficial tastes of the object of our misguided affection. Moreover, we convince ourselves that we really don't want what we can't have: that high-paying job would have forced us to abandon our principles; winning that award would have required us to sit through a boring awards banquet and endure endless pompous speeches.

Sometimes the need for self-esteem trumps even the desire to succeed. We create barriers to our own success so we can use them as ready-made excuses in case we fail. "Of course my presentation bombed this morning," one of our students might say to himself, "I was up all night partying with my friends; and it's no surprise I got a D on that test. I skipped half the classes and didn't bother to do the assigned readings."

Most people, however, are more judicious in their use of self-deception. They make excuses to blunt the immediate impact of their shortcomings, but later step back and try to make adjustments. Navigating through the ups and downs of life requires a delicate balance between self-deception and honest objectivity.

But achieving such balance is especially difficult for people who are unable to form secure attachments, the building blocks of stable self-esteem, as we've seen. Distant, unresponsive, or overly demanding parents can create barriers to self-esteem that cripple a person for life. Being considered an outsider or a loser in a culture that values insiders and winners makes it difficult to get out of bed, stand up straight, and go to school or work. And sometimes really bad things do happen. Losing a job or a relationship can challenge even the most robust self-concept.

THE COSTS OF LOW SELF-ESTEEM

The list of problems associated with low self-esteem is almost endless: poor physical health, depression, anger, hostility, suicidal thoughts, psychosis, alcohol and substance abuse, adolescent smoking, risky sexual behavior, suicide attempts, eating disorders, self-harm, compulsive gambling, compulsive buying, and cheating. Regardless of how or why self-esteem is compromised, the result is the same. Suffering from high levels of anxiety, people with low self-esteem do what they can to reduce it.

Some compensate for a loss of meaning and self-esteem by adopting an entirely new worldview. Michael John is one of millions who found a completely new identity by becoming an evangelical Christian. Raised in a Jewish household, Michael grew his hair long in high school and moved to Humboldt County, California. He grew large quantities of marijuana until he was arrested on drug charges and incarcerated, where he discovered the Bible and Jesus and was "born again." Released from prison, Michael joined a Christian commune in Ohio, where he still resides, reporting that "I am very content now in the love of the Lord." Following such religious conversions, people like Michael report feeling that they have a greater meaning in life, higher self-esteem, and lower fear of death.

Others cope with low self-esteem by assuming a rebellious stance. They take refuge in gangs, cults, fringe groups. They become self-appointed outcasts, alienated from the mainstream. In fact, countercultural groups and cults often have their own elaborate system of beliefs and values. They don't transcend the "mainstream" so much as create a new one, providing social consensus to those "in the know" enough to find the "truth" they have to offer. They reserve for themselves that special sense of righteousness that comes from rejecting a corrupt, unfair, or constraining system. Although such groups are often harmless—they can even be helpful in fermenting constructive social change—some can create terrific harm. Think of the Bloods and Crips, the People's Temple, Heaven's Gate, Aum Shinrikyo.

Korean-born Seung-Hui Cho, who had a long history of mental health problems and social isolation, demonstrated how rebellion against compromised self-esteem can also be a solo affair. In middle and high school in Virginia, Cho was routinely bullied and ridiculed. In an English class where students were asked to read aloud, Cho reluctantly started to read with a Korean accent. According to a classmate, "As soon as he started reading, the whole class started laughing and pointing and saying, 'Go back to China.'"

On the morning of April 16, 2007, Cho entered a dorm at Virginia Tech, where he was a student. He killed Emily Hilscher, a young student whom he may have been stalking, and Ryan Clark, a resident hall aide who tried to help her. Cho then returned to his room and grabbed video and written materials detailing his view of things, as well as another gun and more ammo. He left Virginia Tech to mail his videotaped and written rants to NBC News from a nearby post office, then returned to campus, entered the engineering building, and opened fire on faculty and students in a classroom, killing an additional thirty people before shooting himself to death.

Do you know what it feels like to be spit on your face and have trash shoved down your throat? . . . Do you know what it feels like to be humiliated . . . ? You had everything you wanted. Your Mercedes wasn't enough, you brats. Your golden necklaces weren't enough, you snobs. Your trust fund wasn't enough. Your vodka and Cognac wasn't enough. . . . You had everything.

Cho's effort to express himself through the national media attested to his desire for recognition, to be sure. But he wanted more than that. He sought self-esteem as well as eternal fame—a point to which we will return later—by portraying himself as a martyr who represented the meek, even comparing himself to Jesus. And he wanted to be immortalized—as the most prolific school shooter ever.

Although most people with low self-esteem do not become mass murderers, research confirms that low self-esteem is associated with delinquency and violent antisocial behaviors. In one particularly large-scale study of thousands of adolescents in New Zealand, low self-esteem at age eleven was predictive of a higher incidence of disobedience, lying, bullying, and fighting at age thirteen.

GENUINE AND FALSE SELF-ESTEEM

Self-esteem does not ensure a successful life or great achievement; that requires innate abilities, excellent training, high levels of motivation and commitment, and persistent exertion. But self-esteem is a key to psychological security: as we have seen, it helps buffer anxiety, blunts defensive reactions to thoughts of death, makes people more resilient, and fosters physical, psychological, and interpersonal well-being.

What do people with genuine and durable self-esteem act like? First of all, they are steady; they score high on self-esteem measures over a long span of time. They don't claim high self-esteem one day and low self-esteem the next. Barring extreme events such as running a red light and killing someone, this overall positive self-view is not easily shaken and does not wildly fluctuate from day to day. Such people accept change as it comes and don't spend a lot of time comparing themselves to others. When you meet them, they seem to be emotionally calm and fulfilled, confident but humble, often putting themselves in service to others or to a cause.

The great cellist Yo-Yo Ma appears to be an example of someone who has this kind of genuine self-esteem. He is respected—adored, really—but he never seems to translate this into self-adoration. He seems to prefer thinking of himself as a cello-like instrument himself, a "vessel" through which music flows. "I'm glad I have a job," he has said, as if he were a happy waiter. "I'm grateful every day that I have that opportunity to be wanted and needed someplace."

Sometimes you may not recognize people with genuine self-esteem because they aren't necessarily famous or working hard to get themselves noticed, but those who embody this kind of stability and wisdom are out there. People with durable self-esteem are like big, strong oak or redwood trees; with their roots firmly in the ground, they can bend with the wind. They love openly, laugh at themselves, and savor the moment. They know they have made plenty of mistakes and own them, but they don't brood over them; they have enough self-compassion to understand that mistakes are an opportunity for learning. If they miss their flight, they don't get nasty with the person at the ticket counter; they get another ticket and wait for the next plane. In conversation, they are more interested in talking about you than about themselves.

Some people, however, never develop a secure sense of self-worth in childhood and come to rely on excessive boasting and extreme defensive distortions to try to dampen existential dread. This leads to an inflated but fragile self-image that provides momentary security but requires constant reassurance and is vulnerable to the slightest challenge.

An inflated, unrealistic self-conception is usually referred to as *narcissism*. Sigmund Freud (following the German psychiatrist Paul Näcke) named this personality type after Narcissus, the mythical figure who wasted away staring at his reflection. Narcissus was so handsome that everyone loved and desired him, but Narcissus was too proud to love anyone else. One day, Narcissus came by a clear pool and knelt down to drink from it. He had never seen his reflection before, and he fell in love with what he saw. He tried to kiss the image, but he didn't feel it kiss him back. Eventually, he realized that he was in love with his own reflection and, knowing that his love could never be requited, starved to death, pining after the image in the pool.

How do psychologists sort people with durable, high self-esteem from those with a narcissistic personality disorder? The most highly regarded and widely used measure of self-esteem, the Rosenberg Self-esteem Scale, contains sentences such as "I feel that I am a person of worth, at least on an equal plane with others," "I feel that I have a number of good qualities," and "On the whole, I am satisfied with myself." The more people agree with these statements, the higher their self-esteem; but they don't report feeling superior to other people or a need to be admired. By contrast, the Narcissistic Personality Inventory includes the following statements: "I really like to be the center of attention"; "I am apt to show off if I get the chance"; "I insist upon getting the respect that is due me"; "I can make anybody believe anything I want them to"; and "I like having authority over people." The more strongly people agree with such statements, the more narcissistic they are. People who score high on this scale also tend to think that terms like "perfect," "glorious," and "genius" accurately describe them.

While narcissists sometimes report high opinions of themselves on self-esteem inventories, their self-esteem fluctuates wildly and they make more rapid connections between words like "I" and "myself" and negative words such as "hatred," "evil," and "filth"—which psychologists use as a measure of "implicit" or unconscious self-esteem. By contrast, people with genuine self-esteem score high on both conscious and unconscious self-esteem measures. Narcissists are thus "legends in their own minds" consciously, but at the same time, deep down in the psychological bedrock of the unconscious, they really don't like themselves. Beneath their façade lurk deep self-doubts and feelings of inadequacy.

Narcissists' unrealistically high feelings of grandiosity and low levels of self-esteem make them prone to violence and aggression when their self-views are threatened. Lacking the resources for fending off such attacks that a realistic sense of their value would provide, they lash out at others to restore their damaged sense of pride. Studies have shown that people high in narcissism but not in self-esteem are especially likely to act aggressively toward a person who they feel insults them. Other research shows that narcissistic self-esteem is associated with bullying and perhaps other forms of antisocial behavior.

Moreover, narcissists are overly competitive, resent others who are successful in the same pursuits, and are disconcerted when others are clearly superior to them in some way. And they desperately cling to unrealistic images of themselves by carefully avoiding experiences that challenge their inflated self-image. For example, a narcissist who fancies himself a great runner might be at the track every day with the casual joggers from the neighborhood. He goes to great lengths to ensure the joggers know he can run faster than they can, and he works hard to solicit their admiration, but he's not likely to be found anywhere near the track when aspiring Olympic athletes drop by. Facing more able competition would paint a much less flattering picture of his actual skill and would fail to elicit the adulation that comes from zipping past the locals. In contrast, a runner with secure self-esteem would be proud of her accomplishments but more interested in self-improvement than winning. She would be eager to run with Olympic athletes; that way, she could get inspired, learn from them, and get an accurate gauge of her skills.

"THE FOOD IS GOOD"

As self-conscious animals aware of the inevitability of death, we humans "do not live by bread alone." Self-esteem, like the sturdy, graceful columns of the Parthenon in ancient Greece, is the foundation of fortitude. The psychological nourishment we get from self-esteem is no less vital than the physical nourishment we get from our daily bread.

Lacking self-esteem, we are like Harry Harlow's poor monkeys raised in isolation by wire mothers. We are persistently apprehensive, terrified by novel and unexpected events, in poor physical health, and prone to self-destructive and aggressive outbursts. Conversely, braced by self-esteem, we are encouraged and enthused—and thereby able to parry both psychological and physical adversity. Our experiment with the electrical shocks showed how self-esteem is a powerful vaccine against fear, not just psychologically, but also on a deeply physiological level. And many of us will fight to preserve our self-esteem in the same way that worms and bats will fight to stay alive, because for us humans self-esteem is our symbolic protection against death.

All of which raises the question: What can we do to acquire it?

One tactic is to encourage individuals to cultivate diversified self-concepts. After all, each of us is multifaceted: the same person can be an American, Christian, lawyer, Republican, father, golfer, Indiana Hoosier booster, and volunteer fireman. Different aspects of our identity correspond to different social roles, each with its own associated standards. Some of these standards are more attainable for particular individuals than others. Sure, other lawyers in the firm have more billable hours and your golf game is lamentable, but you're a great father, the go-to guy for driving the fire truck in tight spaces, and a highly regarded trustee at your church. We are all more worthy in some regards than others. By placing our psychological eggs in many different baskets, we increase the odds that we'll have durable ways to feel good about ourselves. Knowing which baskets are right for us is also important. You shouldn't aspire to become a professional opera singer if you can't carry a tune.

Another approach is to foster the development of social roles and opportunities for people who would otherwise be marginalized or ostracized. Consider the case of nineteen-year-old Kendall Bailey, a cognitively challenged autistic American with cerebral palsy. Kendall had not fared well in conventional schools or organized sports. But life got a lot better for Kendall when he started swimming. He practiced breaststroking—hard—and after he started winning Paralympic-sanctioned races, his self-esteem skyrocketed. Eventually he became one of the fastest disabled breaststrokers in the world. Kendall swam in Beijing in the September 2008 Olympics for disabled athletes. The Paralympics give Kendall and thousands of others with physical disabilities opportunities to garner a sense of self-esteem previously unavailable to prior generations of disabled individuals.

A RECENT STUDY OF COMMUNITIES around the world with the highest concentration of centenarians found that their old people felt like valued members of their extended communities. We have a lot to learn from the ancients; the youth, too, for that matter.

Back at Balboa High School, while Francisco Velazquez and friends went hungry, teenagers from Thailand, India, Myanmar, and Hong Kong, as well as American-born Chinese, happily ate the free chicken teriyaki. Sitting with a friend from Myanmar, Amruta Bhavsar, a senior from India, said she felt no stigma. "It doesn't really matter," she said. "The food is good."

WE HAVE NOW SEEN why and how psychological equanimity depends on maintaining the belief that one is a valuable contributor to a meaningful world. But how did we humans come to rely on these protective resources? And how have worldviews developed over the course of history to help us manage the monumental problem of our own inevitable mortality? In the next three chapters, we will explore these questions by examining human evolution and history.

PART
TWO

DEATH
THROUGH
THE AGES

CHAPTER 4

Homo Mortalis:
From Primate to Human

———

Culture and history and religion and science [are] different
from anything else we know of in the universe. That is fact.
It is as if all life evolved to a certain point, and then in ourselves turned at a right angle and simply exploded in a different direction.

—JULIAN JAYNES,
The Origin of Consciousness in the
Breakdown of the Bicameral Mind

HOW DID WE BECOME THE SELF-ESTEEM-SEEKING CULTURAL ANIMALS WE
are today? Although humans share 98.4 percent of our DNA with chimps,
clearly something radical happened along the evolutionary trail from primates to people. There is, psychologist Julian Jaynes proclaimed, a "yawning chasm" between primate intelligence and the full-blown consciousness
necessary to develop uniquely human cultural creations such as religion,
art, science, and technology. And while any effort to reconstruct our evolutionary trajectory is necessarily somewhat speculative, we believe there is
sufficient evidence to provide a plausible argument that early forms of terror management altered the course of human history.

The awareness of death arose as a by-product of early humans' burgeoning self-awareness, and it would have undermined consciousness as a

viable form of mental organization—hurling our terrified and demoralized ancestors into the psychological abyss and onto the evolutionary scrap heap of extinct life-forms—in the absence of simultaneous adaptations to transcend death. But our ancestors ingeniously conspired to "Just Say No" to reality by creating a supernatural universe that afforded a sense of control over life and death, enabling them to bound over the "yawning chasm" and cross the cognitive Rubicon that triggered humankind's evolutionary explosion.

THE DAWN OF HUMAN COGNITION

Evolutionary theorists agree that our lineage diverged from other primates between 4.5 and 6 million years ago. One major evolutionary innovation was bipedalism. Australopithecines like the famous fossil remnant Lucy walked upright 3.5 million years ago, but they had small brains and used no tools. It's unclear why bipedalism originated, but once it did, it increased the variety of terrains these protohumans could traverse and gave them greater access to resources. Perhaps most important, bipedalism freed their hands to explore and manipulate their surroundings.

Two and a half million years ago, Lucy's descendants began to fashion stone tools. This paved the way for the appearance 2 million years ago of *Homo habilis*, whose brains were one and a half times larger than those of the Australopithecines. According to archaeologist Steven Mithen, alterations in hominid family and social structure ensued. Breast-feeding mothers with immature infants clinging to them could not hunt or avoid large predators without assistance, so our ancestors began living in larger groups to ward off predators and obtain food, including meat, more efficiently. But providing protection and obtaining meat required males to collaborate in killing large, dangerous animals with very crude weapons, and to compete with other scavengers for carcasses.

Such cooperation would have been difficult in typical primate communities where sexual access to females is restricted by dominant males. Biological anthropologist Terrence Deacon posits that our inventive ancestors may have used some primitive precursor of the wedding ring. With the assistance of such a symbol, sexually active males could tend to specific females and their offspring while still cooperating with other males in hunting and scavenging. This would have minimized potentially lethal sexually motivated strife and made for much better social harmony.

Symbols conferred unique cognitive advantages as well, especially language. Our closest cousins the chimps cannot discuss what to do about that pride of lions they spotted the other day by the creek. Nor can they consider where to migrate next Thursday at sundown. With symbols, our ancestors could ponder images not immediately impinging on their senses, thus enabling them to better learn from the past and plan for the future.

Symbols also helped forge social bonds extending beyond face-to-face encounters. Like primates, our hominid ancestors practiced laborious social grooming, picking dead skin, bugs, and dirt off each other, which (besides conferring obvious health advantages) promoted group cohesion and coordination. As their groups expanded in size, it became harder for them to practice this kind of you-scratch-my-back, I'll-scratch-yours kind of mutual grooming. Elementary language may have originated as a substitute for physical grooming, initially serving a primarily social function.

Symbols and rudimentary language in turn stimulated the emergence of a self-concept, according to Mithen (and noted a century earlier by Friedrich Nietzsche in *The Gay Science*). Since communication probably often pertained to others in the group, our ancestors needed a way to differentiate themselves from others, so they came up with something like pronouns: *me* and *her* and *him* and *you*—and *I*. The personal pronoun "I," Becker observed, served as a "symbolic rallying point" for self-consciousness by giving each individual a "precise designation" of herself or himself. Facilitated by the development of language, although it's not precisely clear when, a few of our ancestors became fully self-conscious.

Psychologist Nicholas Humphrey argues that self-consciousness arose as an adaptation to social life. Individuals who could reflect on how they felt could in turn imagine how others felt and were thus in a better position to communicate their wishes to, and predict the behavior of, those around them. And as their ability to communicate through language improved, our ancestors became more self-aware. "The human being inventing [symbols]," Nietzsche contended, "is at the same time the human being who becomes ever more keenly conscious of himself." This stimulated the development of even more sophisticated language, and so a dynamic cycle of language and increasing self-consciousness was born.

These changes in social behavior and cognitive capacities occurred over a span of almost two million years, including another increase in brain size approximately half a million years ago. Then, between 100,000 and 250,000 years ago, our hominid ancestors made the miraculous leap to modern *Homo sapiens:* a new species with enhanced linguistic capabilities able to construct and communicate more elaborate chains of sophisticated ideas and to tell intricate stories.

Symbolizing, self-aware, verbally adroit, anatomically modern humans could now integrate their knowledge of social interactions, natural history, and technical skills to do increasingly useful things. They could exchange and refine their own ideas with others: "What's the best way to cross this river?" They could not just ponder past experiences, but imagine future possibilities as well. They could imagine things that did not yet exist, and they had the audacity to transform their dreams into reality. This capacity to strategize, to make decisions, to design and to plan based on an imagined future represented by words and symbols, is something no other creature on earth was then, or is now, able to do.

Our ancestors had become bipedal, self-reflective imaginative primates who could, as Otto Rank put it, "make the unreal real." How awesome to be alive, and to know it. What was not to like?

Drought, famine, pestilence, or disembowelment by hungry lions was not to like. Drowning and decapitation were not to like. And if you were lucky enough to elude all these catastrophes, witnessing the ravages of time transform an active, vivacious family member into a frail, mentally feeble shadow of his former self, and considering one's inevitable future in light of this transformation, was not to like.

In short, death was not to like.

MORTAL TERROR AND
THE INVENTION OF THE SUPERNATURAL

Symbolization, self-consciousness, and the capacity to contemplate the future were extremely helpful to our ancestors. But these highly adaptive cognitive abilities also gave rise to an ever-present potential for mortal terror. What happened when a life-form, crafted by billions of years of evolution to strive to survive at almost any cost, recognized that it was destined to lose that war?

"As a naked fact, that realization is unacceptable," proposed philosopher Susanne Langer, adding, "Nothing, perhaps, is more comprehensible than that people ... would rather reject than accept the idea of death as an inevitable close of their brief earthly careers." Our ancestors consequently used their imagination and ingenuity to stifle their existential dread. They were already employing their sophisticated intellectual abilities to ask and answer questions about how the world worked. But solving the practical problems of living was of little use or solace to them in the face of death. While mountains and stars apparently persisted indefinitely, our ancestors clearly saw that animate entities, subject to forces beyond their control, all came to an end.

Overwhelming fear of death, argues biologist Ajit Varki (working in collaboration with the late geneticist Danny Brower), would "be a dead-end evolutionary barrier, curbing activities and cognitive functions necessary for survival and reproductive fitness." People terrified by the prospect of their own demise would be less likely to take risks in hunting to increase the odds of landing big game, to compete effectively for mates, or to provide good care for their offspring. So our ancestors made a supremely adaptive, ingenious, and imaginative leap: they created a supernatural world, one in which death was not inevitable or irrevocable. The groups of early humans who fabricated the most compelling tales could best manage mortal terror. As a result, they would have been the most capable of functioning effectively in their environment and thereby most likely to perpetuate their genes into future generations.

Some supernatural beliefs may have developed prior to the knowledge of mortality. Evolutionary theorists such as Pascal Boyer and Paul Bloom propose that supernatural beliefs originated because humans are predisposed to attribute mind and intention to living things. According to this view, our ancestors projected their own subjective experiences of feeling, wanting, and willing onto their surroundings; trees and rocks spoke to them with power and purpose, and rain and lightning were both the language and the playthings of invisible gods. This proposition is quite plausible. But even if it is correct, as our ancestors subsequently faced the dawning awareness of mortality, these rudimentary supernatural ideas clearly formed the basis of more sophisticated belief systems designed to help quell the fear of death by providing a sense of continuance beyond it.

Consider the well-preserved Sungir archaeological site outside Vladimir, Russia, inhabited twenty-eight thousand years ago, consisting of houses, hearths, storage pits, and tool production areas. The remnants of multiple elaborate burials were also found there, including those of two young people and a sixty-year-old man. Each body was decorated with pendants, bracelets, and shell necklaces, and dressed in clothing embellished with more than four thousand ivory beads; it would have taken an artisan an hour to make a single bead. The youths were buried head to head and flanked by two mammoth tusks. By devoting such inordinate amounts of time and effort to generate these elaborate burial constructions, the inhabitants of Sungir seemed to show that the symbolic supernatural world they created took priority over more mundane, here-and-now practicalities. Moreover, the grave sites indicate a belief in an afterlife; after all, why bother getting dressed up for a journey to the void?

Such conceptions of the supernatural world were probably in place around forty thousand years ago, with the advent of what anthropologists call the Upper Paleolithic Revolution, or the Creative Explosion. This era was marked by the simultaneous appearance of art, body adornments, burials, and elaborate grave goods in many different societies. Sophisticated technology appeared at the same time. Campsites and shelters became more complex. Specialized stone blades and bone tools became common. The concurrent emergence of material manifestations of supernatural beliefs and extraordinary technological advances is consistent with the notion that the sophisticated cognitive capacities associated with consciousness could serve our ancestors well only when buttressed by confidence in a supernatural universe in which death could be forestalled and ultimately transcended.

RITUAL: WISHFUL THINKING IN ACTION

Our ancestors received support for their beliefs from one another, but they also needed some tangible signs that the invisible world really existed. Rituals, art, myth, and religion—features of every known culture—together made it possible for people to construct, maintain, and concretize their supernatural conceptions of reality. By making the incredible credible, Becker explained, humans "imagined that they took firm control of the material world," which "raised them over and above material decay and death."

Some scholars propose that rituals came first, and ultimately spawned the development of art, myth, and religion. How did ritual evolve? The Greek word for rite or ritual is *dromenon,* "a thing done." Rituals were unnecessary when a resource was readily available. Thirsty people on the bank of a flowing river do not need to dance for rain; they need only lean over and drink. And where food is plentiful, one need only pluck nourishment from a tree or a bush. But nature is not always accommodating. There was not always water nearby when our ancestors were parched, or food when they were famished. Predators might strike at any time. In the wake of such helplessness in the face of nature's indifference, our ancestors had to do *something* to enhance their chances for survival.

In tenuous circumstances, classical scholar Jane Ellen Harrison argued, human beings must act to ease their worry or grief, even if it means thrashing around and howling like an animal. Such spontaneous, idiosyncratic emotional reactions were probably the basis for the earliest rituals. But to become a ritual, an individual's demonstrative outburst had to be formalized and copied by others. A woman whose mate had been killed by a male from a competing tribe might have haphazardly outstretched her arm and thrust it upright with a clenched fist. Her friend might have copied that motion, refining and elaborating it with a sweeping arc. The two angry women would have moved together, echoing each other's movements. What began as a nervous need to express a deep feeling in one woman morphed into a dance between two; others, catching their contagious emotions, would have joined in emulation with their own danced outbursts. A few catchy or comforting snippets of a mournful moan, repeated and extended with a high or low note at the end for emphasis, turned the whimpering wail into a vengeance-seeking song.

Some combination of dance and song in turn likely formed the earliest rituals. Mithen notes that utterances that monkeys employ to defuse conflict and express emotion have rhythm and melody, and he proposed that early humans may have refined this propensity to strengthen bonds between helplessly immature infants and their mothers. Like modern humans all over the world, our ancestors found rhythmic movement and music and the social unity forged by coordinated activity soothing, even if the movements or sounds had no direct or logical connection to the precipitating event and could do nothing to change it.

And rituals were more than balms. They were also directed toward altering dire circumstances, because the essence of ritual is *wishful thinking in action*. We act out what we want to happen. Everyone does this quite naturally, as when we stamp on an imaginary brake pedal while riding in a car driven by a teenager accelerating toward a stop sign, or lean toward the center of a bowling alley lane to coax the gutter-bound ball to follow suit.

Magical dancing was common in Europe into the twentieth century. Farmers in Transylvania jumped high in their fields to make the hemp grow tall. German and Austrian peasants danced or jumped backward from a table to increase the length of the flax. Macedonian farmers threw their spades in the air after planting the fields, and after catching them, they exclaimed, "May the crop grow as high as the spade has gone."

Rituals almost certainly grew out of past successes. After a productive hunt or victorious battle, proud and happy hunters or warriors would reenact their experiences to an appreciative crowd around the campfire. But since not every hunt or battle ends well, why not start such ventures with the same wishful thinking in action? Instead of waiting for a great bear hunt and celebrating afterward by dancing like a bear, people danced like bears before the hunt to ensure they would not return empty-handed.

SACRIFICE AND DEATH RITES

Song, dance, and symbolic preenactments seemed helpful in making wishes come true, but more difficult circumstances sometimes called for more extreme actions. Archaeologists suggest that sacrificial rituals involving objects of symbolic or practical value, such as holy water, wine, succulent food, sacred animals, and even humans, were probably central to most, if not all, early cultures. If a terrible storm or flood destroyed their village, our ancestors felt that the gods—anthropomorphized entities who presumably oversaw and controlled the supernatural and natural worlds— had been angry with them and that they had done wrong. If the gods were angry, then blood was called for if more death was to be prevented. Given that the ancient peoples believed that their many gods had wishes and feelings much like their own, surrendering something of value to the gods was a sign of both apology and humility.

Sacrifices were fundamentally a trade: if the gods were kind in delivering a successful hunt or a healthy child, then it was only fitting to repay their kindness and increase the chances of future assistance. Lavish sacrifices of valuable resources were also symbols of potency and authority; by holding up their end of the deal with the gods through ritual sacrifices, humans gained a sense of control over life and death, a sense that the spirits would protect them in this life and welcome them to the next one. "The sacrifice of living things," Becker explained, "adds visible life power to the stream of life.... The sacrifice was a means for establishing a communion with the invisible world, making a circle on the flow of power, a bridge over which it could pass." Sacrifice brought death to the few to facilitate survival of the many.

Early humans were aware that plants and animals appeared and disappeared at different times of the year, so people adopted seasonal rituals, some to welcome new life, others to discourage death. For example, May Day celebrations in pre-Christian Europe coincided with planting crops for the coming year. A young boy or girl would carry a heavily budded tree branch into a village to infuse it with greenery and the spirit of life. In Thüringen, in central Germany, a ceremony called "Driving Out the Death" was traditionally performed on March 1. A figure of straw made by youngsters was dressed in old clothes and tossed in the river. Afterward, the children returned to the village and were rewarded with eggs and other treats. In Bohemia, children carried a similar straw puppet away from the village and burned it. While the puppet burned, the children sang: "We have carried away Death, and brought back Life." These rituals were not recreational; they were a matter of survival.

And death rituals are particularly important. The Fante of Ghana provide an elaborate example. The death of an adult male is formally announced by the *abusuapanyin* (the oldest living male on the mother's side of the deceased's family), who then presents a "notification drink" to the *supi* (head of the deceased's family on the father's side). The *supi* accepts the drink and summons the *kyerema* (master drummer) to broadcast a message to the entire community. All the men on the father's side of the family then gather to recount the deceased's achievements and work out the specifics of the funeral. Meanwhile, the *abusuapanyin* oversees the bathing and dressing of the corpse, which is laid in state at the family house. Then the *kyerema* leads a procession of men to the family house. A eulogy is given for the deceased, and the coffin is draped with flags. On the day of the burial, there is singing, dancing, drumming, and libations. Eight days after interment, dates are announced for additional rites in the future, to ensure that the deceased will become an ancestor who thereafter serves as a benevolent intermediary between cosmic primal forces and the living relatives.

Throughout history, and to this day, such rituals have enabled people to endure the loss of loved ones, dampening the dread associated with their own eventual demise to the point where they can continue their daily routines.

RITUALS ARE THE BEHAVIORAL bedrock of human culture. As wishful thinking in action, rituals empower us to sustain life, forestall death, and manage the universe. They assure our success in love and war. They determine who we are. You're not an adult until ritually fashioned into one. Ritual determines when you're married. You are not even considered fully dead until the official ritualizers—doctor, coroner, preacher—declare you to be. And if something goes wrong in our lives, we have an out: The problem is due to a wish or prayer somehow misdirected or gone awry. We must have performed the ritual improperly, or we need to add another step to an existing ritual, or create an entirely new one instead. Rituals, then, help manage existential terror by superseding natural processes and fostering the illusion that we control them.

ART AND THE SUPERNATURAL

On a Sunday evening in December 1994, three weekend spelunkers and amateur archaeologists—Eliette Brunel, Christian Hillaire, and Jean-Marie Chauvet—were exploring the caves of the Ardeche Gorge in southern France. They happened on the opening of one cave and began digging around in it. Suddenly, they felt a slight draft of air coming from inside the cave. With the help of smoke, they discovered the small hole from which the air was coming and opened it up enough for the small woman, Brunel, to crawl through. She discovered a larger hole in the ground. The men dug away rock to join her, and then they lowered a chain ladder into the larger opening. Climbing down thirty feet, they found themselves in a large, humid space with a domed, stalagmite-dripping roof. Looking around with their flashlights, they were amazed by what they saw.

All across the walls were beautiful images of short-maned running horses, so accurately rendered in their charcoal, sepia, and ochre clay hues that they appeared to be three-dimensional in the flicker of the flashlights. A pride of lions hunted a herd of stampeding bison. Hallucinatory figures of rhinoceroses, bears, lions, mammoths, and other fearsome beasts danced on the undulating limestone walls. In one corner, what looked like a woman with a dark vulva straddled an erect phallus. On the floor they saw the imprints of bare human feet and the fossilized remains of now extinct animals.

The three hundred or so etchings and paintings found in what is now called the Chauvet Cave were between thirty thousand and thirty-two thousand years old—the oldest known cave paintings in the world. The artist, or artists, had deftly incorporated the curvature of the walls into their work, so that the necks of the horses and other animals appeared stretched and muscular. "As I studied them, I realized I was in the presence of the work of a great artist," noted Jean Clottes, a leading French authority on prehistoric art. "It was like finding the work of an unknown Leonardo da Vinci. In prehistoric times, as now, great artists were rare."

The Chauvet cave yields something very spectacular: a feeling that one is directly looking through the very eyes of our earliest ancestors, far before the dawn of recorded history. When some aboriginal Australian visitors to the Chauvet cave beheld the art, they thought it must have served a critical ritual function. According to archaeologist David Lewis-Williams, cave art in general (that is, both the art and the caves in which it was painted) depicted the cosmos, consisting of supernatural, death-transcending dimensions and representing different states of human consciousness.

Our ancestors, like us, also noted that a cloud sometimes took the shape of a horse, a bird, a bear, or a rabbit and that the moon had a face on it. With the assistance of ritualistic drumming, chanting, or dancing, they enjoyed new sensations; by singing and dancing to the point of exhaustion, they experienced a kind of wild euphoria. With the ingestion of psychotropic substances, they hallucinated. In the absence of scientific explanations, how were our ancestors to make sense of all these remarkable, mysterious, wonderful, and frightening experiences and sensations? For interpretations, they relied on their shamans. It's possible that many of these shamans were artists themselves, or may have directed artists—in much the same way Pope Julius II directed Michelangelo—to produce images of heaven and earth like those in the Chauvet and other caves.

In many of these images, one saw an earthly sphere typical of experiences based on normal waking consciousness. There was a darkened watery netherworld below based on dreams or hallucinations involving fleeing and falling. Above, a heavenly spirit world depicted images of flying or floating. Cave art included recurrent dots and parallel curved lines, unusual hybrid creatures (part-human, part-animal figures), and animals apparently hovering in the air or coming in or out of rock surfaces. Handprints of ancestors dotted the walls as if to say "We were here," encouraging viewers to follow the marks to spirit realms on the other side. By making the long and often circuitous journey into caves and viewing the arresting images there, perhaps assisted by singing or chanting, Lewis-Williams argues, our ancestors "invested [the supernatural] with materiality and precisely situated [it] cosmologically; it was not something that existed merely in people's thoughts and minds." By visiting these caves, people "traveled" through time and the cosmos and experienced supernatural realms beyond death.

Indeed, recent studies confirm that such supernatural escapades serve to manage existential terror. After pondering their mortality, people fantasized more about being able to fly. Additionally, after visualizing themselves flying above a lush green mountain, people reminded of their mortality had fewer death thoughts hovering on the fringes of consciousness.

LIKE RITUAL, ART HELPED to make the incredible credible by offering concrete signs of a supernatural world. "Without art," mused George Bernard Shaw, "the crudeness of reality would make the world unbearable." Art depicting the supernatural, a feature of every known culture, is fundamental to constructing and maintaining supernatural death-transcending conceptions of reality.

THE MYSTERY OF GÖBEKLI TEPE

Thousands of years after human beings painted images in caves, they began to build architectural monuments. Among the most fascinating and oldest known of these is in southeastern Turkey, at a site called Göbekli Tepe. It is an architectural wonder for its time and attests to the central importance of death and the afterlife to ancient peoples. Some twelve thousand years ago, hunter-gatherers erected seven concentric stone circles on a hill. The site consists of a series of sculpted pillars arranged in circles, similar to those found at Stonehenge. Beautiful, detailed, three-dimensional carvings of animals—including boars, foxes, reptiles, lions, crocodiles, and vultures as well as insects and spiders—decorate twenty T-shaped limestone pillars measuring between thirty and a hundred feet tall. The structures predate the wheel and even agriculture.

*A stone pillar
at Göbekli Tepe*

Though archaeologists found no signs of human habitation or cultivation at Göbekli Tepe, they did unearth human bones mingled with the remains of vulture wings. (Vultures were particularly prominent among the animal carvings.) The bones were coated in red ochre and appeared to be the remnants of ritual burials. Diggers also found an engraving of a naked woman and another of a decapitated corpse surrounded by vultures.

Since each of the sculpted pillars weighs between ten and twenty tons, archaeologists think that it would have taken at least five hundred workers to hew the huge pillars, drag them from their quarries, and erect them. How were they able to accomplish this amazing feat of prehistoric construction? Why did these people erect Göbekli Tepe? How could they have been mobilized and fed? What did the pillars and the carved animals mean? What are we to make of this strange place?

After studying the site, and given the glaring absence of evidence of agriculture or living residents at Göbekli Tepe, German archaeologist Klaus Schmidt proposed that it was the center of a death cult, with the departed laid to rest among the gods and afterlife spirits and the animals carved on the pillars to protect them. "First came the temple," Schmidt concluded, "then came the city." Scientists had previously assumed the march of human progress was based on procuring food: we evolved from hunter-gatherers into farmers, domesticating plants and animals along the way and then building towns and cities around our collective farms. The discovery of Göbekli Tepe cast doubt on this assumption, suggesting that the problem of death motivated architectural advances that had nothing to do with practical concerns. These religious monuments predated agriculture and may have even helped stimulate its development.

Another nearby archaeological site called Çatalhöyük adds further support for this view. Research indicates that approximately ten thousand people occupied the site nine thousand years ago, a thousand years before the first evidence of domestic agriculture. The residents of Çatalhöyük lived in meticulously clean mud-brick houses clustered together in apartment-like honeycombs. They had some interesting funerary customs. Anthropologists found decapitated skeletons; the skulls were again painted with ochre. Also interesting was the presence of carved vultures, which also appear prominently in the carvings at Göbekli Tepe.

All of this is clearly at odds with the widely held view that human beings' transition from small bands of seminomadic hunter-gatherers to larger groups of permanent town dwellers resulted from the advent of agriculture. As Schmidt suspects, it may well have been the reverse. Living in and around monuments constructed for ritual and religious purposes may have encouraged people to learn to farm, which would not have occurred as readily if they continued to maintain a more nomadic lifestyle.

Alternatively, agriculture may have arisen, or been abetted, as an unintended consequence of burial practices. By this account, advanced by science writer and novelist Grant Allen in his 1897 *The Evolution of the Idea of God*, digging graves tilled the soil and got rid of weeds. Burying the best grains (along with other grave goods) with the corpses was the first planting of seeds; the decaying flesh may incidentally have provided fertilizing nutrients for the seeds. When new plants grew on the grave site the next year, people likely attributed their good fortune to the goodwill of their ancestors or the gods with whom they were believed to be dwelling. Eventually they would have figured out that seeds, sans corpse, would suffice to grow food.

The existing evidence strongly suggests that rituals surrounding death and the afterlife led to large gatherings of people and impressive technological developments that contributed both to farming and to other cultural advances that follow from the development of larger settlements and a less nomadic lifestyle.

MYTH AND RELIGION

As their language evolved from its original crude social function, our ancestors began using it to address the questions that can only arise, and must inevitably arise, in self-conscious creatures: *Who am I? Where did I come from? What is the meaning of life? What should I do while I'm here? What happens after I die?* Narrative depictions of supernatural conceptions of reality became possible, and necessary. Myth, like art and ritual, lends form to abstract notions like the soul, or the idea of immortality. Myth making, according to cognitive psychologist Merlin Donald, may have been the original function of elaborated language, rather than providing answers to pragmatic "how-do-I-milk-this-goat?" questions. Indeed, all human societies, even the most primitive and technologically impoverished ones, have sophisticated creation myths, ideas about the structure of the universe, and explanations for what happens after death.

The Tewa Indians of the Rio Grande Valley in New Mexico say that in the beginning their ancestors dwelled with spirits and animals in a dark and deathless world beneath Sandy Place Lake in the north. The first mothers of all Tewa were two spirits, Blue Corn Woman Near to Summer and White Corn Maiden Near to Ice. These two spirits asked one of the men to go aboveground to find a way for the people to leave the underground lake. Traveling "above," this man was first attacked by predatory birds and animals. But then the animals and birds befriended him, and they provided him with weapons and clothing for his return as the Hunt Chief.

Upon his return underground, the Hunt Chief created a Summer (Blue Corn) Chief and a Winter (White Corn) Chief, and he divided the people between the two chiefs. The Tewa then emerged from beneath the lake and, led by their respective chiefs, headed south along both sides of the Rio Grande River to their homeland. This epic journey had twelve stops along the way, with periodic pilgrimages back to the lake and surrounding sacred mountains. After death, Tewas return to dwell with the spirits, happy in the place "of endless cicada singing."

Myths provide the narrative justification for rituals and, embellished by art, form religion, which serves to regulate all aspects of social behavior. Religions delineate how we should interact with and treat each other by providing a purposeful, moral conception of a life in which individuals' souls can exist beyond their physical death. And religion gave our ancestors—as it gives us—a sense of community and shared reality, a worldview, without which coordinated and cooperative activities in large groups of humans would be difficult, if not impossible, to sustain.

Sociologist Emile Durkheim and evolutionary biologist David Sloan Wilson argue that the only reason religion originated and flourished was that it fostered social cohesion and coordination. Summarizing this view, science writer Nicholas Wade asserts that "religious behavior evolved for a single reason: to further the survival of human societies." While religions provided such benefits by shoring up extant social structures and interpersonal bonds, we believe it was their psychological appeal that enabled them to serve as social glue in the first place. In short, these spiritual belief systems thrived because they quell existential terror (and we will present evidence in support of this claim in the next chapter).

BOUNDING ACROSS
THE "YAWNING CHASM"

Rituals, art, myth, and religion likely developed more or less sequentially. But once in place, they all functioned, and still function, simultaneously and synergistically. Myths provide narrative explanations of the supernatural; art and rituals serve to embody and enact the myths. Taken collectively, all of these were essential elements of the development of cultural worldviews and how they became central features of human life.

Ritual, art, myth, and religion thus play a much more significant role in human affairs than it is currently fashionable to acknowledge. Many evolutionary theorists view art and religion as superfluous by-products of other cognitive adaptations that have no adaptive significance or enduring value. This view is simply wrong. These products of human ingenuity and imagination were essential for early humans to cope with a uniquely human problem: the awareness of death. The striving for immortality—universal to all cultures—forestalls terror and despair. Consequently, humans do not have agriculture, technology, and science *despite* ritual, art, myth, and religion; rather, humans developed agriculture, technology, and science *because* of them. Although "in their developed forms, phantasy-thinking and reality-thinking are distinct mental processes," wrote psychoanalyst Susan Isaacs, *"reality-thinking cannot operate without concurrent and supporting...phantasies."* We might not have calculus without grave goods, or dentistry without the tooth fairy.

The same cognitive capacities that enabled our ancestors to be self-aware—not to mention to live in large groups, imagine and create sophisticated tools, and plan and execute elaborate hunting and foraging forays—also brought the potentially paralyzing realization of death to mind. And paralysis was a recipe for extinction; so early humans, instead of succumbing to existential despair, placed themselves in the center of an extraordinary, transcendent, and eternal universe. Psychologically fortified by the sense of protection and immortality that ritual, art, myth, and religion provided, our ancestors were able to take full advantage of their sophisticated mental abilities. They deployed them to develop the belief systems, technology, and science that ultimately propelled us into the modern world.

CHAPTER 5

Literal Immortality

———

The charm of history and its enigmatic lesson consist in the fact that, from age to age, nothing changes and yet everything is completely different.

—ALDOUS HUXLEY,
The Devils of Loudun

Tablet 11 of The Epic of Gilgamesh

THE FIRST KNOWN WRITTEN STORY, INSCRIBED ON TABLETS AND BASED on an epic poem from ancient Sumeria, is a tale of a consuming passion for immortality that springs from an overwhelming fear of death. Gilgamesh was a spirited young king who lived in Uruk, an ancient city not far from Göbekli Tepe and Çatalhöyük. Strong, attractive, arrogant, and spirited, Gilgamesh was fond of pummeling the young men and seducing the young women of Uruk. When the beleaguered citizens appealed to the gods for relief from the young king's excesses, the gods created the wild-looking, colossally strong Enkidu to challenge him. Gilgamesh and Enkidu engaged in furious combat. Gilgamesh prevailed, but the two became fast friends after recognizing and respecting each other's power and skill.

Gilgamesh and Enkidu then set out in search of adventure and fame. Along the way, Gilgamesh rejected the advances of the goddess Ishtar. Furious, she sent the Bull of Heaven to wreak her vengeance. The bombastic duo defied divine law by killing the sacred animal. In response, the gods decreed that Enkidu must die. Enkidu fell ill and suffered immensely before he expired. Devastated by his best friend's death, in part because it made him realize that he, too, would die, Gilgamesh roamed the desert, weeping bitterly and lamenting: "How can I rest, how can I be at peace? Despair is in my heart. What my brother is now, that shall I be when I am dead. . . . I am afraid of death."

Obsessed with becoming immortal, Gilgamesh set out to find Utnapishtim, who was granted eternal life by the gods in the aftermath of a great flood. After an arduous journey, Gilgamesh located Utnapishtim, who promised Gilgamesh the secret of immortality if he stayed awake for six days and seven nights. Exhausted by his travels, Gilgamesh fell asleep. However, he got one more chance when Utnapishtim revealed that there was a thorny plant at the bottom of the sea that had the power to rejuvenate anyone who consumed it. Gilgamesh found the plant, and he intended to share it with the elderly men of Uruk. But on the way home, while Gilgamesh bathed in a pool of cold water, a snake appeared and ate the magical plant. Gilgamesh wept bitterly, for his journey was ending as it had begun.

———

ELABORATE BURIALS WITH EXTRAVAGANT grave goods from the Upper Paleolithic era suggest that our oldest ancestors harbored hopes of life after death. *The Epic of Gilgamesh* dates back at least five thousand years and is thought to have been a major influence on the Old Testament. In Chinese artist T'ang Yin's sixteenth-century painting *Dreaming of Immortality in a Thatched Cottage*, a sage asleep at a table imagines himself as an immortal floating over the landscape. The mission statement of the twenty-first-century Immortality Institute states that its primary goal is "to conquer the blight of involuntary death."

When it comes to efforts to transcend death, not much has changed in the last forty thousand years. This project has preoccupied great and not-so-great minds of every generation. Many ingenious approaches to immortality have arisen and endured. Some are of more recent vintage. All serve the same purpose: to diminish existential dread by denying that death is either inevitable or the end of one's existence.

Historically, people have aspired to become immortal in two often overlapping ways. One path is *literal immortality,* which is the promise either that one will never physically die, or that some vital aspect of the self will survive death. People have pursued literal immortality through spiritual paths that include belief in an afterlife and the soul, and also through scientific paths: first in the ancient practices of alchemy, and later through techniques for age reversal and postmortem resuscitation, such as cryonics.

A second means of achieving immortality is to assure that some aspect of one's identity, or some legacy of one's existence, will live on after death. This *symbolic immortality* promises that we will still be part of something eternal after our last breath, that some symbolic vestige of the self will persist in perpetuity.

To fully understand how people manage their existential concerns in the twenty-first century, let's take a brief look at the earliest historical forms of immortality striving and see how they have developed over time into the modes of death transcendence we presently rely on.

TREAT DEATH AS LIFE

In cultures across the globe and across the ages, people have believed that they could cheat death and have taken extraordinary measures to go on living after they died. Chinese nobles, following the proverb "Treat death as life," had their servants, artisans, concubines, and soldiers buried alive with them when they died. This tradition continued through the reign of Qin Shihuangdi (from 221 to 210 B.C.), the first emperor of unified China and the builder of the Great Wall. Qin was fiercely devoted to living forever and ruling eternally, and toward this end, he diligently planned and erected a great tomb. Constructed under a mountain-sized mound, the giant underground palace complex took thirty-six years and seven hundred thousand men to build. More merciful than earlier nobles, Qin was buried with an entire army of life-sized terra-cotta warriors and horses to protect him in the thereafter. The army was precisely positioned in burial pits to protect the tomb; the soldiers were fully equipped with chariots, bows and arrows, spears, and swords. Besides the army, terra-cotta servants and civil officials were entombed with him to help run the world: there were acrobats, strongmen, and musicians to provide entertainment, eye-pleasing natural scenes of gardens and life-sized water birds to soothe him.

The ancient Egyptian royals were perhaps the most well-known devotees of living well after death, an obsessive pursuit that lasted almost three thousand years, from approximately 3000 B.C. to the beginning of the Common Era. Egyptians' belief in resurrection was connected to the goddess Maat, who caused the sun to rise and set each day and the Nile to flood its banks each year and rejuvenate the soil. Maat also caused the dead to be reborn in the next world. However, these cycles of sunset and sunrise, flood and rejuvenation, death and rebirth, had to be continually maintained by the concerted efforts of benevolent supernatural forces, as well as by the pharaohs and Egyptian citizens. Each sunset signaled the death of the sun god Re, who descended into a dark underworld on a cosmic journey. If Re overcame myriad dangers along the way, he was reborn the next day, symbolized by the rising sun. Resurrection resulted from symbolically reenacting Re's nightly voyage.

A view of the famed ancient terra-cotta figures built to join
Chinese emperor Qin Shihuangdi in the afterlife

For the journey to the afterlife, royalty and nobility were entombed in the magnificent pyramids we're all familiar with, along with life-sized wooden boats for magical transport through the netherworld. Clothing, furniture, toiletries, food, and especially drink provided sustenance, and sanctified artifacts including statues of gods and goddesses and special jewelry provided protection. Sacred funerary texts called the Book of the Dead described the layout of the netherworld, the malevolent demons lurking there, and magical formulas for banishing them.

The journey through the netherworld included a stop in the Judgment Hall, where those who abided by the principles of Maat became immortal. Others were incinerated by the fiery breath of serpents in the Place of Destruction. Inscriptions from King Pepi I's tomb (2300 B.C.) describing the course of a successful passage include "Raise yourself. You have not died. Your life force will dwell with you forever" and "I have come forth in this day time in my true form as a living spirit. The place of my heart's desire is among the living in this land forever."

THE ANCIENT SUMERIANS, CHINESE, and Egyptians epitomize humankind's long-standing pursuit of immortality. While the grave goods at Sangir and the monuments at Göbekli Tepe suggest that our much earlier ancestors were devoted to transcending death, it has been abundantly clear since the advent of writing that humans have been extraordinarily preoccupied with living forever.

And the quest for literal immortality has persisted to this day. In the Islamic tradition, the afterlife is located in the heavenly (literally and figuratively) Gardens of Delight (Jannat Al-Na'im). Many Islamic texts portray seven different gardens devoted to different groupings of the faithful. There are gargantuan banners of praise hung above the heavens. "In the Name of God, Lord of the Worlds," "Praise be to God, Lord of the Worlds," and "There Is Only One God, Muhammed Is His Apostle/Prophet" appear in the first row. Each row has seventy thousand banners and extends for a thousand years. Miraculous trees in the gardens are made of silver or gold, with roots in the air and branches in the ground. Magical animals and songbirds abound. Temperate and chaste men are rewarded with houris—virgins devoted solely to providing pleasure. Men and women are resurrected in bodies of perpetual youth, unsullied by pubic and armpit hair or mucus and saliva. Food is plentiful and sumptuous; people eat a hundred times more than on earth with commensurate enjoyment. Alcohol and music are enjoyed by all, but without intoxication.

Nietzsche's famous declaration "God is dead" was premature in twenty-first-century America as well. In a 2007 survey of more than thirty-five thousand Americans conducted by the Pew Forum on Religion and Public Life, 92 percent reported belief in the existence of God. Two thirds viewed their faith's sacred texts as the word of God; 74 percent believe in heaven and an afterlife. More than two thirds (68 percent) believe that angels and demons are active in the world, and 79 percent believe that miracles still occur today as in ancient times.

Religious faith does indeed serve to assuage concerns about death. Strong faith in God is associated with emotional well-being and low death anxiety. Additionally, after a reminder of their mortality, people report being more religious and having a stronger belief in God. Death reminders make people more confident that God exists, and that God answers prayers; they also make people more interested in, and accepting of, supernatural phenomena in general. (This is also true for atheists, who, following death reminders, make more rapid connections between the word "real" and words such as "God," "heaven," "angels," and "miracles," which psychologists use as a measure of "implicit" or unconscious religiosity.) Moreover, reminding devoutly religious people of their faith enables them to think about death without reacting defensively.

A BRIEF HISTORY OF THE SOUL

Common to virtually all conceptions of literal immortality is the idea of the soul. Otto Rank proposed that the soul is one of humankind's earliest and most clever inventions, enabling humans to dodge death by perceiving themselves as more than just physical beings. As Rank's translators put it, "the soul was created in the big bang of an irresistible psychological force—our will to live forever—colliding with the immutable biological fact of death." Unencumbered by finite flesh, the soul's existence was not only conceivable, it was also certainly more welcome than the alternative prospect of total annihilation. Throughout history, humans everywhere have had souls, although the specific nature of them varies considerably across time and space.

For some, the soul is a physical entity with mass and volume, ranging from a full-sized shadow to a miniature replica of the body. For others, the soul is immaterial, but no less real. In some cultures, only humans have souls. In others, all living things have souls. In still others, all living things and minerals have souls. Some souls are completely independent of their body; they can come and go as they please, and they often appear in dreams and ritually enacted spiritual experiences. Others are connected to bodies to some degree. When bodies die, souls depart, either wholly or in part, depending on how the relationship between soul and body is construed by the culture. Some have an autonomous ethereal existence of their own.

Others join a general pool of ancestral "soul-stuff." Some souls are reincarnated into other life-forms. Others are reunited with their resurrected bodies. Regardless of the differences, all soul concepts render the prospect of immortality feasible because souls are detachable from their corporeal containers.

Some of history's most brilliant minds have tried to use logic and reason rather than faith to convince themselves and their fellow humans that the soul is everlasting. Socrates, for example, offered four very rational arguments for the immortality of the soul:

1. Everything comes into being from its own opposite: cold results when hot things cool off, hot results when cold things warm up. This implies that death comes from life and life from death. Dead people were formerly alive, but by the same token, living people must have been formerly dead, suggesting a soul of some sort that predates birth.

2. Because babies possess some knowledge at birth without any prior experience, there must be a soul that existed prior to birth that conveys this information to newborns.

3. There are two kinds of entities in the world, the seen and the unseen. Anything visible is corruptible and changes over time. But the unseen is pure and unchangeable. Bodies can be seen; they decay and die over time. Souls cannot be seen; they must consequently be inexorable and immortal.

4. Finally, everything in the world is caused by intangible and static forms that have always been and will always be. The wheel is a concrete manifestation of the form of a circle; four is a concrete manifestation of the form of even numbers. Wheels and digits come and go, but circles and even numbers, the "forms" that inspired them, exist in perpetuity. Similarly, all bodily activities are caused by the soul, which, as the source of life, persists after death.

The famed seventeenth-century scientist, mathematician, and philosopher René Descartes went through similar mental gymnastics a few thousand years later. Lest there be any doubt of Descartes' intentions, the subtitle of the first edition of his 1641 *Meditations on First Philosophy* was "in which are demonstrated the existence of God and the immortality of the soul."

Descartes started by declaring that only ideas he was absolutely certain of could possibly be true. Any idea subject to any doubt whatsoever he tossed on the metaphysical trash heap. To this end, he made a series of arguments that refuted the notion that "reality" as humans understood it was verifiably true.

He noted, for example, that while the external world certainly seems to exist, we often have vivid visions in dreams that turn out to be illusory upon awakening. How, then, can we know that the world we perceive in waking moments is real and the dream world isn't? Perhaps, he suggested, there is no physical reality. Because the concept of reality was doubtful, onto the trash heap it went.

He also observed that although our bodies certainly seem to exist, amputees often have sensations emanating from limbs they no longer possess. Given such evidence, how can human beings know that our bodies are real? Perhaps the body was also an illusion. This idea of having a body was doubtful, so he tossed it away.

At this point, Descartes realized that the only thing that he could not doubt was that he doubted. And to doubt, one must think, and to think, one must exist. So thinking made him real: *I think, therefore I am.* But you don't need a body to think. That's already been doubted away. Something does the thinking. A disembodied mind, or the soul, does the thinking. Thus, Descartes concluded, "decay of the body does not imply the destruction of the mind." Ergo, the soul exists. Case closed—at least for him.

Not just for Descartes. Soul beliefs are remarkably durable and persistent; almost three quarters of Americans in the twenty-first century are confident that they possess an indestructible soul of some sort.

LONGER LIVING THROUGH ALCHEMY

The ancients also sought to live forever by earthly rather than spiritual means. All over the world, people have cherished the notion that there were certain places where one could live forever, or at least for a very long time. For the Greeks, that place was the Isles of the Blest, located in the Atlantic Ocean and inhabited by a semidivine race that knew no sorrow. Persians longed for the Land of Yima, to the north and underground. The Land of Living Men, north of Teutonic territory, featured a race of giants who never aged or died. And long-sought immortalizing aids in the form of magical fruits and seeds could also help people live forever. For the people of India, the fruit of the magic Jambu tree provided the most fortunate mythical tribe of Uttarakurus with immunity from illness and old age. For the Celts of Western Europe, immunity from aging and death was attained by eating enchanted foods or using a magic vessel to be found at Tir na nÓg, the Land of Youth.

Stories of magical waters abounded as well. On the Japanese island of Horaisan, an eternal spring eliminated sickness, age, or death. The Hindu Pool of Youth dates back at least to 700 B.C., followed by the Hebrew River of Immortality. Alexander the Great searched for the Fountain of Life. In Arabic folklore, el Khidr finds the Well of the Water of Life. Ponce de León stumbled into Florida in pursuit of the Fountain of Youth. Ambrosia and nectar of the gods prolonged life indefinitely for the ancient Greeks; soma did the trick for the Hindus and Persians, and *octli* (an alcoholic drink produced from the sap of the maguey plant) for early Mexicans and Peruvians.

While some scoured the earth for eternalizing places and potions, others hoped to forge their own path to perpetuity through the practice of alchemy. "How happy it would be," mused Duke Ching of Ch'i in 522 B.C. "if there had been no death since ancient times." Fang-shih (necromancers) advised the nobles about how to cultivate "the way of no death" and where to go to find immortals in possession of "drugs of no death." Qin Shihuangdi's alchemists prescribed pills and potions laced with mercury and gold.

The Chinese ingeniously combined religion and life prolongation efforts through Taoism, a belief that promotes living in harmony with the Tao, an ineffable spiritual force that governed all existence. The Taoists worked industriously to prolong their lives. One could also become an immortal spirit, or *hsien*, directly, by perfecting the techniques of longevity.

(*Hsien* were believed to be able to travel at remarkable speed, control the weather, assume the appearance of assorted animals, or become invisible.) By strictly adhering to certain respiratory, dietary, gymnastic, and sexual practices, the Taoists hoped to prolong existence; breathing, in particular, was considered a bridge between the human and the divine, since air, by virtue of touching the heavens, was considered more pure and active than humans. Proper regulation of respiration thus yielded direct physical contact with heavenly realms and the immortality of the gods.

Fortified by proper breathing, diet, exercise, and sex, the Taoists could then devote their attention to formulating the elixir of life, made from gold. In the fourth century A.D., the alchemist Ko Hung summarized the Taoist approach to the elixir of life: "Who eats the elixir of life and guards the One [Tao], lives as long as heaven exists, he revives the constituents of his nature, stores up his breath, and thus lengthens his life indefinitely." Since gold is a noncorroding metal, resistant to chemical change, it was associated with immortality. Not surprisingly then, elixirs of immortality often included bits of gold. The challenge, of course, was to find enough gold, so the early Chinese (and Egyptian) alchemists tried to transform base metals into it.

The alchemists were at the vanguard of striving for literal immortality by not dying in the first place, thus bypassing the need for, and uncertainty surrounding, the existence of heavens, afterlives, resurrections, reincarnations, and souls.

THE MODERN IMMORTALISTS

We moderns have avidly perpetuated the alchemists' ardent disinclination to die. But instead of concocting elixirs of immortality, contemporary "immortalists" use cutting-edge scientific methods to forestall death in order to ultimately render it obsolete, and they take their work very seriously indeed.

Perhaps not surprisingly, René Descartes was an early pioneer in taking a scientific approach to life extension. Descartes foresaw the possibilities of modern medical technology, much of which is now routinely used. Confident that the human body could be understood as "an earthen machine," he reasoned that if the "machine" broke, it should be possible, and one day easy, to locate the dysfunctional part and repair or replace it. Circulatory problems, he insisted, could be eliminated with new blood; respiratory difficulties could be resolved with a new lung. The fact that blood transfusions and organ transplants were not possible at the time did not trouble Descartes. He shared with his Enlightenment-era contemporaries the view that progress was inevitable, and that in the future

> all at present known ... is almost nothing in comparison of what remains to be discovered.... [W]e could free ourselves from an infinity of maladies of body as well as of mind, and perhaps also even from the debility of age, if we had sufficiently ample knowledge of their causes, and of all the remedies provided for us by nature.

Descartes was preoccupied with longevity; he believed he could add a century to his days by studying medicine. He adopted a special vegetarian diet consisting of small but frequent low-calorie meals, believing that this could lengthen the life span by as much as five centuries. Descartes spent his last months in Sweden, where he continued to speak hopefully of extending his life considerably, or, better yet, living forever. He died there at the ripe old age of fifty-four.

By the end of the seventeenth century, blood transfusions had been conducted on dogs, horses, and humans. Although results were inconsistent at best, the occasional success gave researchers hope that rejuvenating techniques to retard or reverse old age were on the medical horizon. During the eighteenth century, bacteria, flies, and fish were among the creatures desiccated or frozen in unsuccessful revivification efforts. Still, by the end of the century, Ben Franklin, by no means a scientific simpleton, regretted being born too soon to witness advances in science that he felt could produce exponential increases in agricultural production, the development of levitation-based transportation, and the cure or prevention of all diseases, "not excepting even that of old age."

Ben was not alone among world-class scientists since the Enlightenment to dream of immortality, and efforts to defeat death began to show more promise in the twentieth century. The French physician and Nobel Prize winner Dr. Alexis Carrel, known for his technique for suturing blood vessels and thereby making organ transplants possible, devoted himself to extending life indefinitely. Carrel had already preserved living tissues for transplants, storing them for two months just above freezing immersed in saline solution or coated in petroleum jelly. He then took cells from the heart of a chicken embryo and attempted to keep them alive in culture flasks. One cell strain persisted for thirty-four years. Reporting these findings after three months, Carrel wrote: "the purpose of the experiments . . . was to determine the conditions under which the active life of a tissue outside of the organism could be prolonged indefinitely." His conclusion: *"La sénescence et la mort sont un phénomène contingent et non nécessaire"* (Old age and death are not a necessary, but merely a contingent, phenomenon).

In 1930, Charles Lindbergh, internationally renowned for his 1927 transatlantic flight from New York to Paris, approached Carrel in hopes of finding a way to repair or replace his sister-in-law's faulty heart valve. Lindbergh was an expert mechanic and, like Descartes, he saw the human body as a machine that could, in principle, be maintained indefinitely by repairing or replacing faulty parts. Lindbergh also had a personal stake in these matters, for as a child, he had been preoccupied with death: "When God first appeared in my memory, he was linked with death," the aviator recalled. "If God is so good, why did he make you die? Why should he not let you live forever? There was nothing good about death; it was terrible."

Together, Lindbergh and Carrel designed a perfusion pump to keep organs—such as the heart, lungs, stomach, intestine, and kidneys—alive after being removed from animals. In 1935, after the pump sustained a cat's thyroid gland for eighteen days, the *New York American* celebrated the achievement with the headline ONE STEP NEARER TO IMMORTALITY.

Although the prospects of "curing" old age are currently dim, mainstream scientists are working zealously on techniques to increase longevity and foster rejuvenation in the service of deposing death from the human experience, just like the Taoist alchemists of yesteryear.

One of these immortalists is a computer scientist turned biological researcher named Aubrey de Grey. A biogeneticist at Cambridge University, de Grey heads the SENS Research Foundation (the acronym stands for Strategies for Engineered Negligible Senescence), which is dedicated to eradicating the diseases of aging by focusing on the main culprit, metabolism. Metabolism, de Grey and other scientists believe, is a two-sided coin: while a fast metabolism is great for burning calories and fat, it also contributes to aging because it makes us wear out faster, analogous to driving your car a hundred miles more a day. Aging, they argue, results from toxic byproducts of cellular metabolism, the process that turns food into energy. So the fix, de Grey and other scientists think, is to slow down metabolism and clean up the age-promoting waste that it produces. The Taoists did this by eating nothing but berries and roots once a day, and it might have worked; the fewer calories you eat, the slower your metabolism runs. Research by these modern immortalists has showed that mice that ate 30 percent fewer calories lived 40 percent longer than mice that ate as they pleased.

To de Grey, "aging is the greatest embodiment of our failure as a species to escape the yoke of nature." And, de Grey argues, "If we are partially rejuvenated, we may live long enough to receive more complete repair as it becomes available." Dr. de Grey believes that sometime within the next thirty years it may be possible to rejuvenate fifty-year-old people so they can live to the age of 130. To encourage such research, the Methuselah Foundation (another group dedicated to extending the human life span, cofounded by de Grey) is offering a "Longevity Prize" for the oldest-ever *Mus musculus* (lab mouse) and a "Rejuvenation Prize" for the most successful intervention to keep an older mouse alive.

In 2004 de Grey declared that the war on aging will vastly accelerate when longevity research gets to the point where mice live long enough for the public to recognize the prospects for human life extension. Viable life extension therapies will then be available to the public, "albeit at a price that only the relatively wealthy can afford," he predicted. Dr. de Grey is on the money, of course; those with significant financial resources have more options than most when it comes to enjoying the fruits of such science. Not only can they pay for the very best in medical care, they can also avail themselves of technologies that promise to return them from the dead.

Consider, for example, Alcor Life Extension Foundation. Inside its square gray building in Scottsdale, Arizona, several nine-foot-tall canisters on rollers stand in a room like a row of stainless steel sentinels. Attached to each of them is a temperature gauge. Once a week, the containers are topped off with liquid nitrogen to keep their contents at a constant temperature of 196 degrees below zero Celsius, or 321 degrees below zero Fahrenheit, making them literally the coolest coffins on the planet.

When a member of the Alcor Life Extension Foundation dies, the team at Alcor springs into action. Doctors place the body in an ice-water bath, put it on a heart-lung resuscitator, and insert an IV to keep up blood pressure and protect the brain. Then the body is cooled to the point where oxygen isn't necessary to keep the organs functioning. The body is infused

A cryogenically frozen body housed at the Alcor Life Extension Foundation, Scottsdale, Arizona

with a preservation solution and cooled down more. Then the body is placed into the canister head downward, where it can literally chill out for decades or centuries. The good people at Alcor will defrost the body at some later date, while molecular nanotechnology makes it possible for the body to recover. The cost? Two hundred thousand dollars per person.

For the fiscally prudent, however, neuropreservation, freezing the head and the brain, starts at $80,000. This is the favored option of the majority of Alcor's many hundreds of members, for whom, according to the company's website, "it makes no sense to preserve . . . a large mass of aged, diseased tissue that may very well be completely replaced during revival anyway." One of Alcor's board members, Saul Kent, famously preserved his old mother's head in hopes that one day someone would grow a new body for it. Kent imagines that when he and his mother are both defrosted, they will be the same age, physically and mentally. "If I were to meet her, I'd say 'Mom, we are now in paradise together. It worked. It really worked.' "

Preserving her head required "cephalic isolation," or decapitation at the sixth cervical vertebra, and disposing of Mrs. Kent's "non-cryopreserved tissue" by cremation. Currently, Alcor's most famous neuropreserved client is baseball great Ted Williams, who died in 2002. Following "the event we now refer to as 'death,' " as Alcor puts it, Williams's body was shipped to the company's facility, where, after neuroseparation, his famous head and body currently reside until a viable cure for old age is discovered. Kent believes that once humankind has mastered cryonics and brought people back to life, "We're going to have powers far beyond Superman. You will be able to change your body like you will change your clothes. In the future, people may have more than one body. Your brain wouldn't necessarily have to be in your body. You could have adaptations, like a smaller body temporarily. By the end of the twenty-first century, there may be more differences between us and the way we are now than between us and the apes . . . we will be a new species."

How else can we use technology to keep going? Raymond Kurzweil, an author, inventor, and futurist who consumes 250 vitamin supplements a day to stay young, predicts that by 2030, human brains will be fortified by computer intelligence. He thinks that tiny robots called nanobots will monitor and regulate circulatory and digestive processes. Other nanobots will serve as minuscule trash compacters, replacing bowel functions. For his part, de Grey anticipates "non-invasive static uploading" to transfer all of the information in a human brain to a computer as a backup in case of memory loss, including one's sense of self, during maintenance or repair of the body. Sociologist Dr. William Bainbridge goes a step further to question the wisdom of returning a person's knowledge and identity to a physical body. Why not dispense with the body entirely and move the information into a more durable robot or just keep it in an external storage device?

Is a digitized remnant of a former human stored on a flash drive or computer cloud a person? What will "life" be like when, instead of posting images of your escapades on your Facebook page, "you" are a Facebook page? What kinds of interactions will you have with fellow virtual people "tweeting" and "digging" you in cyberspace? We will leave it to philosophers to ponder the status of such an entity and the "interpersonal" dynamics of this kind of society. Meanwhile, the fact that some scientists have no qualms about abandoning the body entirely in order to sustain a self in perpetuity reveals an implicit affinity for the religious concept of an immortal soul. This digitized self idea makes sense only if you believe that there is some essence that is not inherently tied to the physical body. What would that be, if not a soul?

Thomas Malthus recognized this surprising convergence of religious and scientific beliefs back in 1798. Best known for developing the idea that populations always increase more rapidly than the means to sustain them (a notion central to Darwin's theory of evolution), Malthus observed that scientists reject "the light of revelation which absolutely promises eternal life in another state" as well as "natural religion, which . . . has indicated the future existence of the soul. Yet so congenial is the idea of immortality to the mind of man, that they cannot consent entirely to throw it out of their systems."

WE HUMANS HAVE BEEN in dedicated pursuit of literal immortality since the birth of our species. Even if unsuccessful, such efforts have contributed mightily to human progress, technological development, and scientific discovery. Sophisticated mathematics began in ancient Greece, when Pythagoras attempted to find invariant aspects of life to confirm his belief that souls migrate from one body to another after death. The engineering skills necessary to construct the enormous stone pillars at Göbekli Tepe and the remarkable pyramids of Egypt were developed for religious purposes surrounding death. The search for a fountain of youth inspired epic treks to foreign lands and voyages across distant seas, leading to accurate accounts of the earth's geography. Chemistry and physics sprang from the alchemists' rigorous observation and measurement of metallic reactions; their experiments led to techniques for purifying water, producing modern drugs, and synthesizing plastics. The modern immortalists' contributions to medicine and nutrition have helped double the average life expectancy for people in first-world countries.

And while we cannot know for sure if Qin Shihuangdi or King Pepi ever made it to the afterlife, or if their souls are still roaming around in the ethereal mist, the fact that more people know about them today than in their own time attests to the fact that they at least attained a modicum of symbolic immortality. As the Egyptians like to say, "to say the names of the dead is to make them live again." Humans have always pursued immortality "by any means necessary." Toward this end, symbolic yearnings for immortality have accompanied our ardent efforts to literally dodge death since antiquity.

CHAPTER 6

Symbolic Immortality

———

The impact of death is at its most powerful (and creative) when *death does not appear under its own name;* in areas and times which are not explicitly dedicated to it; precisely where we manage to live as if death was not or did not matter, when we do not remember about mortality and are not put off or vexed by the thoughts of the ultimate futility of life.

—ZYGMUNT BAUMAN,
Mortality, Immortality, and
Other Life Strategies

This Grave
contains all that was Mortal,
of a
YOUNG ENGLISH POET,
Who,
on his Death Bed,
in the Bitterness of his Heart,
at the Malicious Power of his Enemies
Desired
these Words to be engraven on his Tomb Stone
"Here lies One
Whose Name was writ in Water.
Feb 24th 1821

SO READS THE TOMBSTONE OF JOHN KEATS, ONE OF THE GREAT ENGLISH Romantic poets. Far from family and friends, dying a slow, choking death of tuberculosis in Rome at the age of twenty-five, Keats was tormented by the thought that he would expire without having achieved the fame that he felt was his destiny. So he requested "Here lies One Whose Name was writ in Water" for his epitaph (his friends added the rest). If you visited the Protestant Cemetery in Rome, you would never know that Keats was buried there unless you were familiar with this gloomy memorial.

Keats's story is a particularly pitiable one. The son of a stable keeper, he lost his father in a riding accident when he was eight. He then nursed both his mother and his younger brother when they died of tuberculosis. He earned a license to work as an apothecary, but a small inheritance allowed him to abandon the trade and dive headlong into poetry. The work he managed to publish was roundly rejected and ridiculed. "It is a better and wiser thing to be a starved apothecary than a starved poet," advised *Blackwood's Magazine* in a review. "So back to the shop Mr. John, back to 'plasters, pills and ointment boxes.'"

Keats didn't give up. In the short span of five years, he produced many timeless poems including the astonishing "Ode on a Grecian Urn" and "Ode to a Nightingale." Before he became desperately ill, he was confident that his verse would live on after him, despite the bad reviews. He predicted, "I shall be among the English Poets after my death." And indeed, Keats was obsessed with death, which seemed to hover over his shoulder and dictate to his pen. At twenty-one, he was already imagining what it would be like to lie in his grave. "If I do fall, at least I will be laid / Beneath the silence of a poplar shade," he wrote in the poem "Sleep and Poetry," "And over me the grass shall be smooth shaven; / And there shall be a kind memorial graven."

The memorial he might have imagined then was not the one that ultimately came to be. His experience of life was too short. His body of work was too small and too immature. His experience of love was too truncated to have produced a child that could carry on his name. Mortally ill, Keats felt his life had been worthless. His self-esteem had fallen so low that he asked to be buried anonymously.

In the end, he did not believe his work would survive him, and he asked the eternal question that all mortals ultimately ask themselves. "Is there another Life?" he inquired in one of his last letters home. "Shall I awake and find all this a dream?" He came to the conclusion that there must be, for "We cannot be created for this sort of suffering."

But he did live on, at least in his poetry. He did, in the end, join the canon of the great English poets. And he continues to speak to readers through his art nearly two hundred years after his death.

John Keats's tombstone in a quiet corner of the Protestant Cemetery, Rome, Italy

THE QUEST FOR LITERAL immortality helps us manage the terror of death. But people also yearn to view themselves as part of an enduring culture tied to the past and the future: "symbolic immortality." A symbol stands for something: Keats's verses are not the physical man, but they represent the best of his unique imagination. Like him, we all want to leave a mark: we want to feel that something of us will persist long beyond our physical death. Otherwise our names indeed have been written in water.

"Modern man," Ernest Becker observed, "is denying his finitude with the same dedication as the ancient Egyptian pharaohs, but now whole masses are playing the game, and with a far richer armamentarium of techniques. . . . The hushed hope is that someone who can do this will not die." Keats's disdain for death and his desire to feel he would endure beyond it through his poems are obvious—he himself made them explicit in his work. As kids, many of us likely aspired to the kind of transcendent fame sought by Keats in his day or, say, LeBron James today. However, most of us, eventually figuring out we're not going to make it that big, deploy more modest, subtle, and even disguised routes to symbolic immortality.

Let's peruse these various paths and expose their existential underpinnings.

FAMILY IS FOREVER

In cultures throughout history, individual identity has been defined by ancestry. Knowledge of our ancestors keeps the past alive, and if those who have already died are still with us, then we, too, can continue to exist in the minds of future generations after our own death. This is one reason why the dead figure prominently in so many cultures. Recent excavations have found decorated skulls of dead ancestors in homes in the ancient city of Jericho. Today, in Japanese homes, you can often find a *butsudan,* or family altar, which displays tablets inscribed with ancestors' names. Americans now devote considerable resources to searching for distant relatives on websites to flesh out their family trees. Indeed, thanks to DNA sequencing technology, you can now spit in a cup and find out if you are a descendant of Genghis Khan, Thomas Jefferson, or even a nameless Neanderthal.

Our families offer us the promise of living beyond our bodies through our offspring as well as through their memories of us. Parents throughout the ages have beamed with pride when a cousin says that their child has "his mother's singing voice" or "her father's sense of humor." This delight reflects the hope that a part of you, be it a fondness for mirth or a twinkling gaze, lives on in your child. Your own body may rot under the ground or turn to ash, but those looks and mannerisms will endure in your bloodline as your own children pass those eyes and singing voice on to theirs.

Knowing that we are not the last of our ancestral line, we can better accept our own transience by believing that we live on through our children, and our children's children. Research around the world confirms that reminders of death increase the desire for children in the service of symbolically transcending death. Germans who wrote the first sentence that came to mind while thinking about their own death subsequently reported a greater desire to have children, and to have them sooner, than those who wrote about being in pain. After being primed with death thoughts, Chinese participants were more resistant to the nation's one-child-per-family policy, and Americans indicated that they were more likely to name future offspring after themselves. And after thinking about having children, Israelis reminded of their mortality completed fewer death-related words on a Hebrew version of our word-stem task, signifying that death was less troubling after the prospect of progeny was brought to mind.

But children are more than a physical amalgam of their parents. We cultivate our cherished beliefs and values in them in hopes that they take root and get passed on in turn. One friend of ours seriously laments that his son, though a successful attorney and fine family man, doesn't share his love of Wagner's operas and Kafka's stories. We don't just want our children to move our genes forward in time; we want them to move our beliefs, values, and group identifications into the future as well. In one incident that made the news, a Malaysian father shouted, *"Aku tak mengaku anak"* (I disown you), when his son came home for lunch merely wearing a badge of support for a rival political party. The fact that some parents disown, abandon, or even murder offspring who stray from their own beliefs suggests that passing on the symbols we cherish can even be more important than passing on our genes.

FAME AND CELEBRITY

Keats attained the recognition he sought posthumously, but like the rest of us, he would no doubt have preferred to secure that renown in his lifetime. Indeed, human beings have sought fame at least as far back as Gilgamesh. After he failed to gain literal immortality, Gilgamesh focused on enhancing his own reputation through deeds that "all the world shall know of" in order to "leave behind me an enduring name." He took solace in the idea that his deeds and accomplishments would live on after his death, as indeed they have.

Throughout history, extraordinary men and women who scaled remarkable military, political, economic, scientific, athletic, literary, or artistic heights became famous, not just in their time but after; for most of them, achieving fame for their accomplishments was a large part of the goal. Alexander the Great, for example, toted a copy of Homer's *Iliad*—in which heroic behavior in war was rewarded by "imperishable fame"—along with him on military campaigns. He also made sure that scribes accompanied him along on these exploits to record his unprecedented military exploits.

The word "fame" comes from the Roman goddess Fama, the personification of popular rumor. Fama repeated what she heard, first in a whisper to a few others, then louder and louder until all heaven and earth were informed. As this etymology suggests, fame has more to do with celebrity than anything else. It doesn't necessarily have to be conferred on superior or even good people. Those who lack the talent, skill, or prowess to achieve lasting, centuries-long greatness can also claim a measure of "fama" for themselves through other means.

In China, for example, an undistinguished minor official during the Jin Dynasty, Ge Hong (A.D. 283–343), desperately wanted to be immortal. He figured out a way to live beyond the grave by writing about himself. A literary wannabe, he was an avid practitioner of Taoist longevity techniques, and he was especially keen on developing a gold-based elixir of immortality. He also viewed fame as a viable alternative to literal immortality if his elixir proved elusive, observing that while "physical forms sink into the earth, praise [of good men] continues to circulate and be recorded. Thus, whether a hundred or a thousand generations pass, people still remember [great men] this way."

However, Ge Hong was painfully aware that he was unlikely to attract the attention of historians. Consequently, he wrote an autobiographical account of his life with the explicit hope that he might be remembered by future generations. (Our mention of him here reveals that his effort to immortalize himself was not in vain!) Ge Hong was thousands of years ahead of his time in thinking that he could achieve lasting fame without any noteworthy achievements. By the sixteenth century, the invention of the printing press and the increasing popularity of portrait painting enabled many more people to have their life stories and physical images preserved for the future.

Celebrities are known for being known, even if they have never done anything particularly noteworthy or productive. In the 1960s, Andy Warhol famously predicted, "In the future everyone will be famous for fifteen minutes." Less known, but perhaps more prescient, was Warhol's conjecture a decade later: "In fifteen minutes, everybody will be famous."

What a perfect depiction of the twenty-first century. In 334 B.C., Alexander the Great took ten years to conquer the world and earn enduring fame. In 2009, Joey "Jaws" Chestnut took ten minutes to devour sixty-eight hot dogs and garner international renown. Today, anyone with a cell phone who is camera-savvy enough to document himself stumbling around in a drunken stupor is a YouTube upload away from notoriety, albeit quite fleeting. The more sublimely ridiculous, the better: a sexy blonde named Justine Ezarik, known as a "lifecaster," has posted more than seventeen hundred videos on YouTube. She is so popular that her video story about trying to order a cheeseburger in a posh restaurant (featuring nothing but her Barbie-like face in different expressions) garnered six hundred thousand views in a week, earning her star status and guest TV appearances.

CELEBRITY CAN EVEN HAVE a psychologically uplifting effect on others. Try this thought experiment:

You're boarding a morning plane from New York to London, and you have a ticket in coach. The first-class passengers have already boarded and are sipping their coffee and orange juice, and as you walk by them you enviously check them out. There is one square-jawed fellow wearing sunglasses, a baseball cap pulled low, and a one-day grizzle who is reading a newspaper. He clearly doesn't want to be recognized, but he looks a little familiar. You know you've seen him before.

The liftoff goes smoothly, and soon the flight crew is coming around to take drink orders. Then the pilot's voice comes over the PA system. "Folks, it looks like we're going to get some severe turbulence up ahead. Please return to your seats and fasten your seat belts."

You tighten your seat belt a little anxiously. A few minutes later, the plane feels like it's been walloped on the right side. It bucks for a bit, stabilizes, and then it feels like the bottom has fallen out. As you go down, people start to scream. Babies cry. The woman next to you has gone white, and she is fingering the crucifix around her neck. The thought occurs to you that the plane will end up in the Atlantic. You remember that the people on the American Airlines flight that flew into the Twin Towers called their loved ones on their cell phones to say goodbye. You start to reach for yours, then think again. "Hold on," you tell yourself. "Breathe."

You breathe, and the plane stops dropping, but it continues to buck like a rodeo horse. Then, mercifully, the bucking stops and the plane smooths out. You and everyone else on board breathe a huge sigh of relief. A cheer goes up. "Sorry, folks," says the pilot. "That was a big one. We're going to raise our elevation, and hopefully we'll be able avoid more turbulence."

People are talking all around you. The person in the seat behind you says, "Wow. Did you know George Clooney is on this plane? He's sitting up in first class. Maybe that's why we didn't go down."

If this sounds superstitious, it is; but research has shown that in fact, people believe that a plane is less likely to crash if a famous person is among the passengers, because proximity to a famous person confers upon you some magical sense of your own immortality.

Thoughts of death also increase admiration for famous people and belief in the lasting nature of their work. After a death reminder, Americans viewed abstract paintings reputedly created either by Johnny Depp or by a relatively unknown artist, and they found the paintings "by" Johnny Depp more admirable. Death enhances our regard for celebrities because they provide proof that being remembered "forever" is possible.

Continuing the thought experiment, imagine you get to London and settle in at your hotel. You're still rattled, and you can't quite get the feeling of having had a near-death experience out of your mind. You call your spouse and tell him or her all about it, and about what the passenger behind you said about the movie star on the plane.

Then you turn on the television and absentmindedly start flipping through the channels. You run across an ad for a website called Namestar .net, which says that for the low, low price of $28.95 you can name a star after someone. "Looking for a unique, personalized gift?" the voice-over asks. "Give a star a name for someone! Don't let this opportunity to immortalize a loved one pass you by! Buy the Name a Star gift package for that special someone now! The perfect gift for all occasions." "What a great idea," you think. "I need a star for me."

One of our studies confirmed the plausibility of this anecdote. Participants were shown an advertisement for "YourStar.com," a now defunct Internet-based service, where people could pay to have a star named after them. YourStar.com claimed to work with an outfit called the Universal Star Council to ensure that each star is permanently registered with only one name, allowing the person to "own" a star for billions of years. After thinking about dying, people reported greater interest in having a star named after them, and a willingness to spend more money to do so.

In short, if you can't be a star, at least you can have one named after you that will be around for billions of years. And if you are utterly desperate or mentally unstable, you can seek lasting renown by committing horrible crimes. In a special Secret Service project conducted in the 1990s, psychologists studied case reviews of eighty-three people who attacked or threatened a prominent public official or popular figure. Achieving notoriety topped their list of motives. As a murderer in Wichita, Kansas, put it in 1978, "How many times do I have to kill before I get my name in the paper

Celebrities get their own stars on the Hollywood Walk of Fame,
although, perhaps like all forms of symbolic immortality, up close
and over time they look a bit dingy and lose their luster.

or some national attention?" Keats and a vicious murderer could not be
more dissimilar, yet the same underlying desire motivated their sublime
and egregious accomplishments.

LIVING LARGE: THE ALLURE OF WEALTH

If you can't pray your way into heaven, wait until science conquers death,
feel sufficiently fortified by your place in an ongoing ancestral line, or become famous, money and stuff offer another gateway to immortality. The
trappings of wealth are about much more than comfort and aesthetics.

They are also about feeling special and therefore immune to life's normal limitations.

Traditional economists assume that money was originally created, and still serves, only to facilitate the exchange of goods and services. As the Nobel economist Paul Krugman depicts this view, "The hypothetical Economic Man knows what he wants [and] his choices are driven by rational calculations ... whether consumers are deciding between corn flakes or shredded wheat, or investors are deciding between stocks and bonds." From this perspective, all economic activity, and human behavior in general, results from considering the costs and benefits (although not always consciously) of existing options and choosing the best—that is, the most useful—alternative. However, we humans behave like *Homo economicus* only on occasion, and this über-rational conception of money and consumption does not tell the whole story, for money serves an archetypal role in human ritual and religion in direct service of transcending death.

Thousands of years ago, money originated in religious rituals as consecrated tokens with immortal connotations. The sacred value of the exchange was its primary purpose. In ancient Greece, families held communal feasts in honor of their heroic ancestors. The families believed that ancestors had the character and power of immortal gods and could thus provide protection, advice, and direction for their living progeny. So the living relatives sacrificed bulls (the word "capital" comes from "cattle") and roasted them on spits. Then they distributed the pieces of meat to everyone in attendance, withholding only the "surplus," a piece left on the spit to be "consumed" by the fire as an offering to the heroic ancestors.

The "surplus" meat on the spit was called the *obelos,* or "coin" (related to the word "obligation"). *Obeloi* were also made from pieces of metal, bearing images of individual ancestors. Outsiders could use these coins to join the feasts. People would eagerly trade goods in order to obtain these highly valued coins. Because they attributed magical qualities to the coins, people began to worship them. Carried as amulets, the coins derived their power from "basking in reflected glory" of the heroic ancestors depicted on them. In this way, the coins used in the communal feast kept the ancestors' sacred power circulating. Sacrificing the bulls and giving the surplus to the dead ancestors showed reverence for the past. Sharing one's food with ancestors imbued the living with supernatural attributes to ensure prosperity in the future.

Originally, then, people didn't want money to buy stuff. They wanted stuff to exchange for money. Money was a tangible repository of supernatural clout. It still is. In Fiji, money is called *tambua*, derived from the word *tambu*, which means "sacred." In New Guinea, the Wodani of Irian Jaya use shell money; each shell is different and perceived as an immortal person. Gold has always been both a highly valued religious symbol of immortality and cherished coinage in many cultures throughout history. Then take a look at the back of an American dollar bill: *In God We Trust.* On the left of the bill is a pyramid, with an enlightened (literally) eyeball embedded in the top. According to Joseph Campbell, this symbolizes the eye of God opening at the apex of the pyramid conferring immortality to those who reach the top.

Although early humans valued money and possessions, they disdained having to work to get them. In the biblical story of Genesis, Adam and Eve lived an idyllic leisurely life until they were cast out of the Garden of Eden as punishment for their sins: "By the sweat of your brow you will eat your food until you return to the ground, since from it you were taken; for dust you are and to dust you will return." The Bible explicitly linked work to both sin and death. The ancient Greeks also viewed manual labor as beneath the dignity of upper-class people. Plato and Aristotle emphasized that the majority of men labored "in order that the minority, the élite, might engage in pure exercises of the mind—art, philosophy, and politics."

Money, like fame, also confers the kind of laurel wreath that Keats was after—being well regarded by those still living. In *The Theory of Moral Sentiments,* the less well known complement to his canonical work *The Wealth of Nations,* Adam Smith observed that people pursue wealth not to "supply the necessities of nature" so much as to procure "superfluities" that satisfy the fundamental psychological imperative to be thought well of by others: "It is not wealth that men desire, but the consideration and good opinion that wait upon riches."

The physical stuff we accumulate may well last longer than we do. And, along with DNA, some fortunate people also inherit money and physical stuff. Amassing wealth marked the beginning of an ancient transition from relatively egalitarian seminomadic hunter-gatherer communities—in which people were valued for their actual abilities—to agricultural and industrial societies, in which people were measured less by actual achievement and more by prestige, which itself was largely based upon the acquisition and exhibition of wealth.

For aboriginal people, one way to secure power was to hold gift-giving festivals called "potlatches," which were their versions of extravagant holiday parties. As anthropologist Sergei Kan put it, a primary objective of the potlatch "was to create an impression of an endless supply of wealth." Members of Native American tribes of the Pacific coast from Oregon to Alaska have for centuries held potlatches on special occasions to display their wealth and thereby establish superiority over their peers. After months or years accumulating excessive resources, the wealthiest families would host festivities that began with dancing, singing, speeches, and feasting. The host then distributed gifts to the guests, including fish, meat, berries, skins, blankets, slaves, and copper shields. This process could take several days. Guests were often cajoled to accept more gifts than they could carry and eat more food than they could stomach. As gracious recipients of their neighbor's display of wealth, they were obliged to hold potlatches of their own, at which they tried to give gifts of greater value than those they had received in order to flaunt their own affluence. It was a competitive besting.

For those in larger societies, the accumulation of property and material goods also signaled royalty and privilege. In America, the term "conspicuous consumption" was coined during the Gilded Age to describe the profligate spending of moneyed families such as the Rockefellers, Carnegies, and Vanderbilts. In the 1890s, when 92 percent of Americans earned less than $1,200 a year (with an average income of $380), Newport socialite Mamie Fish held an extravagant dinner party in honor of her dog, who came decked out in a $15,000 diamond collar. Not to be outdone, Theresa Oelrichs decorated her estate with white flowers and swans, and commissioned a flotilla of white ships to hover offshore. Grace Vanderbilt brought the cast of a popular Broadway show to Newport to play at a theater she had specially constructed on her property.

And just before the economic meltdown instigating the current recession, the Robb Report's 2007 Ultimate Gift Guide for Christmas included a 459-foot six-story "giga-yacht" for $250 million, a 300-carat diamond necklace for $16 million, and a $1.4 million "man cave" equipped with an antique pool table, two vintage pinball machines, and giant plasma television screens. In Singapore, $1,200 Jimmy Choo shoes and $850,000 Lamborghini sports cars sold briskly. Affluent Australians paid up to $2 million for special car license plates with one, two, or three digits; the lower the number, the higher the price. At Russia's second annual Millionaire Fair, "regular" Swiss GoldVish cell phones went from $18,000 to $150,000; the $1.27 million diamond-studded phone in a white gold case included a plaque certifying it was the world's most expensive mobile phone. Saudi Prince Alwaleed bin Talal, who already owns a Boeing 747, ordered an Airbus A-380 with a base list price of $320 million before modifications including bedrooms, a bar, and a gym.

Gratuitous spending is hardly confined to the wealthy, because we all like to feel rich, at least once in a while. In 2007, during the three days after Thanksgiving, 147 million Americans, almost half of the population and more than the number who voted in the 2004 presidential election, spent $16.4 billion shopping for stuff, mostly paid for by their soon-to-be-underwater home mortgages.

Bear in mind, however, that for many people the connection between fortune and immortality is fundamentally anchored in religious belief. Just like the ancient Greeks, in America, the early Protestants, especially the Calvinists, sought wealth as a sign of God's benevolent intentions toward them. Those who were not Chosen were (and still are, in many Calvinist minds) condemned to poverty.

Today, those in Pentecostal religious movements who subscribe to prosperity theology, also known as "Word of Faith," "Health and Wealth," or "Name It and Claim It," pursue wealth and spend lavishly because they believe God wants them to be rich. According to Edith Blumhofer, director of Wheaton College's Institute for the Study of American Evangelicals, "You don't have to give up the American Dream. You just see it as a sign of God's blessing." For example, George Adams, a car salesman who subscribes to this theory, sold a Ford F-150 pickup truck with a leather interior. "It's a new day God has given me!" he shouted. "I'm on my way to a six-figure income!" The implicit message is, and has long been, that wealth means we are favored by the gods (if not that we are gods ourselves).

One of us got this sense from a mere car rental while attending a pair of conferences in Seattle and Spokane, Washington, with a friend. They arrived at the Seattle airport to pick up a Ford Taurus, in keeping with the humble nature of their own cars, an old Dodge Caravan and Chevy Cavalier. As luck would have it, at the rental car counter, they were given the option of either an SUV or a Cadillac for a mere $5 more per day.

They looked at each other and blurted out simultaneously, "The Caddy." For seven glorious days, they were treated like superior beings. When they pulled up to hotels and restaurants in a shiny, sleek, leather-seated chariot, people seemed eager to see them. They were complimented on their "ride" everywhere they went. Giving up the keys to the Cadillac provoked a deep sadness. They felt demoted or thrown out of an exclusive club; in the Caddy, they felt "big," but in surrendering it, they shrank back down to their normal, merely human size.

Although neither of them was particularly materialistic or especially fond of cars, that week made them feel like emperors rather than measly mortals. If you can afford the finer things in life, people pay attention to you. You feel special. Your self-esteem, that critical bulwark against the fear of death, rises.

BUT JUST HOW CLOSELY is the desire for money and nice stuff related to the fear of death?

Let's say researchers ask you to complete a survey about depression, rating statements such as "I have trouble sleeping through the night," or you complete a survey about death, rating statements such as "The idea of never thinking again after I die frightens me." Then you peruse the following print advertisements:

A shiny new Lexus RX300 SUV, described as "remarkably powerful, stronger than the average beast," with "3,500 pounds of towing capacity.... It's like no other vehicle on earth."

A cylinder of Pringles potato chips, featuring a Pac-Man figure happily consuming some Pringles accompanied by the slogan "Once you pop, YOU CAN'T STOP" at the top of the page.

A tiny, squat, energy-efficient Chevy Geo Metro shown on a highway in front of a city skyline. "It's stingy," reads the copy. "Geo Metro has the highest mileage in America.... It's smart. Geo understands the value of the dollar.... It's protected. A Bumper to Bumper Plus Warranty protects Geo for 3 years/50,000 miles."

A pink-gold Rolex watch featuring a display "Oyster Perpetual Day-Date."

How do you rate these ads? How effective are they? How interested are you in buying the product after reading the ad, and how likely would you be to purchase a Lexus, Pringles, a Chevy Geo Metro, or a Rolex?

The researchers who conducted this experiment found that after the people in the study thought about death, it didn't change their opinion of Pringles or the Chevy. But they were much more interested in owning a high-status, self-esteem-boosting Lexus or Rolex. Other studies have shown that people who view death most negatively are most attracted to high-status material possessions, especially if they have shaky self-esteem. And after thinking about their mortality, people estimated that they would make more money in the future and spend more of it on luxuries like clothing and entertainment. Death reminders also spurred those with low self-esteem to plan more extravagant parties. Thoughts of death led people in

Poland to overestimate the physical size of coins and paper money; and Poles asked merely to count monetary notes rather than pieces of blank paper of the same size reported a reduced fear of death.

The findings of these experiments are inexplicable if people make economic decisions based solely on rational considerations. Rather, they confirm that managing existential terror underlies our insatiable desire for money and the urge to splurge, and they corroborate Tennessee Williams's observation in *Cat on a Hot Tin Roof* that "the human animal is a beast that dies and if he's got money he buys and buys and buys and I think the reason he buys everything he can buy is that in the back of his mind he has the crazy hope that one of his purchases will be life everlasting."

HEROIC NATIONALISM
AND CHARISMATIC LEADERS

People also gain a sense of symbolic immortality from feeling that they are part of a heroic cause or a nation that will endure indefinitely. Homer's epic poems and Thucydides' account of the Peloponnesian War described the feeling of transcendence that comes from being part of a powerful tribe, a great city, or a thriving, dominant empire. Through identification as an Egyptian, Mexican, Nigerian, or American, people can conceive of themselves as part of a stable and ongoing community united by a common background, conception of the world, and future destiny.

Nationalism acquires a sacred dimension when group identity is strengthened by the sense of being "chosen people" of distinctive character and origin who inhabit a hallowed homeland with a heroic history and a limitless future. And those who die for their country are immortalized in song and story, ceremony and monument. As the Roman rhetorician Cicero noted, *"Nemo unquam sine magna spe immortalitatatis se pro patria offerret ad mortem"* ("No one could ever meet death for his country without the hope of immortality"). "Every group, however small or great," Otto Rank observed, "has an 'individual' impulse for eternalization, which manifests itself in the creation of and care for national, religious, and artistic heroes."

Moreover, according to the great German sociologist Max Weber, charismatic leaders—those who possess, or are viewed by their followers as possessing, "a certain quality of an individual personality by virtue of which he is set apart from ordinary men and treated as endowed with supernatural, superhuman, or at least specifically exceptional powers or qualities"—often emerge during periods of historical upheaval. In a remarkable chapter in *The Denial of Death,* "The Spell Cast by Persons—The Nexus of Unfreedom," Becker provided a potent psychodynamic account of why people find charismatic leaders so alluring in troubled times and, more important, why and how particular individuals are able to capitalize on this proclivity to rise to power and alter the course of history.

Becker began by observing that charismatic leaders rarely assume power unilaterally without the enthusiastic assent of their followers. He then made the now familiar point that we humans procure psychological equanimity by being valued in the eyes of higher powers: at first our parents, and, as we mature, the culture at large. But when protracted difficulties or acute crises arise, when the crops fail and the hunters return empty-handed, when wars are lost, when people are plagued with economic woes and civil unrest to the point where the cultural scheme of things no longer seems to provide a reliable basis for feeling significant and secure, they will look elsewhere to fulfill that need.

Under such conditions, people's allegiance may shift to an individual who exhibits an "unconflicted" personality—in the sense of appearing supremely bold and self-confident—and offers a grand vision that affords a renewed prospect of being a valuable part of something noble and enduring. Furthermore, Becker noted, this charismatic individual typically performs a striking initiatory act that shines a magnifying light on him, makes him seem larger than life, and enthralls followers who wish they had the courage to follow suit. Teeming with admiration and sensing a way to feel significant again, people join the cause of the seemingly larger-than-life leader as a revitalized basis of self-worth and meaning in life. Nationalism, and passionate affection for, deference toward, and identification with, charismatic leaders, therefore supplies what Rank aptly dubbed "collective immortality" to satisfy our aching need for heroic triumph over death.

Becker's analysis explains the well-documented rise to power of Adolf

Hitler, the most notorious charismatic leader of the twentieth century. After the brutal suffering and humiliation of World War I and the Versailles Treaty, German national pride was shattered, along with trust in its leaders. Hitler's initiatory act was the failed "beer hall putsch" plot to overthrow the Weimar Republic government by kidnapping three of their leaders who were guests of honor at a gathering of three thousand businessmen in a Munich beer hall on November 8, 1923. Hitler burst into the room with his storm troopers, fired a pistol into the ceiling, and yelled "Silence!" at the stunned crowd. "The National Revolution has begun!" Hitler proclaimed, "The Bavarian and Reich governments have been removed and a provisional national government formed.... I am going to fulfill the vow I made to myself ... to know neither rest nor peace until the ... criminals had been overthrown, until on the ruins of the wretched Germany of today there should have arisen once more a Germany of power and greatness, of freedom and splendor."

Quite astonishingly, the crowd in the hall roared in approval and sang *"Deutschland über Alles"* (Germany above all). Professor Karl Alexander von Mueller of the University of Munich, who was in attendance, later reported: "I cannot remember in my entire life such a change in the attitude of a crowd in a few minutes, almost a few seconds.... Hitler had turned them inside out, as one turns a glove inside out, with a few sentences. It had almost something of ... magic about it." Although the putsch was quickly suppressed, Hitler gained national attention in his highly publicized trial for treason. The sympathetic German tribunal gave him a relatively light prison sentence. While incarcerated, Hitler refined and articulated his grandiose worldview in *Mein Kampf,* declaring himself Germany's divinely chosen savior and leader of the vastly superior Aryan master race who would attain their destiny as world rulers when the impurities within, especially the Communists and Jews, were eliminated.

The Nazis remained a marginal force until the Great Depression, when, with political dissatisfaction and economic fears on the rise, the party garnered 230 seats in the Reichstag, culminating in a deal with President Hindenburg to make Hitler chancellor as part of an elected coalition government in 1933. Once in power, he took complete control, and with the global economy on the mend, his approval by the German public soared.

Hitler's unconflicted personality was subsequently on full display in his grand speeches, in which he alternately soothed and exhorted the admiring and enthusiastic crowds with his absolute conviction and utter certainty about restoring German power and potency. And his rhetoric clearly revealed the central role of assuaging death fears and providing hope of death transcendence in the Nazi worldview. Hitler urged Germans to replace the worship of God for the worship of Germany, declaring in 1923, "We want no other God except Germany." The Führer became Germany's infallible, omnipotent messiah. The SS and other party organizations resembled religious orders; their ceremonial halls looked like secular monasteries. The Nazis established their own national holidays. On January 30, for example, they celebrated Hitler's assumption of power in 1933. Nazi ceremonies supplanted Christian baptisms, weddings, and funerals.

The Nazis venerated their dead. Indeed, like other fascist movements, they seemed to have a pathological affection for death. "Long live death" was a famous fascist slogan. However, they believed that "the dead are never really dead" and that they could be revived by the faithful exhortation of the living. In *Mein Kampf,* Hitler wrote that Germans lost in previous wars could be resurrected: "Would not the graves of all the hundreds of thousands open, the graves of those who with faith in the fatherland had marched forth never to return? Would they not open and send the silent mud- and blood-covered heroes back as spirits of vengeance to the homeland?" In a 1935 speech commemorating the death of sixteen of his followers in the 1923 putsch, Hitler affirmed their symbolic immortality: "These sixteen soldiers have celebrated a resurrection unique in world history.... They are now attaining German immortality.... Yet for us they are not dead.... Long live our National Socialist Germany! Long live our people! And may today the dead of our Movement, Germany and its men, living and dead, live on!"

Of course Hitler wasn't the only prominent twentieth-century leader who came to serve as the prophet of symbolic immortality for an entire nation when turbulence and death were in the air. Vladimir Lenin was the Russian Communist revolutionary and political theoretician who in 1917 took the helm of what would become the Soviet Union. In the wake of the Russian Revolution, the Communists outlawed religion, choosing to worship Lenin instead. Russians viewed Lenin as a messiah and savior who would make life on earth as it was purported to be in heaven. In 1918, Lenin ordered the Commissar of Enlightenment to construct giant monuments throughout the Soviet Union to serve as constant reminders of great revolutionaries. Busts of Lenin were installed in twenty-nine major cities in the next two years, along with numerous political posters with Bolshevik icons and images of Lenin and Marx. Routinely praised for his superhuman powers, Lenin was often depicted as larger than the sun and the earth, with his outstretched raised hand conferring a benediction or blessing in ways that were reminiscent of Russian Orthodox images of Christ or saints. In this way, Lenin seemed to be promoting both his own immortality and that of those who followed him.

After his death in 1924, Lenin's body was embalmed and placed in a sarcophagus inside a gleaming red granite mausoleum on Red Square abutting the Kremlin for public viewing. This was in accord both with the Russian Orthodox belief, like that of the Egyptians and Chinese before them, that the body of a saint did not decay after death, and with the expectation of eventual scientific resurrection of the dead—ancient and modern versions of immortality coexisting. Russian peasants and workers were devastated by the news of Lenin's death. Many refused to believe it. For decades to come, legend had it that Lenin, like Elvis, was still alive, traveling incognito, observing the work of the authorities, and taking notes to ensure the emancipation of the proletariat.

And around the same time Hitler seized full control in Germany, Mao Zedong emerged as the leader of the Communist Party in China, following the 9,600-kilometer Long March in 1934–1935. Only one tenth of Mao's followers survived the trek as they retreated from Jiangxi province to escape from Chiang Kai-shek's Kuomintang army. The fact that he had survived the ordeal gave Mao an aura of prestige and invincibility that contributed to his deified status in the years to come. Like Lenin and Hitler, Mao promised a revolutionary transformation resulting in an earthly paradise of infinite duration. The Chinese Communist slogan *May the revolutionary regime stay red for ten thousand generations* says it all. Ten thousand generations is longer than the current age of the human race. And "ten thousand" in Chinese numerals connotes infinity, so it's pretty clear that Mao, like Hitler, was digging in for the long haul. The revolution would be "eternal and indestructible." And in his 1957 poem "The Immortals," Mao wrote that those killed in battle would "soar lightly to the heaven of heavens."

To demonstrate experimentally that charismatic leaders become more appealing when existential concerns are aroused, after a reminder of death or an aversive control topic we had participants read campaign statements by three candidates in a hypothetical gubernatorial election. One candidate was task-oriented and emphasized the ability to get the job done: *"I can accomplish all the goals that I set out to do. I am very careful in laying out a detailed blueprint of what needs to be done so that there is no ambiguity."* A second was relationship-oriented and emphasized the importance of shared responsibility, relationships, and working together: *"I encourage all citizens to take an active role in improving their state. I know that each individual can make a difference."* The third candidate was charismatic, bold, self-confident, and emphasized the group's greatness: *"You are not just . . . ordinary citizens, you are part of a special state and a special nation."* Participants then selected the candidate they would vote for. The results were striking. In the control condition, only four of ninety-five participants voted for the charismatic candidate, with the rest of the votes split evenly between the task and relationship oriented leaders. However, following a reminder of death, there was almost an eightfold increase in votes for the charismatic candidate. Intimations of mortality amplify the allure of charismatic leaders (and, as we will see in the next chapter, this is true for real candidates in actual presidential elections as well).

"HISTORY," ERNEST BECKER CONCLUDED, can be viewed as "a succession of immortality ideologies." Passionate devotion to our tribe or nation and steadfast allegiance to charismatic leaders, particularly in unsettled times, mitigates existential terror by infusing us with a sense of pride and power accompanied by the assurance that our group will persist in perpetuity.

"AS LONG AS WE ARE NOT ASSURED OF IMMORTALITY, WE SHALL NEVER BE FULFILLED"

Mao's revolutionary minions soared to the heavens. The ancient Egyptians went by boat. Contemporary immortalists are happy on earth as long as they can stay there forever. The particulars vary from place to place and time to time, but the underlying eternalizing urge remains potent, persistent, and intact. We crave literal immortality, and the symbolic kind, too. Forced to choose, most would agree with Woody Allen that literal immortality is preferable: "I don't want to achieve immortality through my work. I want to achieve it through not dying." We like long shots at the track and in the lottery, but when it comes to the immortality sweepstakes we'll take the sure thing every time. Only by not dying can immortality be unequivocally assured.

It has always been this way. During a battle in the *Iliad*, Hector's ally Sarpedon said to his cousin Glaukos, "could we . . . live forever deathless, without age, I would not ever go again into battle, nor would I send you there for honor's sake!" But when it comes to something as pressing as immortality, people will take whatever they can get, so long as one's name is not "writ in water."

WE HAVE NOW SEEN how expanding consciousness gave rise to potentially debilitating and demoralizing terror. Such fear would have rendered our ancestors quivering piles of biological protoplasm on the fast track to oblivion save for their ingenious construction of a supernatural dimension of reality in which death was literally and symbolically averted. Consciousness became a viable form of mental organization, unleashing a torrent of imagination and creativity, resulting in some of our finest discoveries and inventions. And thanks to effective terror management—the belief that one is a valuable member of a meaningful universe—life for many of us is generally pleasant and productive, and sometimes even noble and heroic.

However, the supernatural cultural scheme of things that we humans embrace to manage existential terror is nevertheless ultimately a defensive distortion and obfuscation of reality to blot out the inevitability of death. And as Ernest Becker explained, this "necessary lie" about the nature of reality invariably sows interpersonal strife and undermines our physical and psychological well-being. Next we will consider why and how such complications arise.

PART THREE

——

DEATH IN MODERN TIMES

CHAPTER 7

The Anatomy
of Human
Destructiveness

———

Perhaps the whole root of our trouble, the human trouble,
is that we will sacrifice all the beauty of our lives, will im-
prison ourselves in totems, taboos, crosses, blood sacrifices, steeples, mosques, races, armies, flags, nations, in
order to deny the fact of death....

—JAMES BALDWIN,
The Fire Next Time

ACCORDING TO TERROR MANAGEMENT THEORY, THE COMBINATION OF A
basic biological inclination toward self-preservation with sophisticated
cognitive capacities renders us humans aware of our perpetual vulnerabili-
ties and inevitable mortality, which gives rise to potentially paralyzing terror. Cultural worldviews and self-esteem help manage this terror by
convincing us that we are special beings with souls and identities that will
persist, literally and/or symbolically, long past our own physical death. We
are thus pervasively preoccupied with maintaining confidence in our cultural scheme of things and satisfying the standards of value associated
with it. But preserving faith in our cultural worldviews and self-esteem becomes challenging when we encounter others with different beliefs. Sinis-
ter complications almost inevitably ensue.

—————

WHEN DUTCH AND ENGLISH settlers arrived in the lower Hudson Valley in the seventeenth century, they marveled at the sheer beauty and prodigious natural bounty of the New World. They were also intrigued by the natives. The Lenapes, who had inhabited the land for thousands of years, were happy, peaceful, welcoming, and eager to trade furs for blankets and tools. Moreover, according to firsthand accounts by Dutch settlers, the Lenapes were "well-fashioned people, strong and sound of body, well fed, without blemish. Some have lived 100 years. Also, there are among them no simpletons, lunatics, or madmen as among us."

At the same time, the Europeans found the Lenapes very unsettling. They lived in communal long houses big enough for a dozen families. They relocated seasonally. They traced their kinship through their mothers, and women had considerable power in communal affairs. They divided themselves into clans identified by animals such as wolves, turtles, or turkeys. They refrained from hunting excessively because their religion stressed that all life was interrelated and interdependent. They weren't interested in enriching themselves beyond what was necessary to survive.

Eventually, the settlers felt that something had to be done to dispose of these "most barbarous" *wilden* (savages). So the Dutch and the English proceeded to exterminate the Lenapes and other Native American tribes. They had a good time doing it, too. In 1644, the director of New Netherland, Willem Kieft, "laughed right heartily" as soldiers tortured and butchered Lenapes in their villages. The soldiers took one captive, "threw him down, and stuck his private parts, which they had cut off, into his mouth while he was still alive, and after that placed him on a millstone and beat his head off," while Dutch women amused themselves by kicking the victims' heads around like soccer balls.

While it might be tempting to view the Europeans' slaughter of the Lenapes as aberration, it's in full accord with the long record of human barbarism. History has been marked by an ongoing succession of genocidal atrocities, ethnic cleansings, and brutal subjugation of domestic inferiors. Assyrian bas-reliefs from 1100 B.C. depict the populace of captured cities impaled alive on stakes running through their groin and out their shoulders. Assyrian kings boasted of their conquests and tried to outdo one another's brutality. Ashurbanipal, who reigned from 668 to 627 B.C., proudly described his treatment of one captive king: "I took him alive in the midst of the battle. In ... my capital, I slowly tore off his skin."

Attila the Hun, Caligula, Ivan the Terrible, Peter the Cruel, Rasputin, Robespierre, Adolf Hitler, Joseph Stalin, Mao Zedong, François Duvalier, Idi Amin, Nicolae Ceaușescu, Pol Pot, Saddam Hussein ... the list goes on. But demonic despots are never singularly responsible for virulent hatred and genocidal atrocities. It takes "normal" people—those who see themselves as doing "God's work," their patriotic duty, or "just following orders"—to stoke the gas chambers at Auschwitz, to sow the killing fields in Cambodia.

More recently, United Nations peacekeeping forces have had their hands full in more than a dozen countries around the world. In Gaza and throughout Europe, the Hamas satellite station Al-Aqsa broadcasts a children's show in which Farfur, a Mickey Mouse clone, teaches Muslim children to hate Jews. It's working quite well. Three-year-old Shaima called the show to joyfully tell the host, "We don't like Jews, because they are dogs! We will fight them!" In Israel, "Arabs to the crematoria" and "Arabs—subhuman" are among the slogans spray-painted by Jewish graffiti artists in Jerusalem. In America, youngsters in Fred Phelps's Westboro Baptist Church carry signs at rallies proclaiming God's hatred of Catholics, Muslims, "fags," "Jews," and "niggers" and disrupt funerals of American soldiers killed in Iraq and Afghanistan with chants that God killed them to punish the nation for its (modestly) tolerant treatment of homosexuals.

Such inflammatory rhetoric is accompanied by increasingly destructive weapons and tactics meant to maximize physical harm (machine guns, shoulder-fired rocket launchers, napalm showers, fertilizer bombs, improvised explosive devices) and psychological harm (anthrax-laced letters, suicide bombings, grisly beheadings posted on the Internet). And today's nuclear weapons make "Little Boy" and "Fat Man"—the atom bombs dropped on Hiroshima and Nagasaki in August 1945—seem like firecrackers by comparison.

Human hatred and violence are, in part, a residual hangover from our tribal primate heritage. Chimps are aggressive in defending and expanding their territory, and they occasionally murder other chimps that do not belong to their group. Early human hunter-gatherers evidently fought wars over ten thousand years ago for the same reasons: to preserve and enhance their regional influence in pursuit of resources such as food, water, and mates. Only humans, however, hate and kill other humans with righteous exuberance for symbolic affronts: worshipping different gods, saluting different flags, or humiliations hundreds or thousands of years in their past. And the increasing mastery of technologies of death does not inspire confidence in the future of our species.

> If those weird individuals with beards and funny hats are acceptable, then what about my claim to superiority? ... Does he, that one, dare hope to live forever too—and perhaps crowd me out. I don't like it. All I know is, if he's right I'm wrong. So different and funny-looking. I think he's trying to fool the gods with his sly ways. Let's show him up. He's not very strong. For a start, see what he'll do if I poke him.
>
> —ALAN HARRINGTON,
> *The Immortalist*

Our longing to transcend death inflames violence toward each other. While our cultural scheme of things keeps a lid on our mortal dread, others cling to very different sets of beliefs to manage theirs. Acknowledging their "truths" inevitably calls ours into question. We have to believe in our own truths to sustain the precarious view that life is meaningful and that we are significant, enduring beings. "One culture is always a potential menace to another," Becker observed, "because it is a living example that life can go on heroically within a value framework totally alien to one's own." If the Aborigines' belief that magical ancestors metamorphosed into humans after becoming lizards is credible, then the idea that God created the world in six days, and Adam in his image, must be suspect.

And the threat posed by different belief systems runs much deeper than mutually exclusive creation stories. Our entire way of life, everything we believe in and everything we strive for, can be challenged by alternative worldviews. For example, in his 2002 song "Outside of the Inside," the Muslim singer/songwriter/guitarist Richard Thompson tried to convey (in part to express his opposition to) the Taliban's fundamentalist view of the world. The song referred to Einstein, Newton, and Shakespeare as childish, senseless, and corrupt, and Van Gogh and Botticelli as offensive madmen scraping colors on a board. Hearing the song for the first time, we were dumbfounded and outraged. Einstein and Newton, surely among the greatest scientists in the history of earth, pointless and senseless? We grew up wanting to be like them. Shakespeare small-minded and childish? We think he's the greatest writer of all time! Painting is blaspheming madness? That's shocking nonsense.

It is deeply disturbing to have one's fundamental beliefs called into question. Take our meanings and purposes away, characterize them as juvenile, useless, or evil, and all we have left are the vulnerable physical creatures that we are. Because cultural conceptions of reality keep a lid on mortal dread, acknowledging the legitimacy of beliefs contrary to our own unleashes the very terror those beliefs serve to quell. So we must parry the threat by derogating and dehumanizing those with alternative views of life, by forcing them to adopt our beliefs and co-opting aspects of their cultures into our own, or by obliterating them entirely.

Moreover, people's sense of meaning and significance cannot completely alleviate mortal terror. Symbols are extremely powerful. Indeed, they are the underlying basis of human imagination, creativity, and the uniquely human capacity to transform reality in accordance with our desires. But no symbol is sufficiently commanding to completely overcome the terror of death. There is always residual death anxiety, a "rumble of panic" that is projected onto other groups of people designated as all-encompassing repositories of evil. And when those in one group bolster their psychological security by imposing their will and venting their animosity on another, this frequently produces a backlash by the "others," resulting in a vicious cycle of bitter acrimony.

DEROGATION AND DEHUMANIZATION

Our first line of psychological defense against those whose conceptions of reality are different from our own is to derogate or belittle them, diminishing the threat their beliefs pose to our own. They are ignorant savages (like the Lenapes), or servants of the devil, or they're brainwashed by evil masters. Perhaps they are not even human. The Nazis portrayed Jews as rats. In the Inuit, Mbuti, Orokawa, Yanomamo, and Kalili cultures, the word for their own group means "man" or "human," implying, of course, that members of other groups are *not* human. Traditional Arabs from Nejd in Saudi Arabia are blunter; they refer to all outsiders as *tarsh al bahr*—"vomit from the sea."

Americans are no less prone to such dehumanization. For example, during the first Persian Gulf War, General Norman Schwarzkopf declared that Iraqis "weren't members of the same human race as the rest of us," and flyers circulated among the troops likening Iraqis to ants and cockroaches. Meanwhile, back stateside, Americans put bumper stickers on their cars declaring, "I don't brake for Iraqis."

This tendency to belittle others is particularly pronounced in the wake of death reminders. Studies have demonstrated that after pondering their mortality, Christians denigrate Jews, conservatives condemn liberals, Italians despise Germans, Israeli children dislike Russian kids, and people everywhere ridicule immigrants. And death reminders cause us to see members of such out-groups as less human and more animalistic. Sadly, these tactics work; it's easier to dispose of troublesome thoughts of death when one disparages "different" others.

CULTURAL ASSIMILATION
AND ACCOMMODATION

Besides denigrating those who are different, we can show these ignorant, misguided, or sinful people the light, thereby assimilating them into our worldview. What better proof of the validity of our view of the world than for others to come around to our way of thinking? For example, David

Bogue, a Scotsman born in 1750, was famous for his evangelical zeal. Known as the "father" of the London Missionary Society, Bogue exhorted the faithful to head to points afar to divest the heathens of their misguided beliefs:

> We are commanded "to love our neighbour as ourselves"; and Christ has taught us that every man is our neighbour. Ye were once Pagans, living in cruel and abominable idolatry. The servants of Jesus came from other lands, and preached His Gospel among you. Hence your knowledge of salvation. And ought ye not, as an equitable compensation for their kindness, to send messengers to the nations which are in like condition with yourselves of old, to entreat them that they turn from their dumb idols to serve the living God, and to wait for His Son from heaven?

Buddhist missionaries spread their doctrine centuries before Jesus' birth. Islamic missionaries followed Allah's command to engage in *da'wah* ("to summon"): "Call unto the way of thy Lord with wisdom and fair exhortation, and reason with them in the better way." Mormon missionaries do the same around the world today.

And such proselytizers have plenty of company in the secular realm. Devout atheists hold seminars and distribute pamphlets to rid the world of religion. Rush Limbaugh's "dittoheads" exhort Americans to escape the thrall of what they see as creeping American socialism. Vegetarian zealots show schoolchildren films of slaughterhouses to encourage them to adopt their tofu-based dietary preferences.

Why? The answer is simple: cultural worldviews gain strength in numbers. For beliefs to serve as effective bulwarks against existential terror, people must be absolutely certain of their validity. However, most of the core beliefs we depend on for psychological security are based on faith rather than fact; they cannot be unambiguously proven. Consequently, the more people who share our beliefs, the more sure we feel that they are correct. If just one person believed that God spoke to Moses in the form of a burning bush, antipsychotic medication would be sought to relieve this poor soul of his florid delusion. But when the same belief is shared by millions of people, it becomes unassailable truth.

Since our sense of being more than mortal animals is dependent on these unassailable truths, our desire to have them validated is especially strong when death is close to mind. Reminders of death make Christians more intent on persuading atheists to embrace Jesus and make evolutionists more determined to persuade creationists to embrace Darwin. Furthermore, studies show that proselytizing is prophylactic: if I learn that you have adopted my beliefs, I feel more confident of their validity and consequently don't worry so much about my own death.

IN ADDITION TO TRYING to convince others to adopt our own customs and beliefs, we humans also tend to "tame" the views we find threatening by incorporating attractive aspects of them into our own cultural worldview. We refer to this as "cultural accommodation" because people are altering their own worldview to include something appealing from another worldview, but in a manner that does not undermine their most cherished beliefs and values. Consider the counterculture movement in the United States in the 1960s, when young people began to "tune in, turn on, drop out." Sparked by support for the civil rights movement and opposition to the escalating war in Vietnam, the "hippies" railed against the military-industrial complex and the greed, materialism, sexism, racism, and sexual repression that went with it. There was a call to be more respectful of other cultures, minorities, women, and the environment, and to move toward a simpler and more peaceful lifestyle.

Young people also rejected the clean-cut "Ozzie and Harriet" look of their parents and older siblings. They donned blue jeans to show their sympathy for Woody Guthrie's workingman. They turned away from meat and started eating granola and other natural health foods. Sex, drugs, and rock and roll were the cultural linchpins of their lives. At the time, these affectations were viewed as a serious threat to traditional American values, earning the scorn of upstanding citizens everywhere. "A hippie is someone who looks like Tarzan, walks like Jane and smells like Cheetah," quipped then California governor Ronald Reagan.

Yet by the time Reagan became president, the hippies' "peace and love" values had morphed into an insipid Coke commercial: "I'd like to teach the world to sing in perfect harmony / I'd like to buy the world a Coke and keep it company." After commercialism crashed into Woodstock, designer blue jeans sold for $100, grocery stores sold chocolate-covered granola bars with fifty ingredients, and elevator-music versions of classic sixties protest songs gently rocked dentist-office waiting rooms. One could then enjoy the appealing looks, tastes, and sounds without being disturbed by those worldview-threatening messages about a simpler, less status-conscious, healthier, and more peaceful lifestyle.

OUR FEAR OF PEOPLE who differ from us is also quelled by putting them into neat little boxes where they can serve the stereotypic cultural roles members of certain groups are expected to inhabit: the athletic, rapping black man; the amiable, family-oriented Mexican; the brainy, studious Asian; the angry, jihadist Arab; the effete Northeastern intellectual clinging to his Marx and Pinot Grigio; the redneck Southerner clinging to his guns and Bible. In fact, when death is close to mind, people prefer their out-groups to fit simple stereotypes. Following a death reminder, Americans prefer Germans to be neat and organized, male homosexuals to be effeminate, men to pay for dinner, and women to babysit the neighbor's kids.

To the extent that such stereotypes are part of the cultural scheme of things, out-group members who confirm them validate the worldview, while out-group members who violate them threaten it. Accordingly, when the need for faith in one's worldview is high, people may actually prefer out-group members who are radically different from the in-group over those who are closer to the cultural mainstream. This could account for the popularity of, and affection for, fictional figures such as Amos and Andy, Jack Benny's sidekick, Rochester, and actors such as Stepin Fetchit among white Americans in the twentieth century. It could also explain why racists who fear and dislike African Americans nonetheless venerate well-known black athletes, musicians, and entertainers.

In one experiment, reminders of death led white American college students to prefer an African American "gangsta" to a straitlaced black person. White American college students met Michael, an African American male posing as a fellow participant for a study. Michael dressed and behaved in a way that either confirmed or violated the cultural stereotype of African American males. In the "stereotype confirmation" condition, he wore long baggy short pants and a backward Atlanta Braves baseball cap. In the "stereotype violation" condition, he was dressed in khaki pants, a buttoned-down shirt, and a sports coat.

Escorted into a supposed getting-acquainted study, the real participants were reminded of their own death or a neutral topic, and then exchanged essays with Michael about what they had done over the summer. When Michael was dressed in his "gangsta" costume, he wrote about "hanging with his homies," "drinking 40s," doing "serious clubbing," and "cruising for honeys." But when Michael showed up looking like a serious job interviewee, he wrote in formal English about "taking computer science classes" for his business degree, reading "classic novels," and "playing chess."

The participants then evaluated Michael. In the control condition, the white students strongly preferred the studious stereotype violator to the "clubbing" and "cruising" Michael. However, those who had been reminded of death far preferred the "gangsta" Michael to the "buttoned-down" African American. When existential terror is aroused, we fortify our cultural scheme of things by encouraging others to conform to socially sanctioned cookie-cutter molds.

DEMONIZATION AND DESTRUCTION

When derogation, assimilation, and accommodation are insufficient to secure a sense of equanimity, psychological push often comes to physical shove. "Might" becomes "right" in the service of eliminating the threatening other entirely, in part because our symbolic solutions to death are never psychologically sufficient. Cultural worldviews are embodied in powerful beliefs, symbols, and icons like flags and crucifixes. However, death is a very real physical problem, and there is always lingering death anxiety that humans project onto other groups of people whom they designate as evil that must be destroyed.

People in the ancient world often used animals as a tangible locus of their death anxiety. For example, on the ancient Hebrew Day of Atonement, two goats were chosen by lot: "the Lord's Goat" was offered as the blood sacrifice for the sins of Israel, and the second, "Azazel," or scapegoat, was cast out into the wilderness bearing the sins of God's people. In ancient Greece, the scapegoat was not an animal but a person. When a community was in the grip of an infectious disease or famine, the *pharmakos*, or human scapegoat, was the object of the village's scorn. The *pharmakos* was usually a person regarded as lowly—a criminal, a slave, or a cripple—who was either beaten or stoned and then ejected from the city.

Throughout history, individuals and entire groups have served as psychological lightning rods for death anxiety. Often the "evildoers" are unambiguously worthy of such depiction; Attila the Hun and Adolf Hitler make just about everyone's list of the top ten most evil people in history. Sometimes, however, evil is in the eye of the proverbial beholder. Barack Obama and Walmart are each vilified by their detractors while glorified by their supporters. Even superficially benign groups like vegetarians, country music enthusiasts, and New York Yankees fans can serve as objects of evil incarnate for some.

Famines, plagues, economic upheaval, political instability, educational deficiencies, power outages, illiteracy, youthful insubordination—you name it: it's *their* fault. *We* are good and pure and right and made in God's image with his countenance shining upon us. *They* are the problem, and the solution is clear: derogate, dehumanize, demonize, destroy. Eradicate the evildoers; purify the world; prove that God is on your side; make life on earth as it is in heaven.

The disquieting point here is that because people need some tangible and potentially controllable cause of their residual death anxiety, they will identify or create different "others" to serve this purpose. "If we could only get rid of those [fill in the blank: terrorists, infidels, socialists, globalists, homosexuals, liberals, Tea Party Republicans, Jews, Muslims, illegal immigrants, or what have you], then all our problems would be solved!"

ALTHOUGH FINDING EVIL OTHERS provides a focus for disposing of residual death anxiety, this strategy usually backfires by increasing the actual threat posed by the others. Attempts to eradicate the evil other fan the flames of conflict by arousing death fears in those on the receiving end, not only through direct threats to their physical existence but also by the psychological humiliation of being belittled and dehumanized. How can people maintain their sense of being significant contributors to a meaningful world while having their homeland appropriated and being forced to relinquish traditional beliefs and adopt an alien way of life? Or while witnessing treasured traditions and artifacts absorbed into the dominant culture in demeaning ways? Or while serving as a cultural caricature? Or while being treated as animals, like the naked and tortured prisoners at Abu Ghraib?

Humiliation strips people of their self-esteem and reduces them to vulnerable creatures rather than significant beings in a world of meaning. According to a Somali proverb, "Humiliation is worse than death; in times of war, words of humiliation hurt more than bullets." Bullets slay your body. Humiliation slaughters the sense of death-transcending significance that shields you from the terror of being just an ephemeral creature. And history is replete with wars of vengeance fought to repair wounded pride. The Trojan War (depicted in the *Iliad*) began after Menelaus, king of Sparta, was humiliated when his wife, Helen, was seduced by Paris, who took her away to the city of Troy. In response to this insult, Menelaus's troops besieged the city for the next ten years, burning most of it to the ground, killing all the men, and raping and/or enslaving the women and children.

And there is no shortage of efforts to avenge and overcome humiliation and shame in modernity, generally with tragic consequences. In the twentieth century, Hitler was elected by promising to wipe out the "shame of Versailles." In World War II, Japanese kamikaze pilots sacrificed themselves to alleviate feelings of shame aroused by the prospect of defeat at the hands of their enemies; these martyrdom operations became more frequent as Japan's losses mounted toward the end of the war. A 1965 Defense Department memorandum stated that the United States' primary aim in the Vietnam War was "to avoid a humiliating U.S. defeat." And in the twenty-first century, after interviewing al-Qaeda supporters and right-wing American Christian militia members, sociologist Mark Juergensmeyer reported that "almost everyone ... who was a supporter of, or involved in, religious violence ... said that they felt an enormous sense of frustration and humiliation." Although each of these examples varies considerably, occurring in dissimilar cultural contexts with different histories, they all involved intense feelings of humiliation that fueled egregious acts of violence.

The humiliation that arouses lethal violence often stems from unresolved conflicts from the distant past that serve as rallying points for feelings of victimization and the need for heroic redemption. For example, the bloody conflicts in Kosovo and Bosnia in the 1990s were fueled in part by exhortations to avenge the Serbians' loss of the Battle of Kosovo in 1389.

Humiliated people attempt to restore their pride and dignity by berating and eradicating their oppressors. "When a humiliated mind is left to reflect on its own destruction," writes Dr. Evelin Lindner, "it may become convinced that it must inflict even greater pain on the perpetrator. So begins a vicious cycle of violation and vindication that both sides believe they are obligated to pursue.... Neither side can break free because being the first to back down would be a further humiliation, so they remain trapped in a self-perpetuating cycle of mayhem and murder."

SEPTEMBER 11, 2001:
THE LASH AND THE BACKLASH

The September 11, 2001, al-Qaeda attacks on the Pentagon and the World Trade Center and ensuing events poignantly illustrate how death fears provoke reciprocal cycles of hatred and violence in pursuit of a heroic triumph over evil.

In the 1980s, Osama bin Laden's goals were allegedly political. He wanted to dislodge Russian troops from Afghanistan and subsequently to evict American troops from Muhammad's "holy land" of Saudi Arabia. However, in 1998, bin Laden joined radical Islamic clerics declaring jihad against America, in part to avenge humiliating affronts to Islam dating back to the Crusades in the eleventh century and the dissolution of the Ottoman Empire in 1918:

> The United States has been occupying the lands of Islam in the holiest of places, the Arabian Peninsula, plundering its riches, dictating to its rulers, humiliating its people, terrorizing its neighbors and turning its bases in the Peninsula into a spearhead through which to fight the neighboring Muslim peoples. We...call on every Muslim who...wishes to be rewarded to comply with Allah's order to kill the Americans and plunder their money.... We also call on Muslim ulema, leaders, youths, and soldiers to launch the raid on Satan's U.S. troops and the devil's supporters allying with them....

Concrete political goals—the dispatching of foreign troops into Saudi Arabia—had metastasized into a humiliation-fueled, divinely ordained duty to destroy Satan's emissaries. What better way to infuse a conflict with cosmic significance and attract adherents willing to sacrifice their lives than to declare a holy war against American evildoers?

The events of 9/11 delivered a powerful one-two death-threat punch to Americans. First, they witnessed potent images of death. Millions were horrified as the Twin Towers collapsed, staggered by the knowledge that the Pentagon was ablaze and another plane had crashed in Pennsylvania. Second, beyond the literal carnage, they were mortified as three of the foremost symbols of Americans' scheme of things had been endangered or assaulted. One symbol of the United States' financial and business prosperity (the Twin Towers) was wholly destroyed; another symbol of its global military domination (the Pentagon) was badly damaged. The third target, presumably the White House or the Capitol, symbolized American democracy itself.

In the immediate aftermath of 9/11, Americans behaved with extraordinary compassion and efficiency. Police and firefighters streamed in from around the country. Blood banks and food banks overflowed. Doing one's part restored a sense of national pride; people responded to the existential threat with assertions of their own value as well as that of their homeland.

But lingering death fears also intensified Americans' zeal to derogate, dehumanize, demonize, assimilate, and destroy. Christian evangelist Franklin Graham denounced Islam as "a very evil and wicked religion." Lieutenant General William Boykin, the U.S. Deputy Undersecretary of Defense, portrayed the conflict with Islamic radicals as a fight against the devil: "The enemy is a spiritual enemy. He's called the principality of darkness. The enemy is a guy called Satan." Former secretary of state Lawrence Eagleburger said, "You have to kill some of these people; even if they were not directly involved, they need to be hit."

The nation's leaders also stepped in to fulfill Americans' need for heroic transcendence. On September 17, 2001, President George W. Bush declared, "This is a new kind of evil, and we understand, and the American people are beginning to understand, this crusade ... is going to take a while.... We will rid the world of the evildoers." Vice President Dick Cheney added that nations that failed to join the crusade would face the "full wrath of the United States."

Prior to 9/11, Bush's presidency was viewed as ineffectual and uninspired, even to many of his Republican supporters. However, the president's approval ratings reached historically unprecedented heights a few weeks thereafter. That Bush's tremendous popularity was in part a result of the dramatic and ongoing reminders of death and vulnerability provoked by the attacks was confirmed by experiments we conducted in 2002 and 2003 showing that following a reminder of death, Americans felt more supportive of President Bush and his policies in Iraq. Then, as the standing president, confidently purveying the classic charismatic message that "we are divinely ordained to defeat the forces of evil," Bush served Americans' terror management needs far better than his opponent, Senator John Kerry, in the 2004 presidential election. In a control condition in which we reminded participants of intense pain, Americans rated Senator Kerry more favorably than President Bush. But after a reminder of death, Bush was more favorably evaluated than Kerry. Six weeks before the election, control participants reported that they would be voting for Senator Kerry by a 4-to-1 margin. But other participants, after thinking about death, favored President Bush by an almost 3-to-1 margin.

Bush's terror management value was likely enhanced by the military operations he initiated in Afghanistan in 2001 and in Iraq in 2003. Saddam Hussein was dispatched in short order; the Taliban took major early hits. These events paved the way for an influx of missionaries into both countries, where they felt it their duty to disabuse the natives of their misguided religious and political convictions. Christian fundamentalists built churches and distributed Bibles along with anti-Islamic diatribes, unperturbed by Muslims' vigorous objections. Occasionally, these missionaries met with violent resistance to their efforts, but they believed that their death would have been for a good cause. "Our activities can lead to people dying," said Todd Nettleton, director of media development for the evangelist group Voice of the Martyrs, "but, the reality is an eternity with Christ in heaven is so far better than an eternity in hell that it is a good deal."

Simultaneously, political and economic emissaries served the mission of the 2002 National Security Strategy to "extend the benefits of freedom across the globe" by designating democratic capitalism as the "single sustainable model of national success."

IN THE IMMEDIATE AFTERMATH of the 9/11 attacks, most Muslims quickly denounced the attackers as a lunatic fringe of religious zealots misrepresenting Islam. Shortly thereafter, however, Muslims were mortified and humiliated by Americans' blanket condemnation of Islam, religious and political proselytizing, and President George W. Bush's declaration of a "crusade" to rid the world of evil, followed by the invasion of Afghanistan and Iraq. The "shock and awe" military attacks killed tens of thousands of innocent victims as "collateral damage." The looting of Baghdad and the humiliations at the Abu Ghraib prison served as powerful symbolic and literal reminders of death to Muslims everywhere, just as the 9/11 attacks

had been to Americans. Lingering death fears intensified their zeal to derogate, dehumanize, demonize, assimilate, and destroy. As was the case in
the United States, the Islamic merchants of humiliation took to the airwaves and the Internet to spread fear and outrage against Americans. Polls
told a chilling story of increasing hostility toward the West: almost a third
of those polled in Turkey, half in Pakistan, and three quarters in Morocco
and Jordan said that suicide bombings against Israelis, Americans, and
Europeans in Iraq were justified. Many Muslim children yearned to become martyrs (*shahid*). At the Jabalia refugee camp in Gaza, an eight-year-
old boy showed a reporter "a portrait his family had taken of him clutching
an AK-47 rifle ... and said that his older brother was a shahid—then he
hung his head and admitted that no, his brother is alive and never did anything so grand." At the Jenin camp in the West Bank, a thirteen-year-old
girl said that although her father wanted her to become a doctor, "she
would prefer to study nuclear physics so she could blow up America."

There was also a lot of lethal backlash. The *Wall Street Journal* reporter
Daniel Pearl (a Jewish American) was kidnapped in Pakistan in January
2002 and subsequently decapitated. The gruesome spectacle was taped
and widely circulated throughout the world. In October 2002, a car bomb
exploded outside a popular tourist nightclub in Bali, killing more than
200 civilians and wounding 100. On March 11, 2004, a series of coordinated bombings on commuter trains in Madrid, killing almost 200 people
and wounding almost 2,000. On July 7, 2005, a similar attack on trains
and a bus in London killed 52 people and 4 suicide bombers, and injured
700.

Meanwhile, Muslim missionaries funded by Saudi Arabia espousing
the teachings of the Wahhabi sect became more active in Europe and Asia,
seeking new converts to their fundamentalist version of Islam.

NOW, MORE THAN A DECADE after the 9/11 attacks, the lashes and back-
lashes continue, as each side continues to disparage, dehumanize, demonize, humiliate, and destroy the other.

Anti-American and anti-Israeli sentiment remains high in most Islamic countries. In 2010, the Muslim Brotherhood leader Mohamed Morsi, former president of Egypt, gave a speech imploring fellow Egyptians to "nurse our children and our grandchildren on hatred" for Jews and Zionists, "these bloodsuckers ... these warmongers, the descendents of apes and pigs.... They are hostile by nature." Morsi declared America and Europe as Zionist supporters; thus, they were enemies, too. Lethal violence continues in Iraq, Afghanistan, Syria, Saudi Arabia, Pakistan, India, Mali, Somalia, and elsewhere.

In America and Europe, homegrown hatred of and violence toward Islam persists. One in three Americans believe that Muslims should be barred from running for president, and a substantial minority of Americans still worry that President Barack Obama is a Muslim. Many Americans remain opposed to building mosques in their neighborhoods, and such opposition increases following reminders of death.

DR. STRANGELOVE IN THE LAB

George Bernard Shaw observed that "when the angel of death sounds his trumpet, the pretenses of civilization are blown from men's heads into the mud like hats in a gust of wind." Sadly, laboratory studies show how just a slight turn of the existential screw is sufficient to tilt people in this direction. Death fears inflame violence toward others with different beliefs, especially those whom we designate as evil.

To demonstrate this propensity, we put together an experiment based on a "hot sauce attack" that occurred in 1995. In February of that year, a breakfast cook at a Denny's restaurant in Lebanon, New Hampshire, decided to play a little joke on a couple of Vermont state troopers who'd crossed over into the state for breakfast. He didn't like police much, so he decided to douse their food with a generous helping of Tabasco sauce. The troopers weren't happy. They said the eggs burned their mouths and upset one officer's stomach. "We've got enough trouble without people screwing around with our food," said Lebanon police lieutenant Ken Lary. Weeks later, the cook was arrested for assault and faced a punishment of up to two years in jail and a $2,000 fine. This was not an isolated incident. Teens have been known to pour hot sauce down each other's throats in fights, and parents have been charged with child abuse for making their children drink hot sauce as punishment.

Inspired by such episodes, we brought politically conservative and liberal students into the lab for a study of "personality and food preferences." We had them either think about death by answering our standard questions, or think about their next important exam. They also wrote a bit about their background, interests, and dietary preferences—purportedly to exchange with a student in the next cubicle with whom they would be working during the food preference portion of the experiment. Participants received materials from their partner that were either consistent or inconsistent with their liberal or conservative identities. (The materials were concocted; there was no actual partner.) Their "partner's" statement contained sentences such as "The best place for a liberal [or alternately, conservative] is out of my sight," and "Liberals [or conservatives] are the cause of so many problems in this country, it's not funny." They also learned that their partner strongly disliked spicy foods.

We then asked them to pour some painfully hot salsa into a cup and said, "Your partner in the next room has to consume this sauce entirely before rating its culinary qualities." How much hot sauce would they allot to their partners—knowing they disliked spicy foods and that they would have to consume all of it? We found that students who wrote about their next exam didn't care one way or the other about their partner's political beliefs. Liberal or conservative, they doled out a modest amount of hot sauce for their partner to consume. Students who wrote about their own mortality were similarly restrained when their partners shared their political views. But students who disagreed with the views of their partner poured out more than twice as much hot sauce (often filling the cup to the brim) after they'd thought about death.

This was the first direct evidence that fear of death magnifies the desire to physically harm those who challenge and insult our beliefs, but it was not the last. In a 2006 experiment, American conservatives reminded of their mortality or the events of 9/11 were more supportive of preemptive nuclear and chemical attacks on countries that posed no immediate threat to the United States. They also felt that capturing or killing Osama bin Laden was worth such a risk, even if thousands of innocent civilians were killed or injured in the process. Another study found that death reminders made Americans more accepting of U.S. intelligence using brutal and humiliating interrogation techniques (torture) on foreign suspects. Parallel studies in Israel found that reminders of mortality led politically conservative Israelis to view violence against the Palestinians as more justified. These participants were also more supportive of a preemptive nuclear attack on Iran. And after pondering their mortality, Iranian college students increased their support for martyrdom attacks on the United States; they were also more interested in becoming suicide bombers themselves.

Finally, in a particularly ominous study, Jeff Schimel and his colleagues at the University of Alberta asked devoutly Christian participants to read either a nonthreatening article about the aurora borealis or an article entitled "Islam Poised to Swallow Jesus' Boyhood Home," concocted from actual news reports and designed to be threatening to Christians. The article said:

> Tens of thousands of residents looked on while leaders of the Islamic Movement—the main Muslim political party in Nazareth—paraded down the main thoroughfare. While the march was billed as a celebration, its militant virtues were clearly visible. The event seemed more a show of force than a street party. Dressed in battle gear, Muslim celebrants beat drums and brandished their party's green flag as a man on a loudspeaker repeatedly exclaimed in Arabic, "Allah is great" and hundreds of activists strutted screaming Islamist epithets, including "Islam is the only truth" and "Islam shall rule all!"

Half of the participants also read an additional paragraph describing a plane crash: "In related news, 117 devout Muslims passed away today en route to the Feast of the Sacrifice in Nazareth.... There were no reported survivors." Then everyone in the study was given a word stem completion task to measure how readily death thoughts came to mind.

Not surprisingly, the Christians who just read "Islam Poised to Swallow Jesus' Boyhood Home" had much higher levels of death thoughts than those who read about the Aurora Borealis, showing that the idea of Muslims occupying sacred Christian territory raised the specter of death. And here is the scary part: those who also read that Muslims had died in a plane crash had the same low level of death thoughts as those who read about the Aurora Borealis. The death of "evildoers" reduced their own mortal terror.

NOTHING NEW UNDER THE SUN

We have now seen how "man's inhumanity to man" stems from humankind's fundamental intolerance of, and propensity to humiliate, those who subscribe to different cultural worldviews. This is compounded by the need to dispose of residual death anxiety by projecting it onto "evil" others. Surely disagreements over territory and access to scarce resources also play a central role in human discord. But such pragmatic considerations also reflect deeper symbolic concerns. What one group claims as its God-given right is viewed by the other as a humiliating injustice. What one group views as a righteous reaction to humiliating injustice, the other views as an act of greed and aggression.

As both sides claim the ethical high ground and bemoan the indignities to which they have been subjected, violent confrontations seem not only justified but morally imperative. The strange beliefs, values, customs, and even physical appearance of the others seem to affirm their wrongmindedness and malevolent intent. Material disputes quickly escalate into cosmic battles of Good (us) versus Evil (them). Rather than battling over trade routes or water rights, the individuals who do the actual killing and dying fight for the glory of Rome, to chase the infidels from the Holy Land, to rid the world of Jewish vermin, or to stop the malignant spread of Communism, capitalism, or Islam.

Ironically, then, a good deal of evil in the world results from efforts to rid the world of evil. As Ernest Becker starkly put it, the "natural and inevitable urge to deny mortality and achieve a heroic self-image are the root causes of human evil." Twenty-five hundred years ago, the great Greek historian Thucydides came to strikingly similar conclusions. He had closely studied the events of the Peloponnesian War in a quest "to see the truth of what both has happened, and will hereafter happen again, according to human nature." He noted that above and beyond protecting themselves and their property, people fought most vigorously in defense of their ideological principles, and that those willing to die in zealous devotion to a cause were driven by an overriding passion for revenge that often resulted in escalating savagery and cruelty.

Because people prepared to fight and die for their beliefs are absolutely certain they are right, any threat to or act of violence directed against them must be avenged. Indeed, according to Thucydides, to "avenge oneself against someone was valued more than never to have suffered [injustice] oneself." But if revenge is sweeter than never having been wronged in the first place, then clearly people fight for reasons beyond land rights, self-protection, or a genuine concern for justice.

What reasons? Thucydides contends that through warfare people strive to overcome "their mortal condition," writes political scientist Peter Ahrensdorf, "by living on after their death—either through their city, or through their glory, or in an afterlife—and by winning the gods' favor through the vehement affirmation of their own nobility or piety, or justice." People thus fight, and are willing or even eager to die, for a cause, to garner honor from their compatriots and curry favor with the gods in pursuit of symbolic and literal immortality. Reminders of mortality, so common once sparks fly, will intensify fighting for everlasting glory, and the quest for immortality will go on and on because it can never be indisputably secured.

OUT ON A LIMB?

"Life," wrote biologist Stephen Jay Gould, "is a copiously branching bush, continually pruned by the grim reaper of extinction, not a ladder of predictable progress." While other creatures have succumbed to abrupt climate changes or competition from other plants or animals, we humans are the only species that can prune our own branch from the proverbial Tree of Life.

Although symbolization, self-consciousness, and the capacity to transform figments of our imagination into reality have been of tremendous service to us humans, they have also made us aware of our vulnerability, transience, and mortality. Confidence in a cultural scheme of things and our own self-worth banish the dread. But when someone "different" challenges our core beliefs or sense of significance, we want to derogate, dehumanize, assimilate, demonize, humiliate, and destroy them. Perhaps the only reason humans have survived to date is that until recently, we lacked the technological means to exterminate ourselves.

The twenty-first-century combination of lethal weapons that can wreak unfathomable havoc and kill huge numbers of people with video-game-like remote control devices makes killing easier on the conscience than face-to-face lethal encounters. And because nation-states will use whatever military technology they possess to defend their secular or religious ideologies—whether to "keep the world safe for democracy" or "to rid the world of evil"—there is a very real danger that we humans will be the first form of life to be responsible for our own extinction.

However, we humans have a pretty good track record of solving seemingly intractable problems once we understand their underlying basis. Infectious diseases exterminated millions of people until we figured out that illness was caused by germs, not by evil spirits. This led to the discovery of antibiotics and the practice of modern medicine. Perhaps, once we fully recognize the central role that mortal terror plays in persistent strife, human ingenuity can also find ways of counteracting the destructive potential our fears can, and do, unleash.

CHAPTER 8

Body and Soul:
An Uneasy Alliance

———

The body is the closest that we come to touching any kind
of reality. And yet we have the desire to flee the body: many
religions are based entirely on disembodiment, because the
body brings with it mortality, fear of death. If you accept
the body as reality, then you have to accept mortality and
people are very afraid to do that. . . .

—DAVID CRONENBERG

MEN OF THE CHAGGA TRIBE IN VILLAGES ON THE SLOPES OF MOUNT KILI-
manjaro traditionally wear anal plugs throughout their adult lives, pre-
tending to have sealed up the opening as if they never needed to defecate.
The Kikuyu of Kenya believe that men and women have strong sex drives
and that sex is necessary for health and sanity. However, wives are forbidden to touch their husband's genitals, and husbands must not touch their
wives' nipples with their mouths or hands. A man must lie on top of a
woman with her legs around him. Any violation of these rules is believed
to be fatal.

Weird customs? Not really. People in all cultures go to extraordinary
lengths to deny that they are animals and to regulate activities that remind
them of their corporeal nature. We alter and adorn our bodies in accord
with the latest fashions, exercise to approximate an idealized physique,

and scrub ourselves to eradicate any scents except those emanating from bottles or spray cans. We visit "rest" rooms to discreetly dispose of bodily excretions. We recoil in horror, or convulse in sophomoric mirth, at the sight of animals copulating, while earnestly pursuing our own amorous adventures in the name of love. Why?

Our bodies and animality are threatening reminders that we are physical creatures who will die. To manage our terror of death we have to be much more than that; and a fundamental function of cultural worldviews is to prevent our bodies from undermining our pretentions of meaning and significance. So we transform our bodies into cultural symbols of beauty and power. We hide bodily activities or turn them into cultural rituals. In the following pages, we will explore the arduous efforts we undertake in order to distance ourselves from our visceral natures, to proclaim, as it were, that we are not in fact animals.

DISTANCING FROM AND
DISPARAGING ANIMALS

Animals slobber, defecate where they want to, and copulate when their body dictates. And animals die. They look particularly dead with buzzards picking at their half-eaten corpses, or when their entrails are splattered on the roadside. For humans, it's horrifying to think that, like animals, we, too, are breathing bits of finite flesh. We have already seen that we humans dampen the dread of mortality by viewing ourselves as significant beings who will persist, literally or symbolically, after death. But death cannot be banished so easily when we are conscious of our own creaturely nature. So we must set ourselves apart from animals.

And this tendency is magnified when death is on our minds. The first study making this point began in the usual way, by having people think about death or dental pain. Then the participants read an essay entitled "The Most Important Things That I Have Learned About Human Nature." One version of the essay argued that humans are very similar to animals. It noted that "the boundary between humans and animals is not as great as most people think ... what appears to be the result of complex thought and free will is really just the result of our biological programming and simple learning experiences." The other version stressed that humans are very different from other animals: "Although we humans have some things in common with other animals, human beings are truly unique ... we are not simple selfish creatures driven by hunger and lust, but complex individuals with a will of our own, capable of making choices and creating our own destinies."

Everyone then evaluated the essays and their authors. After thinking about pain, people found both essays equally compelling. However, after a reminder of death, the participants ardently preferred the essay stressing that humans are unique. Death thoughts also prod people to avoid activities that remind them of their animality. After pondering their mortality, men and women spent less time having a foot massage, and women were more reluctant to conduct breast self-exams.

Moreover, distancing ourselves from animals to deny that we share their fate is more readily accomplished by perceiving them and treating them as our inferiors. Indeed, people reminded of death and the similarities between humans and other animals subsequently disparage animals, even pets they don't own. Death reminders also make people more supportive of killing animals for a variety of purposes, including population control, product testing, and medical research. And reading an article suggesting dolphins may be smarter than humans brings thoughts of death to mind.

This disinclination to acknowledge that we are animals lies at the heart of one of our most powerful emotions: disgust. Disgust likely evolved to steer our ancestors away from spoiled meat and other organic materials that carried deadly pathogens that could literally kill them. But as the awareness of death emerged, disgust extended to a broader range of reminders of our animality, such as guts, bones, blood, and bodily emissions. Indeed, people find urine, mucus, feces, vomit, and blood more disgusting after thinking about death, and vice versa: thinking about bodily products like feces brings death thoughts more readily to mind. And after thinking about death, people tend to refer to bodily processes more euphemistically, for example, "number two" instead of "defecation."

To distinguish ourselves from animals and nature in order to transcend death, we humans have, around the world and since time immemorial, responded in surprisingly similar ways.

THE MORTIFICATION OF THE FLESH

We human beings often hold spiritual beliefs that enable us to view ourselves as different from, and superior to, all other forms of life. The best-known example of this outlook comes from the Judeo-Christian tradition:

> And God said, Let us make man in our image, after our likeness: and let them have dominion over the fish of the sea, and over the fowl of the air, and over the cattle, and over all the earth, and over every creeping thing that creepeth upon the earth. So God created man in his own image, in the image of God created he him; male and female created he them.

From this perspective, only humans were created in God's image. For people subscribing to this faith, being God's emissary in charge of the earth felt (and feels) pretty good; it was even better that God was immutable, omnipresent, omniscient, omnipotent, and eternal. Being everywhere, knowing everything, having unlimited power, and lasting forever was an ideal set of attributes to help those of us who believe that we were created in God's image feel immune from death.

But even while we godly humans held dominion over animals, we still had to take care of our bodily needs. Here's how the seventeenth-century Puritan minister Cotton Mather (who played a prominent role in the Salem witch trials) put it, after urinating against a wall next to a similarly engaged dog:

> *Thought I "what vile and mean things*
> *are the children*
> *of Men in this mortal State.*
> *How much do our natural*

necessities abase us and place us in
some regard on the
same level with the very dogs."...
Accordingly I resolved
that it should be my ordinary practice
whenever I step
to answer the one or the other
necessity of Nature to
make it an opportunity of shaping
in my mind some holy,
noble, divine thought.

Another common approach to distancing ourselves from animals is through scourging purifications. For centuries, human beings had flogged themselves and each other as a matter of both punishment and ritual cleansing. The ancient Egyptians beat themselves while worshipping Isis. In later Christian practice, whips eventually came to be an important tool for conquering the flesh. If a human being is to reach spiritual heights, then the corrupt body needed to be dominated and punished like the animal it was. Only through pain could one find salvation. "If you live according to the flesh," wrote Saint Paul in Romans 8:13, "you will die, but if by the Spirit you put to death the deeds of the body, you will live."

FOR BEAUTY, WE MUST SUFFER

Historically, we human beings have also separated ourselves from animals by undertaking other kinds of pain, in order to decorate the flesh rather than to punish it. All human cultures have obscured their kinship with animals by disguising themselves; in so doing, they show that they belong to the world of culture, not the world of nature. Some beautifications are obviously in the service of being more attractive and admired. It is no coincidence, however, that such efforts are almost always directed toward reducing our resemblance to other animals. Equally telling is that people generally favor their own culture's prescriptions for enhancing physical attractiveness and find those of other cultures bizarre and unappealing. Similarly, the youth within a culture often develop their own variants of beauty, perhaps in part to distance themselves from the elderly on the cusp of death.

In most cultures, unadorned and unmodified bodies—like those of animals destined to die—have always been too "natural" and therefore potentially disquieting. The biblical story of Adam and Eve (depicted in the Hans Thoma painting on the title page of this book) makes this point quite eloquently and explicitly. Eating the apple from the Tree of Knowledge reveals the worm at its core, awareness of mortality, which in turn makes the naked human body shameful. The fig leaf was the first body adornment.

Makeup and skin care were soon to follow. Cleopatra bathed in goat's milk, honey, and almond extract to soften her skin. Early Egyptians dabbed a mix of incense, wax, olive oil, cypress, and fresh milk on their faces for six days to ward off wrinkles. The Greeks and Romans continued these traditions and added some of their own. They used steam, sauna, and vapor baths and made face masks from figs mixed with banana, oatmeal, and rosewater. Lead carbonate whitened the face; mercuric sulfide added rose to the cheeks. To avert old age, a filtered mixture of asparagus roots, wild anise, lily bulbs, goat's milk, and manure was applied to the face with soft bread.

Cosmetics remained popular in Europe after the fall of the Roman Empire. Women traveling with their husbands during the Crusades came back from the Middle East with kohl, which they had seen worn around the eyes by Arab women (known today as eyeliner). Seventeenth-century Englishwomen wore red wigs and reddened their nipples with a dye made of dried cochineal beetles to approximate the ideal of beauty of their day.

Cosmetics are still vitally important for "good grooming" in the twenty-first century. Women spend more money on makeup and skin care every year than the United Nations spends for all its agencies and funds. New cosmetics, new styles, and new fads come and go, but they all result in part from the age-old universal human disdain for bodies in their natural state.

But beauty comes at a high price, and achieving and maintaining it often involves both physical and financial pain. Hair receives considerable attention in all cultures. Although human hair grows prolifically, people are nowhere near as hairy as our closest primate relatives. Nevertheless, we have always hated the stuff. Hairy bodies have always been associated with uncivilized, amoral, sexually promiscuous, or perverted animality.

Google "body hair" and you will get about 33.5 million hits, nearly all related to ways to get rid of it. Hair removal or alteration, especially of the face, eyebrows, underarms, legs, and pubic regions, is an ancient and widespread practice in all cultures. Egyptians used razors, pumice stones, and depilatory creams to get rid of body hair. Julius Caesar had his facial hair extracted with tweezers and shaved his entire body (especially before sex). In *Ars Amatoria* (The Art of Love), the Roman poet Ovid advised young women to "let no rude goat find his way beneath your arms and let not your legs be rough with bristling hair." Today, Brazilian waxes and manscaping have become de rigueur for many young women and men.

Hairstyles and makeup are part of the transformation from animal to human, but these are temporary measures. Hair grows back in unruly ways and unexpected places; makeup fades or runs. Consequently more radical and permanent body modifications are also deployed. American parents mortified by the sight of their metal-studded offspring who need ratchet wrenches to get through airport security will perhaps be comforted by the fact that such practices are ancient and universal. Remnants of ear and nose rings from four thousand years ago have been found in the Middle East. Egyptian pharaohs pierced their navels. Roman soldiers spiked their nipples. Aztecs and Mayans pierced their tongues. Genital piercing was widespread for males and females. The "Prince Albert," today's most frequently sported penis piercing, was favored by Queen Victoria's husband.

Tattoos have been around as long, and are now as popular, as body piercing. Tattoos are symbols on our body that convey meaning and significance and thereby reinforce that we are more than mere animals. They date back at least to ancient Egypt and were often used to indicate social status and position in the life cycle. In the fifth century B.C., the Greek historian Herodotus observed that for the Thracians (a powerful group at the time), "To have punctures on their skin is with them a mark of nobility: to be without them is a testimony of mean descent."

In many cultures, tattoos offer good luck, afford protection from accidents, help charm potential mates, preserve youth, bring good health, and assure immortality. In Japan, many men and women had (and some still have) their entire bodies tattooed (*irezumi*) to remove any vestige of animality, in accord with the view that the sight of the naked body does not have the slightest charm. Today, one in four Americans, and almost half of those younger than forty, have at least one tattoo.

People also undertake a host of other permanent body modifications. Scarification—which involves cutting the skin and inserting objects such as beads in the incisions or rubbing the wounds with charcoal or clay—is common in Africa. So are teeth chipping and lip plates. Ornamental rings are worn to elongate necks. Heads are shaped. Ancient Egyptians favored elongated heads, as do the Mangbetu of Central Africa today. To achieve this, they bind an infant's head between two pieces of wood or wrap it tightly in cloth. For the perfect torso shape, women (as well as men) squeezed themselves into tight corsets; Queen Catherine of France introduced waist binding with a torturous invention consisting of iron bands that minimized the size of the waist to the ideal measurement of thirteen inches. And for over a thousand years, Chinese women bound their feet for years to stunt growth and produce a lotus-shape appendage, ideally no longer than three inches. The custom called for the binding of the feet of five-year-old girls so that as they grew, their toes became permanently twisted under their arches and would actually shrink in size. The big toe remained untouched. The more tightly bound the feet, the more petite they became and the more attractive they were considered to be. But it was impossible to walk.

Today, some American women opt for "cosmetic toe amputation surgery" to get into narrow, pointy high-heeled shoes. The surgery can make walking in regular shoes infeasible because toes are needed for balance, and high heels are notoriously hard on the back. But as one fashion observer put it: "So what? Real ladies should never be seen without appropriate, well-chosen footwear, and this dependence on high heels is essentially a survival of fashion's fittest."

Modifications to the feet and body show no signs of abating. The American Society of Plastic Surgeons reported that there were 14.6 million plastic surgery procedures performed in 2012, the vast majority of them on women. Breast, calf, chin, cheek, and lip augmentation, breast reduction (primarily for men), nose reshaping, liposuction, eyelid surgery, tummy tucks, Botox treatments, buttock implants, ear surgery, hair transplants, pectoral implants, and face, breast, buttock, forehead, thigh, and upper arm lifts are currently the most popular options. In America, teenage women, men of all ages, and elderly men and women are having more cosmetic surgeries than ever before. For the elderly, maintaining a youthful appearance is of paramount importance. As a *USA Today* headline noted ironically, "Some [elderly] say they'd just die if they had to look old."

In short, when we are cropped, depilated, pierced, tattooed, and enhanced, we're not animals anymore. We're ambulatory works of art using our bodies to assert our own cultural value.

"SEX AND DEATH ARE TWINS"

Although looking attractive helps us deny our animal nature, it also serves a more obvious pragmatic function—to appeal to the person on the next bar stool, hopefully enough so that he or she will want to mate with you. And why not? Birds do it, bees do it, beasts do it, and we join genitals, too. This oldest, most frequent, and arguably most pleasurable of activities is why we humans exist at all.

That sex is extremely gratifying and that people go to exceptional lengths to obtain it is indisputable. Indeed, the "urge to merge" has been a driving force in human history. Wars have been fought and empires squandered in pursuit of coital connections. The mass media are saturated with it. As satirist Dave Barry put it, "Violence and smut are of course everywhere on the airwaves. You cannot turn on your television without seeing them, although sometimes you have to hunt around." We are also, however, very ambivalent about sex: it's both exhilarating and frightening. Although, for example, the Mehinaku in Central Brazil enjoy sex and have it often, they also believe that sex stunts growth, saps strength, and attracts evil spirits and lethal illnesses.

Why be ambivalent about something so pleasurable? According to Ernest Becker, it is because "sex is of the body, and the body is of death." That is, sex is a potent signification of our creaturely, corporeal, and ephemeral condition. Sex is first and foremost a glaring reminder that we are animals; next to urination and defecation, it is the closest human beings come to acting like beasts. Anyone who has been to a zoo, farm, or dog park would be hard-pressed to deny the unmistakable visual, auditory, and olfactory similarities between themselves enjoying a proverbial "roll in the hay" and barnyard animals taking a literal roll in the hay.

Moreover, sex draws our attention to our bodies in ways that threaten to undermine the symbolic identities we rely on to keep death fears at bay. Maintaining a psychologically comfortable Cartesian distance from our bodies is much easier when we present ourselves as appropriately clothed parishioners at church or hedge fund managers at the office rather than as naked, pulsating pieces of fornicating finite species meat.

Finally, sex in the service of reproduction—Mr. Turkey Baster and Ms. Baby Incubator momentarily conjoined in a biomechanical docking maneuver—makes us anywhere from dimly to painfully aware that we are transient ambulatory gene repositories taking a short lap around the track of life before passing the baton to the next generation and joining the ranks of innumerable iterations of the unknown and unliving.

TO VERIFY THE PSYCHOLOGICAL LINK between sex and death, after thinking about their death or watching television, we gave participants the following survey:

> Please take a few moments and think about what it is about the
> sexual experience that appeals to you. You need not have experi-

enced the actual behaviors listed below, nor do you need to currently have a partner. Please rate how appealing each experience would be "at this moment" and respond with the first answer that comes to mind.

1.   Feeling close with my partner
2.   Expressing love for my partner
3.   Skin rubbing against my own skin*
4.   Expressing love to one another
5.   Opening up emotionally with my partner
6.   Tasting sweat*
7.   A tongue in my ear*
8.   Performing oral sex*
9.   The emotional connection
10. Exchanging bodily fluids*
11. The romantic feelings surrounding sex
12. The smell of sex*
13. Being loved by my partner
14. Connecting spiritually
15. Feeling my genitals respond sexually*
16. Feeling my partner's sweat on my body*
17. Feeling tenderness toward my partner
18. Tasting bodily fluids*
19. Blending of selves
20. Having an orgasm*

The asterisked items describe physical aspects of sex (although they were not identified as such on the survey); the other items describe romantic aspects of sex that make no reference to the body. Thinking about death had no effect on participants' impressions of the romantic aspects of sex. However, they found the physical aspects of sex less appealing after a death reminder.

We then wondered whether thinking about the physical aspects of sex would bring death thoughts more readily to mind. So in the next study we gave some participants the sexual experience survey with just the items about the physical aspects of sex. Other participants received the survey with just the items about the romantic aspects of sex. Death thought accessibility was then measured with the word-stem task in which missing letters for word fragments could be completed with either neutral or death-related words. Although pondering the romantic aspects of sex had no effect on the word-stem task, death-related words were more frequent after considering the carnal aspects of sex.

Ernest Becker was right then when he proclaimed that "sex and death are twins." Thinking about death makes the physical aspects of sex unappealing, and considering the physical aspects of sex nudges death thoughts closer to consciousness.

WE MANAGE OUR DEATH-FUELED anxiety about sex by imbuing it with symbolic meaning, transforming it from the creaturely to the sublime, thereby making it psychologically safer. There is no universal standard of "normal" sexual activity, and cross-cultural variations of what constitutes appropriate sexual conduct are truly astonishing. Most cultures prescribe sex in seclusion, but Formosan natives copulate in public unless children are present. Hopis (Native Americans) have sex only at night in the dark. Chenchus (an aboriginal tribe of India) have sex only during the day.

The particular cultural constraints on sexual behavior are not as important as the fact that they exist. When a culture provides explicit descriptions of proper mating conduct, sex becomes a cultural ritual rather than an animalistic biological imperative. From the ancient Hindu *Kama Sutra* to *The Joy of Sex*, countless instructional texts have been consulted over the centuries in the hope of converting sex into a transcendental act. Animal lust becomes human love. And research confirms that pondering more meaningful, romantic aspects of sex, like "expressing love for my partner," is not linked to, and actually protects people from, concerns about death and their physicality.

LA FEMME FATALE

In virtually all cultures, women's bodies and sexual behavior are especially subject to rules and regulations. Evolutionary thinkers attribute this solely to men's need to control access to females in the service of sexual fidelity, thereby increasing the chances that a male is helping to raising his own offspring. Though that is likely part of the story, it is also about animality and death. Such restrictions exist because men have always made the rules, and women arouse sexual lust in them. They also stem from the corporeal nature of menstruation, pregnancy, and the birthing process. In most societies, "women have been the expression of male loathing of the physical and the potentially decaying," writes philosopher Martha Nussbaum. "Taboos surrounding sex, birth, menstruation—all express the desire to ward off something that is too physical, that partakes too much of the secretions of the body."

Although women are viewed with less contempt than in the past in most of the developed and Western world, vestiges of this disgust with menstruation and lactation remain. For example, let's say you are called, along with an equal number of male and female students, into the lab for an experiment on "group productivity" and told that you will soon try to solve some problems with a partner. When you get to a lab cubicle, your partner, a twenty-one-year-old woman, is already in the room. You both complete some personality scales and hand them to the experimenter, who leaves the room to prepare for the next part of the study.

Your partner fishes in her bag for some lip gloss. In the process, a tampon falls on the table. You stare at it for a second; she grabs it, stuffs it back in her purse, and applies the lip gloss. Then the experimenter comes back into the room and hands you both another questionnaire asking you to evaluate how competent, intelligent, focused, friendly, and likable you perceive your partner to be in anticipation of working together.

If you rated this woman more negatively than you might have had she not dropped the tampon, you would not have been alone, regardless of whether you are male or female. In the experiment, the female student was actually working with the experimenter. During the study, she seemed to inadvertently drop either a tampon or a hairclip out of her handbag while fishing for the lip gloss.

What researchers found was that after the woman dropped the tampon on the table, male and female participants rated her less competent and less likable than they did when she dropped the hairclip. They also chose to sit farther away from her. Perhaps most intriguing, dropping the tampon led both men and women to rate physical appearance as especially important for women. This finding supports the idea that the emphasis on feminine beauty is at least partly an attempt to deny the creaturely side of being female.

Pregnancy and lactation are other reminders that women's bodies are much like those of other female animals. In a pair of studies, participants read essays describing humans as either very similar to or quite different from animals. They were then shown revealing pictures of two celebrities, Demi Moore and Gwyneth Paltrow, either pregnant or not. After reading that humans are special, the participants regarded both Moore and Paltrow highly, regardless of whether they were gestating a baby. However, following the reminder that humans are just like other animals, the celebrities were evaluated more negatively by both male and female participants if the photos showed them pregnant. Similarly, after participants wrote essays about death, they subsequently gave more negative evaluations of, and sat farther away from, a mother they believed was breastfeeding.

Women have historically been viewed by men as dangerous, polluting, licentious creatures, responsible for human misfortunes in general and for coyly eliciting lust-fueled masculine sexual excesses in particular. As noted earlier, this no doubt reflects the fact that men have largely dictated the cultural scheme of things. It is, as James Brown famously declared, "A Man's Man's Man's World." From time immemorial, men have utilized their superior physical strength, political power, and economic clout to dominate, denigrate, and control women, as well as using women to serve as designated inferiors in order to prop up their self-esteem. Moreover, men are more easily and more frequently aroused by visual imagery, and hence prone to be sexually aroused by fleeting and impersonal contact with women; as Mae West is said to have put it to a police escort in 1936, "Is that a gun in your pocket, or are you just happy to see me?"

Women make men hard, and this makes it hard for men to ignore their own animality. This is a psychologically unbearable state of affairs, and "something must be done" to diminish the threat women pose to men's sense that they are not animals, but special beings with souls and enduring identities. When women arouse men or remind them of their sexual feelings, men are forced to remember that they are creatures, too. And when intimations of mortality are involved, the desire to derogate comes to the fore. In one study, after men were reminded of death, they rated sexually provocative women less favorably than wholesome, modestly attired women.

In another study, male University of Arizona students met Dena (who was posing as a study participant but was actually working with the experimenters), a very attractive blond coed wearing tight denim shorts and a form-fitting halter top. After being led to think about death or pain, they struck up a conversation with Dena, purportedly to get acquainted with her; later they indicated how much sexual interest they had in her. Those males who were reminded of death reported less sexual interest.

MANY MAJOR RELIGIONS PORTRAY women as dangerous temptresses, worthy of derogation and subjugation. The Abrahamic creeds, following the Old Testament, hold that when God cursed Eve, he granted Adam complete dominion over her and told her "thy desire shall be subject to thine husband, and he shall rule over thee" (Genesis 3:16). Saint Paul said a woman's role was "to be in silence," imbuing a powerful Christian thought with a powerful antiwoman message.

Derogation and subjugation can quickly turn into abuse—and no wonder, given that both religion and culture tell men that it's part of their job to put and keep women in their place. In cases of American domestic violence—which causes women more injuries than automobile accidents, muggings, and rapes combined—abused women typically say that men use four dehumanizing words when assaulting them: *bitch, cunt, whore,* and *slut.* Violence against women is expressed in rap lyrics that refer to women as "hos" and "bitches" and in pornography that depicts women sodomized and gang-raped.

We think that widespread patterns of violence against women may well be partially rooted in men's sexual ambivalence; the conflict between lust and the need to deny animality makes men uncomfortable with their own sexual arousal. Because men find females sexually alluring, they blame women for their own lustful urges, derogating and abusing them for reminding them of their own corporeal nature.

Do reminders of death increase aggression against women? To find out, we asked American male college students to write first about their own deaths, and then about a time when they experienced intense lust for a woman. Then they had to pretend that they were judges who were meting out punishment in a court case in which a man brutally assaulted his girlfriend. When the young men were reminded of both death and their own lust, they recommended especially light sentences for the abusive boyfriend. This finding suggests that many of the images we receive through the media combining death and sex may contribute to male tolerance of violence against women. The link between death and sex in films, such as the classic slasher scenario of a woman having sex and then being stalked and killed, reflects the ambivalence we have been discussing; men crave sex, but simultaneously they want to punish women for arousing that desire.

BEING AN EMBODIED ANIMAL aware of death is difficult indeed. We simply cannot bear the thought that we are biological creatures, no different from dogs, cats, fish, or worms. Accordingly, people are generally partial to views of humans as different from, and superior to, animals. We adorn and modify our bodies, transforming our animal carcasses into cultural symbols. Rather than thinking of ourselves as hormonally regulated gene reproduction machines bumping and grinding our way toward oblivion, we "make love" to transform copulation into romance. And when women ooze hormones, blood, and babies, men blame them for their own lustful urges, which serves to perpetuate negative stereotypes about, and justify abuse of, women.

Terror of death is thus at the heart of human estrangement from our animal nature. It isolates us from our own bodies, from each other, and from the other creatures with whom we share noses, lips, eyes, teeth, and limbs, everywhere on the planet.

CHAPTER 9

Death Near and Far

———

Not me, not now.

—STEVE CHAPLIN,
The Psychology of Time and Death

HOW OFTEN DO YOU CONSCIOUSLY THINK ABOUT DEATH? PROBABLY NOT much, unless you have just had a near miss with a hurtling cab or are fighting a life-threatening disease. In fact, most of us are generally oblivious to death. Yet, as we have already seen, the awareness of death has a pervasive effect on many aspects of human experience.

How can we reconcile these two facts? First, it's important to recognize that reminders of death are all around us every day, even if we don't really pay much attention to them. Most of these are incidental intimations of mortality culled from the newspaper, television, the Internet (or the book that you're currently reading). Others, however, involve the threat of death to people we know, or even to ourselves: a sick grandparent, your toddler who almost ran out into the street, a teenager caught driving drunk, or a strange lump on your neck. You could probably recall some of these encounters with death if you thought carefully about your experiences over the last twenty-four hours. But to illustrate this point, consider what happened during a single day while we were working on an earlier version of this chapter.

On July 11, 2012, a bloody internal conflict threatened to become a full-blown civil war in Syria, where thousands had been killed by President Bashar al-Assad's backers. At least eight people perished in a suicide bomb attack at the police academy in the Yemeni capital of Sana'a. Fifty-four people died after running out of water while trying to cross the Mediterranean from Libya to Italy in an inflatable boat. In the United States, at least forty-two people were confirmed dead over several days as a heat wave brought record-breaking temperatures to swaths of the central and eastern part of the country. Forty-six new graves were dug in a field outside Krymsk, Russia, following catastrophic flooding. A cholera outbreak in Cuba reached the capital, Havana. In the United Kingdom, the body of American-born Eva Rausing, one of Britain's richest women, was found at her home in London. In Utah, a man was arrested in the death of a six-year-old girl after authorities say he sneaked into her home through a sliding glass door in the middle of the night, then raped and killed her.

To distract ourselves from all this bad news, we often ignore it altogether and instead focus on more entertaining fare. We watch television shows, go to movies, and play video games. But these pleasant pastimes are also inundated with images of death. Fifty-seven percent of all programs contain violence, and by age eighteen, American youth will have viewed dramatic depictions of 16,000 murders and 200,000 violent acts on television alone. Teen or mature-rated video games, another primary source of entertainment (particularly for boys), feature an average of 180 incidents of aggression in a forty-minute play period, adding up to 5,400 incidents per month.

Besides media images of death, there are also plenty of actual fatalities around us. Mortal mayhem reigns on the roads and around the house. Someone expires every thirteen minutes from one of more than six million car crashes that occur every year. One in two drivers have hit animals on the road, and treacherous encounters with larger critters like deer, elk, and moose are on the rise (almost one hundred thousand deer are struck annually in Pennsylvania alone). Besides riding in a car or truck, the most perilous place to be for those who enjoy living is in their own homes, where falls, poisoning, fires, suffocation and choking, and drowning result in eighteen thousand casualties and 13 million injuries in America each year. Of course most of us, along with our families and friends, avoid such mishaps, but it's not uncommon on any given day for someone in our inner circle to experience near accidents, unusual headaches, digestive problems, or a newly discovered skin discoloration. And by middle age, every gray hair, skin wrinkle, and body ache is a glaring reminder of how soon death is coming.

If life is so perilous and people are perpetually pelted with an onslaught of reminders of potentially lethal hazards, shouldn't they be constantly cowering in closets or frantically groping for supersized sedatives? Is death really the worm at the core of the human condition, or is it just an aberrant fixation of sullen artists, philosophers, and psychologists like the three of us?

DEATH: OUT OF SIGHT, OUT OF MIND?

"I am dying of breast cancer," Gisela wrote. "The mastectomy came too late. I have a gigantic slice across my chest, going up under my arm, where my breast used to be. It's horrifying to look at. The cancer has metastasized, the doctors say. It's moved into the lining of my lung, which is why I've been coughing so much. They are still treating me with chemotherapy, which makes me dreadfully nauseous. I'm losing weight. My hair is all gone. I'm beginning to look like a Nazi concentration camp survivor. I'm much too young to die, and I'm horribly frightened."

Gisela wasn't really dying of cancer, but because she had witnessed her mother's awful death from it, she had a pretty clear idea of what such a process entailed. She was a participant in a study conducted in the early 1990s by a German colleague, Randolph Ochsmann. Ochsmann wondered what would happen if, in addition to describing the emotions aroused by thoughts of their own deaths and what they thought would happen when they died, the study participants also spent an additional, torturous twenty minutes writing about what it would be like to have been diagnosed with advanced-stage cancer. Then he asked them to pass judgment on prostitutes and criminals. Would the respondents become more punitive, like the Arizona judges who increased Carol Ann Dennis's bail for prostitution after pondering their own mortality?

Surprisingly, this more potent and protracted death reminder did *not* increase the participants' desire to punish. What was going on?

The most obvious difference between Ochsmann's study and ours with the judges was the greater length of time that participants focused on thoughts of their mortality. So we ran another experiment, in which we compared the effects of a short and more extensive contemplation of death in the same study. Some people responded to our usual two questions about their own death. Others responded to the same questions, but they also were asked to consider their deepest emotions about death and to describe what scared them most about dying. Moreover, they were told that if it would help them get in touch with these emotions, they should imagine that they had been diagnosed as having advanced-stage cancer.

Then, after a short delay, they evaluated the authors of a pro-American and an anti-American essay. As in our earlier experiments, those who just answered the two questions about their mortality had more favorable evaluations of the pro-American target and more unfavorable evaluations of the anti-American target. But those who thought more extensively about their own deaths didn't react more positively to the pro-American target, or at all negatively to the anti-American target.

This, too, was strange. Once again, these findings flew in the face of common sense. Use more dynamite and get a bigger explosion. Hit the car brakes harder and stop sooner. Eat more potato chips and gain more weight. Why not the same for thinking about death? Shouldn't spending a lot of time contemplating one's mortality cause a *more* vigorous reaction rather than none at all?

We thought that these findings might be due to the fact that the people who thought about death more deeply were more likely to *still* be thinking about death when they read the essays. Usually, participants in our studies experienced a short delay between pondering their mortality and having to evaluate the essay writers. For those participants not prompted to think deeply about death, this delay may have given them enough time to get thoughts of death out of their minds. But for those who had to think about their own deaths more thoroughly, the mortal thoughts may have been harder to shake off.

To check this hunch, we redid the study of reactions to pro-American and anti-American essays. This time, some participants experienced a delay after describing the emotions aroused by thoughts of their own death and what they thought would happen when they died. Other people went right from contemplating their death to judging the essays. When a delay followed the death reminder, participants had more favorable evaluations of the pro-American target and more unfavorable evaluations of the anti-American target. However, participants who evaluated the pro- and anti-American essays *immediately* after thinking about death did not show these exaggerated defensive reactions. Our hunch was correct.

Based on this study, and fortified by additional research, we discovered that human beings use two distinct kinds of psychological defenses to cope with thoughts of death. When we are conscious of death, our *proximal defenses* are activated. These are rational (or rationalizing) efforts to get rid of such thoughts. We either repress these uncomfortable thoughts, try to distract ourselves, or push the problem of death into the distant future.

In contrast, unconscious thoughts of death instigate our *distal defenses*. These defenses have no logical or semantic relation to the problem of death. Prescribing harsher punishment for criminals, derogating others who repudiate our cultural values, or attempting to boost our self-esteem has little or no direct bearing on the brute fact that we will someday die. Nevertheless, such reactions muffle mortal terror because they support the belief that we will endure in some literal or symbolic form beyond our death.

Proximal and distal defenses typically work in tandem. A reminder of death prompts a proximal defense as we try to get the unpleasant thought out of our mind. But once we do that, those thoughts linger on the fringes of our consciousness, and then our distal defenses kick in. This explains why most people believe they don't think about death or that they're not affected by such thoughts, despite being bombarded with intimations of mortality every day. In short, proximal defenses enable us to depose death thoughts from the forefront of our mind, and distal defenses keep unconscious death thoughts from becoming conscious.

However, the ongoing operation of distal defenses—in the form of believing that one is a valuable contributor to a meaningful cultural scheme of things—renders proximal defenses viable in the first place. This is a complex idea, so an analogy helps here. Think of psychological security as a way of keeping the inside of a leaky old house dry in a heavy rainstorm. You need to place some buckets around the house to catch whatever raindrops might be coming through the roof. The rain represents death thoughts; the roof represents your distal defenses; and the buckets represent your proximal defenses. If the roof, which serves to keep water from cascading into the house (just as distal defenses function to prevent death thoughts from becoming conscious), has just a few leaks, the buckets (proximal defenses) will suffice to collect the water and keep the house dry. But if the roof leaks profusely, or is blown completely off in the storm, the buckets won't be able to keep up with the influx of water. Your psychological house would then be swamped by a raging river of death fears in exceedingly short order.

In other words, distal defenses keep death thoughts from flooding consciousness. Throughout our lives, proximal defenses help us deal with occasions when death stands at the front and center of our minds. But for most of us, the distal defenses minimize such instances, so we are not preoccupied with our ultimate fate beyond what our proximal distractions and rationalizations can handle.

NOW CONSIDER HOW YOUR PROXIMAL and distal defenses might function on an average day. Let's say you're a middle-aged person living in an apartment in lower Manhattan. Your clock radio, set to wake you to NPR, rouses you with news of bomb blasts that have killed innocents in the Middle East. You crack open your eyes and hear a siren screaming down the street in front of your apartment. You tumble out of bed and go into the bathroom, where the mirror tells you that the hair on your temples is graying, the sacks below your eyes are getting baggier, and a strange-looking new mole has taken up residence next to your nose. You nick yourself and draw blood as you shave.

As you pull on your clothes in the bedroom, you turn on the television. An earthquake has devastated a city, killing thousands of people. You watch the dead being pulled from the rubble. A reporter interviews a rescue worker. Health officials lament the mounting body count and the devastating illnesses likely to follow the disaster. Depressed, you switch channels. Flitting past another channel, you see that climate change may force 100,000-plus people to leave their homes on the tiny island nation of Kiribati to move to the higher ground of Fiji.

Shaking your head, you turn off the television and walk into the kitchen. You eat a bowl of high-fiber cereal and think briefly of your cousin who died of colon cancer. Then you take the elevator down to the street. You don't like elevators; that dropping feeling makes you feel queasy. As you cross the avenue with all of your black-clothed, grim-looking fellow Manhattanites, a speeding taxi nearly clips you on your way to your high-pressure job. You feel a terrible, cold frisson of adrenaline. When you get to the office, you hear a colleague at the coffee station saying something like "Hey, I just read this interesting tidbit. Did you know that people with high tolerance to cold live longer?"

What is happening to you, psychologically speaking, as you face a morning full of terrible news and that rush of adrenaline at the crosswalk? Immediately after the brush with the cab, your brain goes on the defensive in an effort to banish the realization that you could have been hit. When you are *conscious* of death, proximal defenses work to purge death thoughts from your mind as soon as they arise. You tell yourself, "I still have a long time to live."

At the same time, your proximal defenses also tell you to look for tiny, seemingly logical shards of proof that you will go on living for many years to come. Your officemate's telling you that people with high tolerance to cold live longer gets you thinking. Your brain's hungry pincers grasp and hold on to this idea. You believe that you can hold death at a distance if you walk to work without an overcoat. Indeed, in a clever study to demonstrate this point, researchers found that people who were told that having a high tolerance for cold is associated with longevity subsequently kept their hands plunged into a bucket of ice water longer than others who were not informed of this (completely spurious) association.

And as you go about your day, proximal defenses enable you to distract yourself, or suppress or rationalize away the daily reminders of mortality—the bags under your eyes, the news of distant earthquakes and bombings, and so on. As long as you can tell yourself "Not me, not now," reminders of death are like so much white noise. In the absence of such defenses, you could be panicking about death all the time.

Only after death thoughts have been banished from consciousness do the distal defenses kick in. Back at your desk in the office, you daydream about getting the firm's highest bonus this year and imagine your name on the plaque at company headquarters marking this achievement. By shoring up the sense that you are a significant person in a meaningful universe, you become a viable candidate for transcending death via immortality. "Not me," you think. "Not ever!"

THE POWER OF THE UNCONSCIOUS

"But wait a minute," you may be saying. "I just don't see how unconscious death thoughts can influence my judgments. How do you know that distal defenses are launched when death is on my mind but I am unaware of it?"

The fact is, your brain gnaws anxiously on the bone of death more often than you think, but the ongoing operation of proximal and distal defenses keeps you from realizing it. So instead of walking around worrying about dying, proximal defenses first distract you with matters like what you want to eat for lunch and who will be the next contestant to be eliminated from *American Idol*. Distal defenses then direct you to think about how right your beliefs are or how much you are accomplishing.

To see whether distal defenses really occur when people have death thoughts hovering outside consciousness, consider what happens when researchers use subliminal messages. Experiments involving subliminal messages were famously initiated in 1957 when market researcher James

Vicary ran a study at a movie theater in Fort Lee, New Jersey. While the patrons watched a movie, two undetectable subliminal messages ("eat popcorn" and "drink Coca-Cola") flashed on the screen for three milliseconds every five seconds. Vicary claimed that popcorn and Coke sales rose dramatically, but he later admitted that he had fabricated his findings. Nonetheless, subsequent work has shown that subliminal messages are powerful indeed.

In one of our favorite studies, social psychologist Mark Baldwin and colleagues had Catholic women read a short story in which a woman described a sexually provocative dream:

> It was a pleasant, low-key dream. She was in bed with Mike Campbell, except that ... they weren't in bed but outdoors. . . . In the dream, spring had really come. . . . They were lying on a green lawn, the grass springy under their backs, playing with each other's hands. For a time, he watched her without speaking; then slowly his hand moved to the base of her neck. He loosened the pins that held her soft brown hair in place, so that it fell to her shoulders. He leaned forward to brush her lips with a tentative, lingering kiss, then he lifted her into his arms and kissed her again. Carefully, he was undressing her, pausing to neatly fold each garment before he moved on to the next. It was a slow process, but he did it perfectly, so, in time, Janet felt more thoroughly naked than ever before.

Afterward, half of the women were repeatedly exposed to subliminal pictures of the pope (John Paul II) or of an unfamiliar man of similar age and appearance, for five milliseconds every five seconds. Both the pope and the unfamiliar gentleman were depicted as frowning in a decidedly disapproving way. Everyone was then asked to rate themselves on a scale of competence, morality, and temperament. Although none of the women reported seeing any of the subliminal images, those exposed to the frowning pope rated themselves as less competent, less moral, and more anxious. Subliminal stimuli had a potent psychological effect.

To determine whether subliminal presentation of death-related words would activate distal defenses, we once again had American participants evaluate essays by foreign students that were supportive or critical of the United States. But this time, we threw in a sneaky twist. Before reading the essays, we had the students sit in a computer lab and look at pairs of words and judge whether they were similar or dissimilar. If words like "flower" and "rose" appeared on the computer screen, they pressed a right-hand key. If unrelated words like "fajitas" and "sneaker" appeared, they pressed a left-hand key. In between those two readily visible words, we flashed single words: either "death," "field," "pain," or "fail," for 28 milliseconds— not enough time for the conscious mind to notice them.

No one reported seeing anything in between the readily visible words. And the subliminal words "field," "fail," and "pain" had no effect on evaluations of the authors of the essays. But the participants subliminally exposed to the word "death" reported greater affection for the pro-U.S. student and intensified their disdain for the anti-U.S. student. The mere word "death" had a significant impact on people's judgments—even though they were unaware of having seen it.

This experiment, and many others like it, show that unconscious death thoughts instigate distal defenses.

DEATH *CAN* BE HAZARDOUS
TO YOUR HEALTH

Proximal and distal defenses affect the way people deal with the prospect of death in their daily lives, particularly when it comes to their health. Two of our former students, Jamie Arndt and Jamie Goldenberg, have spearheaded research showing how proximal and distal defenses produce both beneficial and detrimental responses to a host of health-related concerns. Although people often do the right things to keep themselves alive and well—dodging oncoming traffic, or getting flu vaccines—they also undermine their health through risky activities such as smoking cigarettes and having unprotected sex. The Jamies proposed that because people's core motivation is to quell their fear of death rather than to take care of themselves per se, conscious and unconscious death thoughts can have different effects on health-related attitudes and behaviors. And while some proximal and distal reactions are good for you, others foster sickness and even death.

Proximal Defenses and Health

Sometimes, proximal defenses—the ones you use to remove thoughts of death from consciousness—can improve your physical well-being. If you've just seen your doctor, and she tells you that you are in danger of getting atherosclerosis, the prospect of a lethal heart attack could move you to eat a carrot stick instead of that fried cheese stick. Eating the carrot gets death off your mind and clumps of fat off the walls of your arteries. What about that phlegm you've been coughing up? Is it due to a bad cold or a cancerous tumor? Making an appointment with your doctor for a physical gets death off your mind, and if you actually get there and the doctor suspects something, early cancer detection dramatically increases your chances of recovery.

Research confirms the potentially beneficial effects of proximal reactions to death reminders. Immediately after writing about their mortality, when death thoughts are presumably conscious, people reported that they planned to exercise more and chose more potent sunblock to use at the beach. Similarly, immediately after writing about their mortality, occasional smokers reported that they intended to cut back on cigarettes. In situations like these, proximal reactions to banish death thoughts from consciousness also serve to enhance physical well-being.

But at other times, proximal defenses can have pernicious consequences. Occasionally we rationalize our bad choices by saying something like, "That fried cheese stick would be bad for me if I was fat, but luckily I'm just big-boned, so I'll have a dozen." This kind of "not-me" tactic gets death thoughts out of mind, but it doesn't do anything to promote one's physical well-being. Not-now tactics work, too: "It's too damned hot to exercise, and it wouldn't be right not to help my neighbors kick the keg at the July Fourth picnic!" or "I'll cut down on my drinking as soon as the wine cellar is empty." Such thoughts drive death thoughts out of mind, but in so doing, they defer effective behavior, often indefinitely.

Shifting focus away from oneself also helps purge death thoughts from consciousness. Research shows that self-awareness—for example, when you see your image in a mirror or notice someone looking at you, and you become aware that you are thinking about yourself—brings death thoughts more readily to mind. Consequently, people are especially eager to avoid focusing on themselves after thinking about death. Overeating, excessive drinking, chain-smoking, and long stints in front of the television all reduce self-awareness. Nothing like a jumbo pizza washed down with a case of Budweiser and topped off by a pack of Marlboros in the midst of (another) James Bond movie marathon to muffle self-consciousness.

So, vowing to slow down on the way home just after watching gory traffic accidents in a driving safety class is an effective proximal ploy to push conscious death thoughts into the unconscious. That's good. A few stiff drinks to muffle self-awareness before hitting the road would serve the same proximal function. That's not good.

Imagine, for example, walking around on the beautiful campus of the Interdisciplinary Center (IDC) in Herzliya, Israel. You are handed a flyer from the (fictitious) Kalima Institute that reads, "Are you concerned about death? We can help! Call us and we can ease your suffering both physically and spiritually." Following the text is a phone number and name of a contact person. Then, just a few seconds later and fifteen meters away, a friendly student in a booth tries to sell you a Caipirinha—a beverage with cachaça (very strong Brazilian rum), raw sugar, and lime—advertised as containing a whopping 30 percent alcohol. How likely are you to imbibe?

This clever experiment was actually conducted by our colleague Gilad Hirschberger and his associates at the IDC. Half of the participants got the flyer described above about death; the others received a superficially similar flyer from the Kalima Institute that read, "Are you dealing with severe back pain? We can help! Call us and we can ease your suffering both physically and spiritually." Then half of all of the participants were solicited to purchase the über-alcoholic Caipirinha; the others were peddled a refreshing, comparably priced nonalcoholic beverage.

When people received the flyers about pain or death and were subsequently offered the nonalcoholic drink, sales were about the same in both cases. There was, however, a whopping difference when booze was on the menu. This time, more than one third of the people who received the flyer about death bought a Caipirinha, compared to less than one tenth of the folks who received the flyer about back pain. Being "comfortably numb" from drugs and alcohol is a great way to banish death thoughts from consciousness, but not so great for staying healthy and alive.

WHEN DO PEOPLE REACT to conscious death thoughts with constructive rather than destructive proximal defenses? There seem to be two basic determinants of more beneficial coping. First, people with high self-esteem are less fearful of death and therefore less in need of distractions and rationalizations when a real death threat arises—say, a serious heart arrhythmia or a cancerous melanoma. They are better able to confront these matters head-on. Second, optimistic people, who tend to believe that exercise, medical care, and healthy living can effectively prolong their lives, are more likely to seek diagnoses and engage in health-promoting behaviors. Pessimists, who tend to doubt that much can be done, are much more likely to seek distractions or deny the threat.

Distal Defenses and Health

What happens to health-related attitudes and behaviors when the problem of death is on the fringes of consciousness? Recall that immediately after a reminder of their mortality, people engage in proximal defenses, such as planning to exercise more, in order to remove death thoughts from consciousness. But a very different picture emerges a few minutes later. Once those thoughts of death have faded from consciousness, your reactions depend on the values from which you derive self-esteem, and on your core cultural beliefs.

Let's say you like to take good care of your body, watch what you eat, and run at least three miles every morning. Your self-esteem is based on looking good and staying healthy. You and others are given our standard essay questions asking you to think about death. Then you're asked to read a mundane passage from a novel for a few minutes, enough time for any proximal defenses to banish death thoughts from consciousness. Finally, you take a survey that includes a question about how much you intend to exercise in the future. Like other study participants who based their self-esteem on being fit, you report that you were going to step up your exercise regimen. But if your self-esteem was based on the quality of your stamp collection rather than on overall fitness, there would be no change in your exercise intentions.

This experiment also highlighted the distinction between proximal and distal defenses. While the proximal defenses usher death thoughts from consciousness, distal defenses shore up self-esteem. When death thoughts are conscious, most people—fitness buffs and stamp collectors alike—say they will exercise more because the health and longevity benefits of exercise flush death thoughts from awareness. However, once death thoughts are unconscious, only those who base their self-esteem on fitness respond to unconscious death thoughts by saying they would work out more regularly.

In another study demonstrating the difference between proximal and distal defenses, after thinking about death or failure, participants read one of two advertisements for "H2O," a new bottled water: one featuring the endorsement of Dr. Jane Watson and one by actress Jennifer Aniston. Participants who read the ad *immediately* after thinking about death rated H2O more favorably and drank more of it if it was endorsed by Dr. Watson. When death is still on our minds, we do what's best for our health by listening to the medical expert. However, other participants who read a short story after thinking about death and before seeing the H2O ad found Jennifer Aniston more persuasive. They liked the water better and drank more of it if Jen endorsed it. With death on the fringes of consciousness, we want to do what's trendy by emulating the rich and famous.

Unfortunately, many of the things that are trendy and boost our self-esteem are not good for our health. And, ironically, we are more likely to do these things when thoughts of death are on the fringes of our consciousness.

For example, although just about everyone intended to buy more powerful sunscreen immediately after writing about death, a few minutes later, people who based their self-esteem on being tan opted for a *less* powerful sunscreen and expressed *greater* interest in going to a tanning salon. In another experiment, fifteen minutes after reading warning labels on cigarette packages that "Smokers die earlier" and "Smoking leads to deadly lung cancer," people who view smoking as part of their positive self-image expressed more favorable attitudes about smoking and claimed that they would be more likely to smoke in the future. (However, if rather than identifying death-related health effects, the warning labels emphasized "Smoking makes you unattractive," then people who view smoking as part of their positive self-image reported being more open to trying to quit.)

Similarly, a few minutes after thinking about death, people who based their self-esteem on their driving prowess reported being more likely to pass cars illegally, run a red light, speed, enter a one-way street from the wrong direction, and drive too fast with a car full of friends after some beers at a pub. They also drove more rapidly and recklessly on a realistic car simulator.

Additionally, a few minutes after considering their own mortality, skin diving aficionados claimed they'd be more likely to dive at night without a light, when the weather was bad, or when they were feeling ill, and to forgo a safety stop to decompress while ascending. Ditto for sex aficionados: a few minutes after thinking about death, males were more eager to engage in unprotected sex, and they yearned for more sexual partners in the future. They also reported being especially eager to engage in all kinds of risky and reckless activities: climb rocks, drive fast, have casual sex, ride a motorcycle, sky-dive, drink large quantities of alcohol, snowboard, try heroin, hang-glide, bungee-jump, and go whitewater rafting.

Affirming important cultural values as a defense against unconscious death thoughts can also have striking effects on health-related attitudes and behavior. People who value modern medicine as part of their worldview embrace such views more ardently and behave in accord with them in response to unconscious death thoughts. But what about people who rely more on religious faith than modern medicine when they are ill? For some groups, such as Christian Scientists, all physical maladies result from fear, ignorance, or sin, and only God has the power to cure them. Consequently, believers are urged to refuse medical treatment for themselves and their families, resulting in fatalities from conditions that, when treated, have survival rates of over 90 percent. In one highly publicized case, a two-year-old boy choked on a piece of banana for an hour while his parents gathered other church members in a circle to pray as he expired. Eleven-year-old Madeline Neumann couldn't walk, talk, eat, or drink due to undiagnosed diabetes; she died on the floor of her home as people surrounded her and prayed.

These are not isolated incidents. In a 2009 survey in Ireland, respondents who reported strong beliefs in faith-based healing were less likely to adhere to their prescribed medications and more likely to be dissatisfied with their doctors. Secular ideology can also foster resistance to medical treatment. In the fall of 2010, conservative pundits implored their followers to steer clear of the H1N1 flu vaccination because they distrusted the federal government. Some claimed the vaccination was a part of a plot by President Obama to infect the masses in order to hasten a socialist revolution, produce infertility, and keep track of the public through nano-sized microchips slipped into the vaccinations.

By now you are quite familiar with the idea that reminders of death increase our tendency to cling to our worldviews and live up to their dictates. Consequently, if you believe that modern medicine is evil, the reminder of mortality that comes with getting sick leads you to deal with your illness in a way that comports with your worldview. Accordingly, research shows that unconscious death thoughts tend to boost ideologically driven medical noncompliance. For example, a few minutes after writing about death, Christian fundamentalists in the United States increased their support for prayer as a substitute for medical treatment and rated prayer as more effective than medical treatment. They were also more supportive of religiously motivated refusals of medical treatment and rated themselves as more willing to rely on faith alone for recovering from a physical ailment.

Like proximal defenses, then, distal defenses are a double-edged sword. Once death thoughts are unconscious, distal defenses help to boost self-esteem and fortify cultural values. People who believe in the overriding importance of obeying the law and take pride in being good citizens might drive more prudently to keep unconscious death thoughts from making their way back into consciousness. That's good. On the other hand, NASCAR fans who measure themselves by their exploits behind the wheel might put the pedal to the metal with reckless abandon to enhance their self-esteem in order to keep unconscious death thoughts at bay. That's not good.

UNDERSTANDING THE DISTINCTION BETWEEN proximal and distal defenses will hopefully help psychologists and health-care practitioners develop more effective strategies to promote physical well-being. When thoughts of death are conscious, advantageous proximal reactions can be fostered by bolstering an individual's sense of optimism and efficacy for healthy behavior. For example, immediately after a graphic depiction of AIDS as a pernicious and fatal disease that also highlights the importance of early detection and the efficacy of pharmacological regimes, and while death thoughts are conscious, people should be more willing to be tested for HIV as a proximal defense. However, if people do not think HIV testing is likely to help keep them alive, they are more likely to deploy ill-fated proximal defenses like denying that they are at risk or using drugs and alcohol to purge death thoughts from consciousness. Moreover, moments later, when death thoughts are on the fringes of consciousness and distal defenses are engaged, a heavy-handed portrayal of AIDS could be ineffective or counterproductive for people who derive self-esteem from their sexual prowess. Half an hour after watching an AIDS prevention video, people like basketball great "Wilt the Stilt" Chamberlain, who notoriously claims to have slept with more than twenty thousand women, may ironically become more inclined to have unprotected sex with multiple partners as a distal reaction to bolster self-esteem and keep death on the fringes of consciousness. The best way to go, then, for health campaigns that make people think about death is to capitalize on both healthy proximal and distal reactions. This can be accomplished by fortifying a sense of personal efficacy of desired behavior, such as getting tested for AIDS, while also appealing to the self-esteem-enhancing implications of responsible behavior, such as emphasizing that people generally frown on indiscriminate sexual promiscuity and value engaging in safe sex.

Enhancing physical well-being by minimizing the adverse effects of proximal and distal reactions to death is a good start. However, according to the World Health Organization, health "is a state of complete physical, mental and social well-being, and not merely the absence of disease or infirmity." Or, as the Roman poet Juvenal put it two thousand years ago, "You should pray for a sound mind in a sound body." And as we shall now see, death fears can also pose challenges to mental health.

CHAPTER 10

Cracks in the Shields

———

We may take for granted that the fear of death is always present in our mental functioning. . . . For behind the sense of insecurity in the face of danger, behind the sense of discouragement and depression, there always lurks the basic fear of death, a fear which undergoes most complex elaborations and manifests itself in many indirect ways. . . . The anxiety neuroses, the various phobic states, even a considerable number of depressive suicidal states and many schizophrenias amply demonstrate the ever-present fear of death which becomes woven into the major conflicts of the given psychopathological conditions.

—GREGORY ZILBOORG,
"Fear of Death"

PAT, A THIRD-YEAR PSYCHOLOGY STUDENT WITH CURLY BROWN HAIR, BLUE eyes, and an impish demeanor, was an exceptionally bright young man in his early twenties. One day, he bounded into my[1] office with a smile on his face and a twinkle in his eyes. "I just wrote something I think you will ap-

---

1 One of us.

preciate," he said. He opened his journal and pointed to a passage that read:

> People are anxiety-avoiding mechanisms, never reflecting. Why must they avoid anxiety—what is the source or "cause" of the anxiety they avoid so religiously? What are they afraid of? That they are afraid of truth is for certain, but the truth about what? Could it be that things are not what they appear to them to be? Could it be that they themselves are not what they think themselves to be?

"Wow, those are pretty insightful musings," I told him. "You might be interested in taking some courses in personality theory and psychopathology."

"Oh, I don't need to take courses like that," Pat said cheerfully. "I already know pretty much everything about psychology. My mission now is to make the world a better place, like Abraham Lincoln, Winston Churchill, John F. Kennedy, and Bruce Lee."

"Bruce Lee?" I asked. "You mean the Chinese martial arts guy?"

"Yes, that Bruce Lee," Pat responded. He went on to tell me that Lee gave him support and advice via messages transmitted through toasters and microwave ovens. At that point, I realized that Pat might be better off seeing a psychologist than studying to become one.

I later learned that Pat had just spent some time in the mental health unit of the local hospital, where he was diagnosed with schizophrenia. From then on, I often found Pat waiting outside my office to chat when I arrived at seven in the morning. Although Pat was disappointed that his co-workers at a local pizza parlor seemed oblivious to his great talents, he chalked this up to their ignorance. He remained confident that it was only a matter of time and continued guidance from JFK and Bruce Lee before he took his rightful place as commander of the universe.

Pat eventually lost his job delivering pizzas after customers complained that they were more concerned about the timely arrival of their dinner than effecting radical changes in planetary conditions. Pat became increasingly agitated for a few weeks, and he looked especially disheveled when he appeared at my office one morning. He had been up all night collecting his thoughts, and he had written more than a hundred pages of disjointed prose, including the following:

STRANGE THINGS: Ethel Kennedy, Emily. * Warren and his dead brother's phone call. * Neal and his question over the phone "are you paranoid?" * When the telephone lines went down. * I knew what card my grandmother was going to throw down. * When I was itching all over from the neck up. * This paper is a recording of all the strange things that have happened to me that I could not and would not make sense of. * When I controlled the world through my TV. * The thoughts that crossed my mind upon entering the mental health unit for the second time. * The thoughts that were not my own, when I left after the second time. * Avoiding the risk of possible spontaneous combustion. * When voices occur, saying "get the fuck out of my mind" has never failed me. *—there are world leaders who know Pat. * Ninja is after me.

Shortly thereafter, Pat was involuntarily committed to a psychiatric facility. Two weeks later, Pat was back in my office, eager to share his journal entry reflecting on his experience at the mental health unit:

For over a week, I had a state of mind where all things were possible. I felt the laws of nature could be defied. . . . I will one day have a mind superior to JFK's and maybe of anyone ever. This, I feel, is a conservative goal. One key to such development is to be my own master of learning. There is going to be a surge of development in Pat like this world has never seen before in any individual. Perhaps I will never need the official platform of the Presidency. Perhaps pen, paper, and lectures will be sufficient. As it is right now, the only thing preventing me from becoming President is the prejudice of the voters. I will no doubt be the man best qualified to handle the job. I feel it will just be a matter of going through the motions. I feel no pressure. I feel no anxiety.

For the next few years, Pat hopped from job to job and put in an occasional stint at various mental health facilities. At one point, he was doing quite well. He liked his job at a local factory, even though his co-workers failed to recognize his brilliance and the president of the company didn't respond to Pat's repeated offers for a face-to-face meeting at corporate head-quarters. Pat wanted to explain how some minor alterations in company procedures, including installing Pat in an executive position, would be tre-mendously beneficial for the company, the country, and the world at large. Pat was quite surprised when he came to work one day and found he had been terminated. I was quite surprised they had kept him so long.

A few weeks after he lost his job, Pat's mother called to tell me that Pat had committed suicide. Pat left a note asking her to be sure to leave me his lamp, his books, and his favorite picture: a giant print of the sixteenth-century Chinese landscape artist T'ang Yin's *Dreaming of Immortality in a Thatched Cottage*, which we described in chapter 5.

WE DON'T THINK PAT'S favorite picture was a coincidence, nor was his nickname for humans: "talking sausages." The worm at the core was gnawing away at Pat, as it does at many suffering from schizophrenia and other mental illnesses.

Psychological disorders are typically caused by a combination of factors, but there is no doubt that death anxiety plays a role in many of them. As long as people's twin shields against the fear of extinction—a view of life as meaningful, and of themselves as valuable—are intact, they can live their lives with relatively minimal psychological turmoil. Yet some people, because of their genetic predispositions, biochemical imbalances, unfor-

This is a partial rendering of T'ang Yin's Dreaming of Immortality in a Thatched Cottage, *circa 1500, Smithsonian Freer Gallery of Art and Arthur M. Sackler Gallery, Washington, D.C.*

tunate upbringing, or other stressful life experiences, cannot successfully deploy these shields to quell their worries about death. So they try, often with admirable courage and imagination, to erect their own defenses. Unfortunately, these "clumsy modes of dealing with terror," as the existential psychotherapist Irvin Yalom put it, often prove inadequate. Dread seeps through the cracks in their shields, and as a result they suffer severely.

Let's briefly survey evidence from the clinic and the lab to see how death fears contribute to, and are manifested in, different psychological disorders, and then consider the therapeutic implications of conceiving of psychological disorders as terror "mismanagement" for helping people better manage their terror of death.

SCHIZOPHRENIA: DEATH DEFIED

Schizophrenics like Pat are unable or unwilling to partake of a shared cultural belief system. Subject to bouts of overwhelming terror, schizophrenics construct imaginary worlds—which are as real to them as this book is to you—to counteract the dread.

These phantasmagorical universes are often peopled with hostile and fearsome forces. "When I was psychotic, the main delusion I had was that someone was trying to kill me," wrote an anonymous contributor to the delusion chat room on a website for schizophrenics. "I started thinking that it was the Mafia, and then everyone I saw on the street became suspicious characters and I managed to work them into my delusions. Pretty soon everyone was out to get me."

To combat these forces, schizophrenics often have grandiose delusions, imagining themselves as magically omnipotent and physically invulnerable. Some, like Pat, feel that they are on a personal mission to right the wrongs of the world. Schizophrenics thus vacillate between feeling imminently imperiled by malevolent powers and feeling gloriously empowered to thwart them. Pat's dread of death was manifested in his frequent concern about spontaneous combustion or being overtaken by ninjas. But he inflated his self-esteem, aligning himself with the likes of Winston Churchill, JFK, and Bruce Lee. Believing that he was able to defy the laws of nature, Pat felt invincible. His homegrown terror shields temporarily relieved his anxiety.

Clinical observations verify that schizophrenics suffer from an overriding fear of, or persistent ruminations about, death. One study of 205 hospitalized schizophrenic men found that 80 patients were overtly preoccupied with death, and that death fears coincided with the onset of the schizophrenic symptoms or with times when the symptoms were magnified. So when Pat wondered in his journal what truth people were afraid of, and whether "they themselves are not what they think themselves to be," he was beating around the psychological bush. In fact, he was getting as close as he could to identifying death as the worm at the core of the human experience, including his own.

Schizophrenics' idiosyncratic worldviews are unlikely to be accepted by others, even if they are no more incredible than the ones to which "normal" people subscribe. If you are schizophrenic and think that ninjas are after you, or that you are the president, being routinely rebuffed by others' skeptical disbelief—if not greeted with outright hostility and ridicule—would surely intensify your already daunting psychological difficulties.

PHOBIAS AND OBSESSIONS:
DEATH DISPLACED

"I'm lying in hospital, shaking with fear," wrote Jessie Hewitson. "There are no familiar faces, only doctors and midwives hovering above me, their mouths moving silently. The contractions keep coming, and I'm horribly confused. How can I be in labour when I would never have allowed myself to get pregnant?"

Describing this recurring nightmare in the UK's *Guardian* newspaper, Hewitson noted that she first began suffering from tokophobia, or fear of childbirth, during her teenage years when the nightmares began. "Some tokophobes think they will die; others imagine something unbearable happening," she wrote. "For many, the idea of a baby growing inside them is deeply unsettling." When Hewitson became pregnant herself, her terrors grew with every passing month.

People like Hewitson suffer from phobias, which are defined as a persistent and excessive fear and avoidance of specific objects, activities, or situations. Intense horror of spiders, snakes, germs, or heights are quite common, though how such specific fears originate is essentially still a mystery.

About a century ago, Freud proposed that phobias and obsessions serve to ward off some kind of imagined disaster, at the bottom of which lies death. We suspect Freud was on to something. Unbridled fear of death is overwhelming; death is always looming and always final. Better to be afraid of *something sometimes* than *everything at all times*. So for people suffering from various phobias and obsessions, death fears are channeled into terror of something more controllable, ranging alphabetically from amathophobia (fear of dust) to zemmiphobia (fear of the great mole rat).

But how closely are thoughts of death related to such phobias? Does reminding phobic people of death increase their fear? To find out, we placed an ad in a Colorado Springs newspaper to recruit people who were afraid of spiders, as well as a comparable control group of people who weren't. When those in the control group were asked, "Can you tell me generally how you feel about spiders?" the most common response was "They just don't bother me." (One woman went so far as to say, "I just love the furry little guys.") But arachnophobes definitely met the diagnostic criteria for their phobia. When asked "Can you tell me generally how you feel about spiders?" the most common response was "I am terrified of them." Others said, "I avoid going to parks because there may be spiders there," or "I could never sleep in a room if I thought a spider had been there."

After answering these questions, everyone completed some personality questionnaires, which included the usual essay questions about their mortality for half of the participants; the others wrote about watching television. This was followed by a "cognitive processing task" in which participants scrolled through pictures of flowers and spiders at their own rate. Afterward, they reported how dangerous they perceived each spider to be and how likely each spider would attack someone who got close to it. Phobic participants reminded of their own mortality spent less time viewing the spiders and reported them to be more dangerous and attack-prone than the phobic participants reminded of watching television, whereas thinking about death had no effect on nonfearful participants' reactions to the spiders.

These findings support the general idea that phobias often entail projecting fears of big, uncontrollable concerns, like death, onto smaller, more manageable problems, like spiders.

OBSESSIVE-COMPULSIVE DISORDER IS ANOTHER prominent anxiety-fueled affliction. People with OCD may constantly wash their hands for fear of contracting germs; others hoard food, mail, or newspapers for fear that something bad will happen if they throw anything away.

Anna, a thirty-five-year-old mother of three, had recurring thoughts that someone had stolen the license plate off her car. "When this happens I am compelled to check the situation," Anna said. "If I don't check it immediately, I worry until I get around to it." Anna's main fear was that "someone" had taken her tag and blamed her for some hideous crime. She was afraid that this person would tell the police that she'd removed the tag to make the car unidentifiable. "Then the police see my car without the tag, and assume the tip is for real," she said. "The police, thinking I am a dangerous criminal, then have to shoot me." If Anna could not check her tag, she suffered terrible panic attacks. Sometimes she would have to get out of bed in the middle of the night to check it.

To examine the relationship between OCD and death fears, we asked compulsive hand washers and nonobsessed control participants to complete some personality measures. Half of the participants responded to the standard questions about death; others were asked to recall a time when other people had shunned them. Then, supposedly to measure nervous system activity, the experimenter dabbed the participants' fingers with sterile electrode cream before attaching electrodes connected to a physiograph machine (like the one we described in chapter 3) for two minutes. Afterward, the electrodes were removed and participants were told that they could wash the goop off their fingers in the lab sink. We unobtrusively recorded how long they spent washing their hands. Compulsive hand washers who had been reminded of death took an especially long time to do this.

It appears that the OCD participants, like the phobics, were focalizing their fear of death, something beyond their control, onto germs, something that could be more readily avoided.

IT IS PROBABLY NOT particularly surprising that death reminders increase phobic reactions and obsessive behaviors, given that certain spider bites and germs can actually kill you. But what about anxieties that have no direct physical connection to mortality, such as social anxiety disorder?

Jim, on his first visit to a clinic, traced his shyness and social anxiety to his early years. "I've suffered with this anxiety for as long as I can remember," he said. "Even in school, I was backward and didn't know what to say. After I got married, my wife started taking over all of the daily family responsibilities, and I was more than glad to let her." His wife made every doctor's appointment for their children, went to all of the parent-teacher conferences at the school, managed every social engagement, and even called in the orders for takeout food because Jim was too fearful and shy to use the phone. Jim worked in a small music store that sells CDs, but he was petrified when he had to talk to customers directly. "When I have to call people up to tell them that their order is in," he said, "I know my voice is going to be weak and break, and I will be unable to get my words out. I'll stumble around and choke up ... then I'll blurt out the rest of my message so fast I'm afraid they won't understand me. Sometimes I have to repeat myself, and that is excruciatingly embarrassing." Jim found just thinking about going to work or an upcoming social event harrowing and exhausting.

For those, like Jim, with debilitating social anxiety, "hell," as French existentialist Jean-Paul Sartre famously wrote, "is other people." Because social anxiety disorders generally have to do with self-esteem and feeling valued by others—and as we've seen, thoughts of death intensify the desire to feel worthy—we hypothesized that death thoughts would amplify social anxiety.

Imagine being in a study of how personality characteristics are related to social interaction. Let's say you're Jim, and you and other study participants (selected because they said they had either high or low social anxiety) are each taken to a private cubicle to fill out the usual questionnaires: some write about death, and the others write about feeling intense pain. Afterward, you're told to take as long as you'd like to write anything that you'd like in your cubicle before coming to a larger room to talk with other participants about your hobbies and opinions about current events. The experimenter explains that you can join the others at any time until the end of the hour, and points to a clock so you can keep track of time. How much time do you spend in the cubicle writing by yourself before going into the large room? How would being reminded of your death affect your behavior?

Our experiment showed that those with social anxiety who wrote about being in intense pain didn't wait any longer to join the group than people who didn't have social anxiety, whether or not they were reminded of pain or death. But people like Jim, who had social anxiety and had written about their mortality, lingered in their cubicles considerably longer.

ANOTHER COMMON ANXIETY DISORDER has to do with food. Because American culture promotes thinness as a basis of worth for girls and women, eating disorders frequently result. Clinicians report that those with eating disorders are often riddled with fear of death. Anorexics tend to view eating as a bestial behavior tied to an animal body destined to decay and die. Aimee Liu put the association of eating with death most succinctly in a memoir of her experiences with anorexia, when she opened a fortune cookie at a sumptuous meal that she read as: "You eat—you die."

Is there a demonstrable connection between eating and the fear of death for women? Imagine that you're a female college student on the varsity swim team. You burn a lot of calories every day, and you are usually lean and hungry, but you try to stick to healthful food and the occasional beer. Your psychology professor asks you to participate in a study that involves taste-testing some delicious and relatively nutritious, "healthful" snack foods—a yummy mix of raisins and nuts, yogurt-covered raisins, and chocolate- and toffee-covered peanuts—for a marketing study by a national food manufacturer. Each bowl of snack food contains 10 grams of tasty stuff. "You have four minutes to sample and evaluate each product," the experimenter tells you. "Eat as much as you'd like." Then the experimenter leaves the room.

Normally, you would wolf down the yogurt-covered raisins, which just happen to be your favorite snack food. But moments before you were invited in to taste the snacks, you had to answer the standard questions regarding your feelings about death. (Your snacking neighbor had to think about dental pain.) How much would you eat?

As it turned out, the men and women who thought about pain ate the same amount from the 10-gram snack bowls, but after thinking about death, the women ate about 40 percent less. And the death-primed men? They ate as much as their pain-primed counterparts. Death thoughts apparently drove women to seek to meet the cultural ideal of thinness.

POST-TRAUMATIC STRESS DISORDER:
THE SHIELD SHATTERED

In March 2004, Mike Nashif set out from Fort Hood for Iraq to scout enemy targets in one of the most war-torn areas of southern Baghdad. Mike and his team went on nightly missions checking houses for weapons or enemy combatants, or patrolling the area in Bradley Fighting Vehicles or Humvees. The vehicles were being hit, or nearly hit, at least once a week by improvised explosive devices (IEDs). Once, a 250-pound bomb blew up in a parked car as he drove by. When the bomb went off, Mike told a reporter, "You feel it, you smell it and you taste it. It's one big beat on your body. It's like somebody slapping you very hard on both sides of your body. You feel it on your toes, chest, head, fingers—all over your body."

When a buddy was killed by an IED, Mike spent four hours cleaning his mangled friend's blood and tissue from the salvaged radio gear inside the Humvee. A sadder, more gruesome job is difficult to imagine. After he returned to the States, Mike suffered from migraines, nightmares, memory lapses, anxiety, and hypervigilance. He became increasingly disengaged from his wife and children. "It was like I was standing outside my house, watching my family through a window," he said. But he was quickly enraged when he felt crossed or disobeyed. When his oldest son wouldn't stop badgering his brother, Mike grabbed him by the throat and held him up against a wall. Another time he picked up a baseball bat and smashed one of his sons' monster trucks to pieces in the living room. Eventually, his marriage fell apart, and he was allowed to see his children only every other weekend.

LIKE OTHERS WHO SUFFER from post-traumatic stress disorder (PTSD), Mike experienced the terror of death in its most immediate, elemental form. Military psychologists estimate that from 17 to 25 percent of American soldiers returning from Iraq and Afghanistan return with some form of PTSD. For others, earthquakes and hurricanes, terrorist attacks, or violent personal assaults such as rape or domestic violence can trigger the disorder. Regardless of how it happens, people with PTSD have been so traumatized by one or more catastrophic events that their sense of reality is shaken to its core—like having the roof of the old house, described in the last chapter to represent distal defenses, blown off in a storm—leaving them vulnerable to buffeting waves of nightmares, flashbacks, severe anxiety and panic, and uncontrollable thoughts.

Mike's feeling that he was standing outside his own life, watching it through a window, is typical of PTSD sufferers. When facing the prospect of annihilation and feeling powerless to fight or flee, people often blank out. Things seem to happen in slow motion. They feel disconnected from their body as they watch themselves from a distance, as if they are in a dream or at a movie. They feel confused and unable to clearly make out what's going on. In psychological terms, this state is known as "dissociation" because the person "dis-associates" himself or herself from the dreadful encounter. For those unable to physically escape, dissociation provides a psychological exodus from the horror of the traumatic event.

Dissociation makes the unbearable less unbearable, at least in the short run. But it also prevents people from coming to terms with their traumatic experiences. People who dissociate during a traumatic event are more prone to subsequently develop PTSD. Thereafter, they feel perpetually endangered and are always anxious and on the lookout for hazards. They repeatedly relive the original trauma in vivid flashbacks while awake and terrifying nightmares while asleep. To cope with chronic anxiety and relentless recollections of the original trauma, PTSD victims often enter a protracted dissociated state that clinicians call *psychic numbing* (often aided by heavy use of alcohol and other drugs).

Research confirms that concerns about death underlie dissociation in reaction to trauma. Individuals who experience intense fear of death during a traumatic event are especially likely to dissociate and subsequently develop PTSD. In 2005, New York college students reminded of their mortality and then asked to recall how they felt during the 9/11 terrorist attacks, or when they watched video footage of the attacks, reported greater dissociative reactions compared to a control group of students who thought about being in pain or an upcoming exam. These dissociative reactions in turn led to more anxieties about the future.

Another study tracked people who had survived a devastating earthquake in Zarand, Iran, in 2005 in which more than seven hundred people perished and almost seven thousand had to evacuate their homes. Survivors of the quake undoubtedly experienced a severe trauma. When reminded of their own death or the earthquake a few months later, survivors who did not dissociate in the aftermath of the earthquake responded without anxiety. They instead tended to express negativity toward foreigners—an unfortunate, but typical, defensive reaction to manage terror. Those survivors who did dissociate during the earthquake, when reminded of the event months later, reported a great deal of anxiety and did not express antipathy toward foreigners. The usual means of terror management, bolstering one's own group at the expense of others, was apparently unavailable to the survivors who had dissociated. And two years later, these high dissociators were far more likely to have developed PTSD than those who had not dissociated. Similar results have been found for Polish soldiers returning from the war in Afghanistan and survivors of a civil war in the Ivory Coast.

Although almost everyone experiences some anxiety in response to life-threatening traumas, most people don't dissociate to a maladaptive extent or develop PTSD. There is much yet to be learned about what makes people resilient in the face of these threats. But we do know that a strong sense of the meaningfulness of life and of one's own value in society provides shields against such mortal terror.

DEPRESSION: DEATH VISIBLE

So far we've seen that schizophrenia, anxiety disorders, and PTSD are, at least in part, maladaptive responses to mortal terror. But what about depression, the common cold of psychological woes, which afflicts approximately 16 percent of the adult population of the United States in a given year?

"THE SHADOWS OF NIGHTFALL seemed more somber, my mornings were less buoyant, walks in the woods became less zestful," William Styron recalled, "and there was a moment during my working hours in the late afternoon when a kind of panic and anxiety overtook me . . . accompanied by a visceral queasiness." His formerly friendly, lively old house felt ominous. Sleep was a blessing that never occurred, except in small increments or with the help of addictive sleeping aids. He lost all sense of self-worth. He nearly stopped talking. He could barely function.

Such was the torture suffered by the brilliant writer of great novels such as *The Confessions of Nat Turner* and *Sophie's Choice*. Styron felt that he was "accompanied by a second self . . . who . . . is able to watch with dispassionate curiosity as his companion struggles against the oncoming disaster" and that his brain became "an instrument registering, minute by minute, varying degrees of its own suffering." He felt his mind slowly drowning "like one of those outmoded small-town telephone exchanges being gradually inundated by floodwaters: one by one, the normal circuits began to drown, causing some of the functions of the body and nearly all of those of instinct and intellect to disconnect."

Determined to shed a light on the curse of severe depression—a condition familiar to too many creative artists and writers—Styron set down, in writhing detail, his own experience in a 1989 *Vanity Fair* essay and 1990 book *Darkness Visible,* whose name he borrowed from John Milton's vision of hell:

> *A Dungeon horrible, on all sides round*
> *As one great Furnace flam'd, yet from those flames*
> *No light, but rather darkness visible*
> *Serv'd onely to discover sights of woe,*
> *Regions of sorrow, doleful shades, where peace*
> *And rest can never dwell, hope never comes*
> *That comes to all; but torture without end.*

In his unstinting portrayal of depression, Styron made it clear that extreme depression "is a form of madness."

People who are depressed are generally dissatisfied with life and see little value in either themselves or the world in which they live. They tend to dwell on gloomy and death-related thoughts that are likely to prolong and exacerbate their state of depression, and they have difficulties perceiving purpose and meaning in life. Depression sometimes results from specific events: if someone close to you dies, for example, or if you get terribly ill, or you lose your job. Other times, depression creeps up on people for no discernible reason.

But regardless of how depression arises, mortal musings and doubts about life's meaning and one's own significance clearly contribute to a downward spiral of anxiety and despair. And regardless of the cause, depressed people no longer confidently subscribe to their cultural scheme of things or believe themselves to be valuable members of their culture.

Given their tenuous faith in the meaningfulness of life and in their own self-worth, we suspected that depressed people would be especially vulnerable to death reminders. Although it would be unethical to induce severely depressed people to think about their mortality, we conducted some studies with mildly depressed individuals. While depressed Americans are generally less demonstrative in their support of America than their compatriots, we found that after a death reminder, mildly depressed people became even more nationalistic than their fellow citizens. And after being jolted into defending their culture by a reminder of their mortality, the mildly depressed people reported that life was more meaningful.

These findings suggest that although the mildly depressed are generally unable to obtain sufficient meaning and self-esteem from their worldviews to muster much zest for life, they have not forsaken their worldviews entirely. However, we suspect that severely depressed people, like those suffering from PTSD, have probably completely abandoned their cultural scheme of things.

SUICIDE: DEATH ENACTED

As we saw with the anguished, schizophrenic Pat, and as is particularly common in response to depression, mental agony sometimes leads to suicide attempts. But why would people hasten the very event that terrifies them, one we all spend most of our lives ardently avoiding? Some suicides are attempted and completed simply because physical or psychological pain is so great that death seems like the only relief. In many of these cases, drugs and alcohol are used to dampen the dread to make the act possible. Other suicide attempts are not intended to succeed, but rather intended to elicit help or some reaction from others.

However, many suicides, rather ironically, result from the horror of mortality itself. Why bother to go on living when death will get you anyway? "The majority of suicides," wrote the great Spanish philosopher Miguel de Unamuno, "would not take their lives if they had the assurance that they would never die on this earth. The self-slayer kills himself because he will not wait for death." Dostoyevsky came to a similar conclusion in *The Possessed*, in which the character Pyotr Stepanovich explained his impending suicide: "I wish to deprive myself of life...because I don't want to have the fear of death."

And then there is that ancient wish for literal immortality. People who commit suicide often genuinely believe that they will outlive their own death. Even children who kill themselves seem to feel this way. Clinical studies find suicidal children are more likely than nonsuicidal children to view death as a continuation of life in which long-standing wishes may be fulfilled. And many share Shakespeare's Cleopatra's idea that in dying they will walk through the door to either literal or symbolic immortality, or both: "Give me my robe, put on my crown," she proclaimed as she took up a venomous snake. "I have immortal longings in me."

In certain instances, suicide is part of a culturally approved script. Devoutly religious people sometimes book their own passage from a transient earthly existence to a heavenly afterlife. Early Christianity had an annual commemoration of eager and willing martyrs to celebrate their "birthday to immortality." In traditional Japanese culture, death transcendence is derived from being part of an immortal ancestral lineage that extends long into the past and projects indefinitely into the future. Committing hara-kiri (ritual suicide by disembowelment) can atone for dishonorable behavior and restore a valued place in the ancestral line. Similar practices continue to this day in various cultures. Mohamed Atta, one of the hijackers in the September 11, 2001, attack on the World Trade Center, left a note behind stating: "Pledge allegiance to die...understand what God had prepared for the faithful—He prepared an everlasting paradise for the martyrs." Immortality: to die for!

Research verifies that death fears contribute to suicidal acts when they can be viewed as heroic efforts to serve one's god or country. As noted in chapter 7, Iranian students were more interested in becoming suicidal martyrs after thinking about dying. Death reminders also increased British citizens' reported willingness to die for "this blessed plot, this earth...this England." So in a variety of contexts, suicides provide a path to literal or symbolic immortality.

ALCOHOL AND OTHER DRUGS:
DEATH DIFFUSED

While suicide is an extreme and irrevocable way to flee the terror and miseries of mortal life, alcohol and other drugs provide a much more common, albeit momentary, mode of escape. Ritualistic use of psychoactive substances has been, and remains, prevalent in virtually all cultures from time immemorial. Children everywhere enjoy spinning around and rolling down hills to make themselves dizzy, suggesting that humans have an innate fondness for alterations of consciousness. People enjoy catching a buzz; and occasional spiritual, recreational, or medical use of drugs and alcohol does not necessarily cause enduring harm, and may even have beneficial effects.

People use drugs for many reasons: to feel good, amplify sensory and sensual experiences, alleviate pain, boost energy, increase feelings of power and self-worth, stimulate creativity, enhance social and spiritual connections ... and to manage terror. It's certainly not a news flash that some people resort to drugs to escape reality and subdue anxieties. By and large, people who lack sufficient meaning and self-worth are most prone to becoming addicted to drugs rather than using them in moderation. Although each psychoactive substance has its own unique biochemical effects, they all can serve to manage terror by reducing the capacity to experience anxiety, dimming self-awareness, distorting perceptions, and altering one's sense of the flow of time.

Recall from the last chapter how people drank more alcohol after thinking about their mortality. Recent studies show that reminders of death increase smoking as well. To demonstrate that addictive behaviors are magnified in reaction to reminders of death, Jamie Arndt and his colleagues had cigarette smokers come into the lab for a study examining "basic personality and smoking behaviors." First, participants responded to questions to determine if they were dependent on nicotine. For example, they rated their agreement with statements such as "I have a desire for a cigarette right now" and "I could control things better right now if I could smoke"—

and reported how soon after waking up they smoked their first cigarette, and whether they smoked even if they were so ill that they were in bed most of the day. Participants were then given a cigarette of their favorite brand, and they took five puffs while connected to a gadget that measured how much they inhaled, how long each puff lasted, and how fast they inhaled. Next, participants pondered either their own mortality or the prospect of failing an upcoming exam. Finally, everyone got another of their favorite cigarettes and took another five puffs while hooked up to the gadget.

The findings were striking. After thinking about death, the highly addicted smokers puffed harder, longer, and faster to jack up the amount of nicotine they inhaled.

OTHER ACTIVITIES, SUCH AS gambling, serve a similar function to drugs and can become problematic when people engage in them compulsively to reduce anxiety, obliterate self-awareness, obtain a momentary surge of self-esteem, and dampen existential dread. Video game addiction has become a particularly serious concern in recent years. Gamers are seduced by the allure of a fantasy world in which they can attain a sense of heroism and, importantly, in which death is not permanent. Avatars can have "infinite lives." If you do die, you just start again. Although, as with all addictions, there are multiple forces at work, pathological gambling and gaming likely result in part from a flight from the terror of mortal life.

MENDING THE CRACKS IN THE SHIELDS

Schizophrenia, phobias, obsessions, social anxiety, eating disorders, PTSD, depression, suicide, and addictions surely have multiple and distinct underlying causes. Individuals suffering from one or more of these conditions are consequently well served by a variety of biochemical, behavioral, and psychosocial interventions. But mental health practitioners, and the rest of us, should be mindful of how the fear of death contributes to and aggravates various psychological disorders in order to cultivate additional ways to help those in need.

Existential approaches to psychotherapy, developed by clinicians such as Otto Rank, Viktor Frankl, R. D. Laing, Rollo May, and Irvin Yalom, address the role of death anxiety and related existential concerns in the etiology and treatment of psychological disorders. The core principles of existential psychotherapy have been most fully articulated by Yalom in his aptly titled 1980 book *Existential Psychotherapy*. Yalom begins by asserting that there is no specific set of techniques employed in existential psychotherapy. Rather, existential psychotherapists emphasize the importance of treating each of their clients as a unique individual and developing deep and authentic relationships with them. This entails becoming intimately acquainted with the client's worldview, personal strivings, and social connections and encouraging the client to get to know the therapist as a unique individual who, like all humans, is not immune to broad existential concerns and his own personal psychological difficulties.

The therapist also stresses human freedom and responsibility: that there is an element of choice in just about everything that people do, and that our choices have consequences that we are accountable for. A strong, genuine relationship, braced by a sense of freedom and responsibility, lays the groundwork for helping the client shore up her terror management resources while tackling the three most common presenting existential difficulties: meaninglessness, isolation, and death.

TO ADDRESS THE PROBLEM of meaninglessness, existential psychotherapists seek to grasp how the client has derived, or seeks to derive, meaning in the world. These meanings can be inadequately formed in youth or undermined in adulthood because of a host of challenges, including neurological impairments, biochemical imbalances, harsh or chaotic upbringing, traumatic experiences, awareness of alternative belief systems, discomfort with our bodies and carnal desires, economic upheaval, betrayal by or loss of loved ones, and physical ailments. And this often results in the tenuous meanings of those suffering from various psychological disorders. The grandiose schizophrenic claims to consort with JFK and defy the laws of nature, or adheres to other idiosyncratic and unsustainable delusions. The obsessive-compulsive becomes preoccupied with stepping over the cracks in the sidewalk, or flushing the toilet three times after urinating—in short, focusing on meanings too narrow and symbolically impoverished to afford a sense of significance. The depressive's gradual and the PTSD sufferer's more abrupt disillusionment are triggered largely by abandonment or obliteration of meaning entirely. Regardless of the specific challenges to meaning, existential therapy focuses on helping individuals reaffirm previous meanings, modify existing beliefs to render them more compelling and sustainable, or fashion entirely new meanings.

A sense of meaninglessness often results from the client's taking a galactic view of the world in which all culture-based meanings fall away, leaving only an absurd, indifferent universe in its wake. No self-respecting existential psychotherapist would argue that life has any inherent or ultimate meaning. Instead, she would try to bring the client down to a less grand perspective on life by encouraging the person to focus on what matters to him in his life.

Yalom uses the example of the nineteenth-century German philosopher Arthur Schopenhauer to illustrate this phenomenological shift. In his philosophical treatises, Schopenhauer argued that nothing matters in the grand scheme of an absurd, indifferent universe; consequently, nothing is worth striving for. But Schopenhauer was personally bothered by this, which means that it mattered to him that there seemed to be no meaning or purpose in life. Further, it was clearly important to Schopenhauer, rather ironically, to convince others that nothing mattered. And he continued to produce philosophical works until the end of his life instead of committing suicide; that evidently mattered to him as well. So, Yalom notes, once individuals relinquish their intellectualized galactic view of existence, there are virtually always aspects of life that do matter to them. The therapist's goal is thus to help clients find those meanings and orient them toward engaging in activities that serve to bolster and affirm them. Such meanings would then serve as a durable foundation for obtaining and maintaining self-esteem. Infused with a new or renewed sense of meaning and value, individuals can better distinguish between who they are and who other people expect them to be, and clarify what they want for themselves. They can then act on their desires, "willing" in existential parlance, making more mature and courageous choices about their current and future concerns (as well as coming to terms with maladaptive choices in the past) and taking greater responsibility for their decisions.

DEALING WITH FEELINGS OF existential isolation is a second frequent goal in existential psychotherapy. Recall from chapter 2 that parental affection provides profoundly immature and anxiety-prone infants with a sense of safety and security. Thereafter, close relationships with friends, family, and significant others based on mutual affection, trust, and respect serve the same function. Indeed, thinking of loved ones reduces or eliminates the defensive reactions that death reminders typically evoke; and thinking about a close relationship being disrupted or dissolved brings death thoughts closer to consciousness. Accordingly, helping people forge new social bonds, fortify existing connections, and restore estranged relationships is often a high priority on the existential therapeutic agenda. Robust interpersonal relationships serve to bolster faith in the cultural scheme of things and help individuals obtain and maintain self-esteem.

However, if a client asserts that he or she is ultimately isolated and alone, existential psychotherapists generally will not take issue with that contention. This is because we are all, according to the existentialists, ultimately isolated from our fellow humans in that we can never communicate with them directly, only indirectly through words and other symbols that, despite their great power, never enable us to completely know another person or be known by another person. "We come into contact with others only through our exteriors," Becker explained, "yet each of us walks about with a great wealth of interior life . . . we are hopelessly separated from everyone else. . . . We touch people on the outsides of their bodies, and they us, but we cannot get at their insides and cannot reveal our insides to them." Even the best relationships cannot fully bridge this gap, no matter how close they are. "Often," as Becker put it, "we want to say something unusually intimate to a spouse, a parent, a friend, communicate something of how we are really feeling about a sunset, who we really feel we are, only to fall strangely and miserably flat." In existential psychotherapy, clients are helped to come to accept this undeniable truth. Only then can they come to understand what can and cannot be obtained from their relationships with other human beings. If you go into a relationship wanting the other person to know you fully, you will inevitably be disappointed and frustrated. By trying to use another person to overcome existential isolation, people are seeking too much and therefore often end up getting too little.

Once the person understands what a relationship with another person *cannot* provide, the person can begin to focus on the positive things that they *can* provide. The key to forging good relationships that reduce feelings of existential isolation and loneliness is to have the goal of getting to know another person rather than the goal of meeting your own needs. And the therapist's relationship with the client should ideally serve as a model of what that endeavor looks like. Yalom, following Austrian-born Israeli philosopher Martin Buber, calls it an I-thou relationship rather than an I-it one. By getting to know someone as a whole person rather than a need fulfiller, you can come to realize that the other person as just as ultimately alone as you are. But you now have that in common. Once you accept the limited knowledge you can have of each other, you can then feel close to and love someone, and be loved by them. Love doesn't eliminate all divides between people, but it allows one to value and be valued, and to feel connected to another person who is in the same existential boat that you are in, thereby minimizing feelings of anxiety and loneliness.

EXISTENTIAL PSYCHOTHERAPISTS RECOGNIZE THAT although clients are sometimes consciously troubled by death, they are more often unaware that inadequate defenses against death anxiety are contributing to their difficulties. Therefore the therapeutic focus is typically on helping the client shore up her terror management resources, her sense that life is meaningful, her self-worth, and her sense of connectedness to other people. But for those clients for whom mortality is consciously viewed as troubling or problematic, existential psychotherapy is devoted to helping them come to terms with their mortality. The fleeting reminders of death we encounter on a daily basis instigate proximal defenses to banish death thoughts from consciousness, followed by distal defenses to shore up faith in the cultural scheme of things and boost self-esteem. The ongoing operation of these defenses keeps existential terror at bay, but it does not foster coming to terms with mortality. This requires a more sustained and intentional, emotionally arduous and tumultuous confrontation and eventual acceptance of "the simple fact," as psychoanalyst Harold Searles portrayed it, "that, for every individual, the whole complex business of living, this whole fascinating, agonizing, thrilling, boring, reassuring and frightening business, with all its moments of simple peace and complex turmoil, will some day, inescapably, end." To facilitate acceptance of this fact, existential psychotherapists sometimes guide clients through sustained contemplation of death and efforts to desensitize them to it.

Consistent with this approach, people who have had close brushes with death, and elderly folks who acknowledge that their remaining time on earth is waning, report a greater appreciation of the present moment, place more importance on close relationships than material possessions, and report being less fearful of and defensive about their own mortality. This of course raises the question of whether it is possible to foster acceptance of one's finitude in the absence of mortal danger and old age, and if so, how—questions that we will address further in our final chapter.

FEAR OF DEATH IS UNIVERSAL, albeit with varying degrees of awareness. Most of us are shielded from existential terror by embracing a cultural scheme of things and striving for self-esteem. But we all have some cracks, or at least some dings, in our terror management shields, resulting in a host of suboptimal attitudes and behaviors. In this sense, many of us are good candidates for existential psychotherapy. And all of us, even paragons of psychological well-being, are destined to die. It behooves us all, therefore, to consider how to make the best of living with death.

CHAPTER 11

Living with Death

———

The two old, simple problems ever intertwined,
Close home, elusive, present, baffled, grappled.
By each successive age insoluble, pass'd on,
To ours to-day—and we pass on the same.
　　　　　　　　　　—WALT WHITMAN,
　　　　　　　　　　Life and Death

AT THE OUTSET OF OUR TREK, WE PROPOSED THAT EXAMINING HISTORY, the sciences and the humanities, findings from laboratory experiments, and people's day-to-day struggles would expose death as the *worm at the core* of the human experience. Our exploration of death's place in the human psyche has taken us from ancient burial sites to futuristic cryogenics labs, from the slopes of Kilimanjaro to a school cafeteria in San Francisco, from the mind of a typical three-year-old to that of a florid schizophrenic. Let's briefly recap what we've learned and then consider how, as individuals and societies, we might all arrive at better ways to deal with death.

We began with Ernest Becker. Although the idea that humans dread death and are preoccupied with transcending it has been floating around since antiquity in both religious and philosophical thought, Becker seized readers by the throat in 1973 with his powerful articulation of this notion in *The Denial of Death*. This book certainly made a substantial splash in its day, bringing death into public discourse, winning a Pulitzer Prize, making a cameo in *Annie Hall,* and impacting the lives of many readers, including the young Bill Clinton. But for the most part, the wave rapidly dissipated, as Becker's analysis did not directly contribute to progress in any specific discipline. In a world where science dominates conversation in the streets and on the Internet, in university classrooms and academic conferences, and in political summits and executive board meetings, the ideas lay dormant.

When three young experimental social psychologists happened upon Becker's decade-old book, they were taken by the idea that the terror of death drove a great deal of human behavior. Energized to get the word out, and hoping to launch a wave large enough to start irrigating the parched fields of social science, we encountered two frustrating—albeit opposite— reactions. Many of our fellow scientists argued that they do not think about death all that much, so it was inconceivable that death fears could pervade just about everything people think, feel, and do. Others were willing to grant in principle that the Grim Reaper weighs in on the scale of human affairs but insisted that there was no way to confirm that notion empirically, and consequently cogitations about mortal matters would never get beyond hipster party chatter.

Once we formalized Becker's analysis of the human condition into terror management theory, we began fashioning experiments to test the many hypotheses that spilled readily out of the theory. Some thirty years and more than five hundred studies later, there is now overwhelming evidence confirming Becker's central claim that the awareness of death gives rise to potentially debilitating terror that humans manage by perceiving themselves to be significant contributors to an ongoing cultural drama. We found, as Becker posited, that self-esteem buffers anxiety in general and anxiety about death in particular. We discovered that subtle, and even subliminal, reminders of death increase devotion to one's cultural scheme of things, support for charismatic leaders, and confidence in the existence of God and belief in the efficacy of prayer. They amplify our disdain toward people who do not share our beliefs even to the point of taking solace in their demise. They drive us to compulsively smoke, drink, eat, and shop.

They make us uncomfortable with our bodies and our sexuality. They impel us to drive recklessly and fry ourselves in tanning booths to bolster our self-esteem. They magnify our phobias, obsessions, and social anxieties.

Many of these findings confirmed very specific ideas that can be found verbatim in Becker's books, even ones that seem at first outlandish, such as the link between sex and death. But it's one thing to propose such a link and quite another to demonstrate it empirically. And as research findings accumulated, they have led us and other investigators in a variety of surprising directions that even Becker and his predecessors had not anticipated, even beyond the domains we have explored in this book.

Remember the first terror management experiment in chapter 1? Municipal court judges had more punitive reactions to an alleged prostitute after thinking about their own mortality. This has some ominous implications for jurisprudence. Intimations of mortality, often prevalent in legal proceedings, decisively influence judicial outcomes independent of actual evidence, and this is especially true for capital punishment cases. Donald Judges (great name for a lawyer!) at the University of Arkansas School of Law argued that "terror management ... may be the driving force behind capital punishment ... in both adjudicative and legislative settings," motivated "by an unconscious defense of one's worldview to ward off incipient death awareness." Indeed, a recent study found that during troubled times, when rates of homicide and violent crimes were high and death fears were likely to be aroused, death sentences and executions increased in conservative states but decreased in liberal ones. Jeffrey Kirchmeier at the City University of New York School of Law concluded that judges, prosecutors, and defense attorneys "should be aware of terror management influences in deciding cases ... in order to seek justice and a fairer death penalty system."

Reminders of death also abound in medical settings, likely affecting how health care providers diagnose and treat their patients. When non-Muslim American medical students reminded of their own death inspected identical emergency room admittance forms for a Muslim or Christian patient complaining of chest pain, they gave more serious cardiac risk estimates for a Christian and less serious estimates for a Muslim, suggesting that diagnostic biases could result if health care providers use their cultural identification to manage their own death anxiety. Medical students in another study reported how they would treat a patient with severe lung disease brought to the emergency room by his family in respiratory distress. Although the patient was supposedly lucid at the time of admission and was opposed to artificial means to keep him alive, those reminded of their own death were determined to extend his life as long as possible; their treatment preferences were driven by their own existential concerns rather than the patient's wishes.

Finally, terror management research has also deepened our understanding of how people respond to intimations of mortality by demonstrating that proximal defenses are triggered by conscious thoughts of death and distal defenses are instigated by death thoughts that occur outside awareness. As we saw in chapter 9, this novel insight has a host of important implications for improving health-related decision making.

Terror management research continues around the globe and will hopefully serve to enhance our comprehension of the role of death in life for years to come.

IF I SHOULD WAKE BEFORE I DIE

One of our goals in writing this book was to help awaken us all from the dream of the life we lead when we are totally immersed in our own cultural worldview. Austrian artist Gustav Klimt depicted a similar idea in his famous 1910 painting *Death and Life.*

Most people are generally asleep to the reality of death, but there is that one young woman in the picture awake with her eyes open to it. But now that we're like the young woman with her eyes open to death, what can we do about it?

IN THE BEGINNING, ACCORDING to the book of Genesis, God created Adam and Eve in His image and installed them as caretakers in the Garden of

Eden. The Beginning was a blissful time and Eden a perfect place. There
was no death, no shame, no sin. Adam and Eve had carte blanche to sample
all the abundant amenities in the garden, as long as they steered clear of
the apples from the Tree of Knowledge and the Tree of Life. Things went
swimmingly until the serpent tempted Eve to grab a bite of forbidden fruit
from the Tree of Knowledge, and she passed the apple on to Adam. God
was not pleased. He expelled Adam and Eve from Paradise and doomed
them—and us, their descendants—to a life of work and pain as the pre-
lude to death.

From a biblical standpoint, the knowledge Adam and Eve gained by
partaking of the apple made them mortal. From a scientific standpoint, the
development of the human neocortex spawned symbolic thought, self-
awareness, the capacity to reflect on the past and anticipate the future, and
the knowledge of our mortality. In this way, the "fall of man," the allegori-

Gustav Klimt's Death and Life, *1910, Leopold Museum, Vienna, Austria*

cal foundation of Western religion, converges with contemporary science: with increasing knowledge came the awareness of death—and that changed everything.

The knowledge of death, rather than death per se, is the worm at the core of the biblical apple. It is that knowledge that made us human and initiated our unrelenting quest for immortality—a quest that profoundly influenced the course of human history and persists to this day.

THOUSANDS OF YEARS AGO, Greek philosopher Epicurus (341–270 B.C.) argued that unacknowledged death fears, and the problems that arise from them, are defining characteristics of our species. In the first century B.C., Epicurus' follower, Roman poet and philosopher Lucretius (94–51 B.C.), explained in *On the Nature of Things,* that death fears make people overly dependent on religious and secular authorities and lead them to adhere to superstitious and irrational beliefs instead of relying on their own experience and critical judgment. Moreover, to avoid self-awareness and the coincident recognition of their finitude, people squander their lives in trivial pursuits, or are obsessed with greedily accumulating money and stuff or blindly lusting for power and honor. Such insatiable desires, Lucretius contended, make humans prone to unhappiness and profoundly dangerous.

Epicurus and Lucretius were both brilliant and prescient. They described the universe as an infinite number of atoms bounding about in space, coming together and breaking apart incessantly without plan or purpose, sometimes veering in unpredictable directions yielding unexpected outcomes. This vision anticipated the foundation of modern physical science, Darwin's theory of evolution, and Einstein's theory of relativity. And their account of humans as powerfully motivated by efforts to transcend death anticipated the existential foundation of modern psychological science that Ernest Becker articulated and that terror management research has verified.

How then can we learn to deal with our inevitable mortality in a way that does not provoke personal distress and hatred and killing of others? How can we, in short, learn to live better with death?

THE EPICUREAN CURE

For Epicureans, including Lucretius, the way out of this psychological co-nundrum was straightforward. First, we must become aware of our fear of death; then, we must recognize that it is irrational to be afraid of death. After all, the Epicureans argued, bad things can only happen to those capable of sensation. Dead people are devoid of all sensations, just as we all were before we were conceived. Being dead is thus no different from never having existed. No one is terrified of the time before they were born, so why fret about death, since it is precisely the same insensate state that prevailed for eons before our time? Once we realize this, death anxiety will be eliminated and we will no longer yearn for immortality. This, Epicurus proposed, will in turn make "the mortality of life more enjoyable."

Indeed, looked at in a certain way, our awareness of death yields a keener appreciation for life. The lilies of the field and the birds in the sky are spared our existential excruciations. Yet they are also denied the unique awe and delight of finite self-reflective creatures. "It is from some obscure recognition of the fact of death," wrote Scottish essayist Alexander Smith in 1863, "that life draws its final sweetness." As children we have hours of fleeting fun that Smith likened to the glee of frolicking animals, but as adults we have "serious joy ... which looks before and after, and takes in both this world and the next." We know, if only vaguely and inchoately, that our finest and most memorable experiences may never, and indeed, ultimately will never, happen again. That is why we cherish them so.

Moreover, add contemporary thinkers such as Martha Nussbaum, Tyler Volk, and Stephen Cave, death is necessary for life to go on. Without it, humankind would be unable to adapt to fluctuating environmental conditions. If nobody died, there would be no room for new humans to provide genetic variation, original discoveries, technological innovations, and artistic creations. Human biological and cultural evolution would come to a grinding halt. Each of us must die to ensure "that future generations may grow," Lucretius wrote. "They, too, having lived out their lives, will follow you. Generations before this perished just like you, and will perish again.

Thus one thing will never stop arising from another. Life is nobody's private property, but is everyone's to use."

In an Epicurean universe, then, God would tell Adam and Eve about Lucretius' *On the Nature of Things* in the Garden of Eden instead of assuming they'd prefer to remain oblivious to the reality of the human condition. And Adam and Eve would be delighted to reside in their earthly paradise, even as temporary inhabitants who leave no footprints in the sands of time.

THE PERSISTENCE OF
THE TERROR OF DEATH

These are cogent arguments, worthy of serious consideration. However, Epicurean efforts to eliminate death anxiety on rational grounds have been spectacularly unsuccessful to date. People have not changed all that much in the last three thousand years; they remain steadfastly disinclined to die, and passionately devoted to acquiring literal and symbolic immortality. Death—"the undiscovered country," as Hamlet portrayed it, from which "no traveler returns"—is, for self-conscious creatures, too terrifying to stop worrying about. Death anxiety may not be rational—but neither are we.

We are animals, and like all living creatures, we are biologically predisposed to resist premature termination. Any life-form that readily acquiesced to death would be eradicated from the gene pool in exceedingly short order. We have a variety of bodily systems that keep us going, including a limbic system that generates terror when our existence is threatened. And we need this fear to survive in a dangerous world. At the same time, our cerebral cortex makes us aware of our perpetual vulnerability and inevitable mortality. We must therefore continually manage the potential to experience that terror.

If death anxiety cannot be summarily deposed, how about banishing death itself? If we didn't die, presumably there would be nothing to worry about. Or would there? Even if the modern immortalists like Aubrey de Grey and Ray Kurzweil figure out how to extend life indefinitely, or replace body parts with robotic components, or upload themselves onto flash drives and computer clouds, they will never be able to completely eliminate random incidents and accidents that have irrevocable and fatal consequences. Perishing in a plane crash is tragic today because decades might be lost from one's life. But being incinerated in an aerial mishap would be even more ominous for beings with a vast or infinite life span, because of the exponentially greater amount of time lost. Ironically, then, death anxiety might not be eliminated, and could even be heightened, in a world where death was not inevitable.

So if banishing death anxiety or death itself is likely impossible, and perhaps not even desirable, what else can be done? Walt Whitman was probably right in his poetic proposition that life and death are age-old problems that, unlike curing polio or getting a rocket ship to the moon, have no clear solution, and that people of each generation must grapple with them in light of current knowledge, historical conditions, and personal experiences. But from a terror management perspective, it seems to us that there are two viable approaches to foster better living with death. First, we can become more aware and accepting of the reality of our mortality. Second, we can strengthen our sense of death transcendence in nondestructive ways.

COMING TO TERMS WITH DEATH

In his *Notebooks*, Albert Camus wrote: "Come to terms with death. Thereafter anything is possible." Since antiquity, theologians and philosophers (and more recently psychologists) have emphasized the importance of accepting our mortality as a means to diminish the destructive effects of unconscious death fears and to enhance appreciation of everyday life.

Let's say you are, today and right now, attempting to confront the raw fact that your wonderful, soft body—the happy one that played as a child, the youth that enjoyed athletics and sex, the adult that perhaps produced children, the same body that holds your miraculous brain that has imparted so many ideas and the beating heart that has loved so much and so many—is going to go the ignominious way of all other animals and humans that have existed before you. It's sad and unwelcome news. How do you begin to face that cold reality?

Many approaches to facing death head on have been practiced in different times and places. Medieval monks kept a human skull on their desks. Tibetan lamas used a ceremonial bowl made from a human skull to remind them of the impermanence of life. Eastern and Western sages slept near or in their coffins for the same purpose. "How-to" manuals, such as the Bardo Thodol (currently popularized as the *Tibetan Book of Living and Dying*) and *Artes Moriendi* (The Art of Dying Well) have also been commonly employed.

In his famous 1580 essay *That to Study Philosophy Is to Learn to Die*, Michel de Montaigne, an enthusiastic admirer of Lucretius, laid out his approach to coming to terms with death. For Montaigne, death is an adversary who cannot be evaded and so must be confronted:

> —let us learn bravely to stand our ground, and fight him. And to begin to deprive him of the greatest advantage he has over us, let us take a way quite contrary to the common course. Let us disarm him of his novelty and strangeness, let us converse and be familiar with him, and have nothing so frequent in our thoughts as death. Upon all occasions represent him to our imagination in his every shape; at the stumbling of a horse, at the falling of a tile, at the least prick with a pin, let us presently consider, and say to ourselves, "Well, and what if it had been death itself?" and, thereupon, let us encourage and fortify ourselves. Let us evermore, amidst our jollity and feasting, set the remembrance of our frail condition before our eyes, never suffering ourselves to be so far transported with our delights, but that we have some intervals of reflecting upon, and considering how many several ways this jollity of ours tends to death, and with how many dangers it threatens it.

Through diligent efforts to become familiar with the prospect (and the inevitable fact) of dying, one ideally becomes psychologically fortified to the point where, as Montaigne put it, "I am at all hours as well prepared as I am ever like to be, and death, whenever he shall come, can bring nothing along with him I did not expect long before." Thus encouraged, Montaigne can agree with Lucretius' counsel: "Why not depart from life as a sated guest from a feast?"

A few centuries after Montaigne, Danish philosopher Søren Kierkegaard recommended enrolling in the school of anxiety as the best way to come to terms with death. He proposed allowing the unbridled fear of death to enter consciousness to the point where all culturally constructed beliefs, including one's own personal identity, are momentarily shattered. At this extremely tenuous moment, one can then experience a "leap of faith"—in Kierkegaard's case, into Christianity. Graduating from the school of anxiety wouldn't completely eliminate death anxiety. Rather, facing the undistorted, undenied fact of death becomes a spur toward a deeper appreciation of life and greater compassion for fellow humans.

For some philosophers and theologians after Kierkegaard, all of the world's religions can serve the same transformative function. Other existential thinkers insist that a deep confrontation with one's own mortality requires no formal religious allegiance. Martin Heidegger argued that every individual must recognize that she or he is a "being toward death," and because everyone dies his or her own death, authentic living by courageous awareness and acceptance of death is of necessity a personal undertaking.

Such openness to a sustained contemplation of death may be easier in societies deeply steeped in religious concepts of soul and afterlife than in more secular settings. Americans are particularly prone to simply avoiding thinking about death and dealing with the dying, and our affluence and technology make it easier for us to keep intimations of mortality at bay. Yet there are at least glimmers of more openness to coming to terms with death in Western cultures.

In 1980, Derek Humphry founded the Hemlock Society to lobby for laws that support a person's right to a peaceful, dignified death. In 2004, Swiss sociologist Bernard Crettaz organized "Mortal Cafés" in Switzerland, Belgium, and France—casual gatherings held in coffee shops and restaurants at which individuals talk about death in a comfortable environment hosted by social workers and chaplains. Jon Underwood exported the "Death Café" to England and the United States in 2011. Participants "are people who definitely want to talk about death," Underwood observed. "For nearly all of them, engaging with dying, even for a short time, is a positive and life enhancing process."

IDENTIFYING WITH THE CONTINUITY OF LIFE: TRANSIENCE VERSUS TRANSCENDENCE

Making peace with one's death is surely a worthy goal with many psychological and social benefits. We humans are, however, not psychologically equipped to fully acquire such equanimity without an enduring sense of significance that extends beyond our own individual existence. In *The Broken Connection: On Death and the Continuity of Life,* Robert Jay Lifton described five core modes of death transcendence (some of which we have already considered in previous chapters on literal and symbolic immortality).

Biosocial transcendence is derived from the literal connection to future generations by passing on one's genes, history, values, and possessions, or by identification with an ancestral line or ethnic or national identity that perseveres indefinitely.

The theological mode entails faith in a soul and the possibility of literal immortality; it can also be a more symbolic sense of spiritual connection to an ongoing life force.

Creative transcendence is obtained by contributing to future generations through innovations and teaching in art, science, and technology.

Natural transcendence is identifying with all life, nature, or even the universe. This is ultimately how Charles Lindbergh found his peace. Recall that Lindbergh was consumed by his fear of death and spent most of his life in urgent pursuit of literal immortality. However, he had a change of heart on a visit to Africa and embraced natural immortality: "When I watch wild animals of an African plain, my civilized values ... give way to a timeless vision in which life embraces the necessity of death. I see individual animals as mortal manifestations of immortal life streams.... In death, then, is the eternal life which men have sought so blindly for centuries, not realizing they had it as a birthright. Only by dying, can we continue living."

Finally, experiential transcendence is characterized by a sense of time-lessness accompanied by a heightened sense of awe and wonder. Certain drugs can foster this kind of experience, as can meditation, various cultural rituals, and activities that provide a sense of flow, of losing oneself in con-templation and enjoyment. And such experiential states are most fulfilling when they occur in the context of one of the four other modes: playing with your children, engaging in spiritual rituals, throwing yourself into creative activity, being immersed in the natural world.

CULTURAL WORLDVIEWS:
THE ROCK AND THE HARD PLACE

These modes of death transcendence are all grounded within a culturally constructed scheme of things, and some cultural worldviews guide us toward more constructive paths of transcendence than others. The ques-tion then becomes, as Ernest Becker put it, "What is *life-enhancing* illu-sion?"

In the classic 1941 horror film *The Wolf Man*, Sir John Talbot, the Wolf Man's father, describes two diverging approaches to life:

> For some people life is very simple. They decide that this is good, that is bad, this is wrong, that's right. There is no right in wrong, no good in bad, no shadings and grays, all blacks and whites.... Now others of us find that good, bad, right, wrong are many-sided, com-plex things; we try to see every side, but the more we see, the less sure we are.

These perspectives reflect two different kinds of worldviews. We call one the rock and the other the hard place.

The *rock* is a black-and-white scheme of things, with explicit prescrip-tions for attaining literal and symbolic immortality. Unfortunately, many people who subscribe to rock views fervently proclaim their beliefs to be absolute truth, and they insist that they can unambiguously differentiate between good and evil. "Isms"—fundamentalism, fascism, communism, and some forms of free-market capitalism—are rock views. According to Protestant theologian Paul Tillich, the fundamental problem with all "isms" is confusing their way with The Way: "It makes its myths and doctrines, its rites and laws into ultimates and persecutes those who do not subject themselves to it."

Because rock worldviews provide clear and simple bases of meaning, self-worth, and immortality, they afford seductive psychological security for those who sustain faith in, and feel valued within, them. "It was a great feeling," recalled former Hitler Youth member Henry Metelmann. "You felt you belonged to a great nation which [found] its feet again. Germany was in good safe hands and I was going to help and build a strong Germany."

Heroically triumphing over evil is a great way to feel transcendent, and not just to Nazis. Nineteenth-century Lord Thomas Macaulay's well-known poem, from *Lays of Ancient Rome*, provides a classic example of such sentiment:

> *Then out spake brave Horatius,*
> *The Captain of the Gate:*
> *"To every man upon this earth*
> *Death cometh soon or late.*
>
> *And how can man die better*
> *Than facing fearful odds,*
> *For the ashes of his fathers,*
> *And the temples of his gods."*

Such gritty acknowledgment of our mortal fate has its appeal, but serving the ashes of ancestors and the temples of one's deities has perhaps led to more atrocities and killing than all other human motives combined. Why? Because the rock-type worldview tends to foster an *us* vs. *them* tribal mentality that, as we have seen, breeds hatred and inflames intergroup conflicts.

The alternative to rock worldviews is the hard place: conceptions of life that accept ambiguity and acknowledge that all beliefs are held with some measure of uncertainty. Hard place worldviews are malleable. Although adherents of the hard place take their beliefs and values seriously, they are open to other ideas and refuse to claim sole ownership of the truth. They recognize that right and wrong, and good and evil, cannot always be disentangled. Consequently, they tend to be more tolerant of those who are different.

The hard place means accepting that meaning and values are human creations. We each combine bits and pieces of our experiences with the ideas and "truths" that we encounter to construct the reality in which we live and to become the kind of people who can make the best of that world. Perhaps there is an ultimate meaning and truth out there, but we can never fully grasp it, because our awareness is constrained by the limits of our sense organs, our mental capacities, and our cultural blinders. This can be a disturbing realization, but it can be a liberating one as well. We do not have to accept the vision of reality that others have given us. Rather, we can strive to fashion meanings that maximize what we can get out of life and minimize the harm we do to others.

Yet because meaning, self-worth, and immortality are never unambiguously certain, the *hard place* is a challenging place to be, psychologically speaking. Anxiety prevails. Death fears are manifested as vague and persistent dis-ease. Those living in the hard place often take refuge in self-medication through drugs and alcohol, self-indulgence through mass consumption and frivolous hedonism, and self-help through dubious books, New Age gurus, and spiritual fads.

So we are caught. The rock provides psychological security but takes a terrible toll on those victimized by angry and self-righteous crusades to rid the world of evil. The hard place yields perhaps a more compassionate view of the world but is less effective at buffering death anxiety. Somehow we need to fashion worldviews that yield psychological security, like the rock, but also promote tolerance and acceptance of ambiguity, like the hard place.

SOME FINAL THOUGHTS ON FINALITY

Come to terms with death. Really grasp that being mortal, while terrifying, can also make our lives sublime by infusing us with courage, compassion, and concern for future generations. Seek enduring significance through your own combination of meanings and values, social connections, spirituality, personal accomplishments, identifications with nature, and momentary experiences of transcendence. Promote cultural worldviews that provide such paths while encouraging tolerance of uncertainty and others who harbor different beliefs.

Ancient wisdom fortified by contemporary science. But is there any chance these ideas might alter the course of human affairs in the foreseeable future? Given that humans are transient creatures in a world that is all too often unpredictable, tragic, and grotesque, misery and strife will almost certainly persist, perhaps even to the point of human self-destruction.

We cannot return to the Garden of Eden; we were never actually there. But the vast knowledge we have now about the pervasive influence of the awareness of death on human affairs may give us some purchase on how we can get better at living out our mortal lives. We believe that the ideas in this book provide a powerful way to understand yourself and the world you live in. And we hope that knowing how conscious and unconscious death thoughts instigate a host of unfortunate psychological and behavioral defenses enables you to monitor and alter such reactions. In turn, you can be more self-determined in the choices you make and the actions you take.

Are you acting out of fear, or being manipulated to do so by others? Are you driven by rigid defenses, or are you pursuing the goals you really hold dear in your life? In dealing with other people, are you considering how their efforts to manage the terror of death are affecting their actions and how your own defenses are influencing your reactions to them? By asking and answering these questions, we can perhaps enhance our own enjoyment of life, enrich the lives of those around us, and have a beneficial impact beyond it.

Acknowledgments

———

THIS BOOK PRESENTS WORK WE HAVE PURSUED COLLABORATIVELY FOR more than three decades. We would like to recognize our many colleagues, former and current students, and students of our students who have vastly enriched our professional and personal lives in general and advanced our theoretical and empirical understanding of the role of death awareness in life in particular. Special thanks to our friends and colleagues Jamie Goldenberg and Jamie Arndt, whose studies are featured in chapters 8 through 10. Beyond the two Jamies, there are too many others to identify their specific contributions, so we list them here alphabetically in order to convey our deep appreciation: John Allen, Alisabeth Ayars, Jack Brehm, Mike Breus, Brian Burke, John Burling, Emanuele Castano, Stephen Cave, Steve Chaplin, Armand Chatard, Florette Cohen, Cathy Cox, David Cullier, Mark Dechesne, Samantha Dowd, Shelly Duvall, Gerry Erchak, Victor Florian, Immo Fritsche, Michael Halloran, Eddie Harmon-Jones, Josh Hart, Joe Hayes, Nathan Heflick, Gilad Hirschberger, Nicholas Humphrey, Eva Jonas, Pelin Kesebir, Sander Koole, Spee Kosloff, Mark Landau, Joel Lieberman, Daniel Liechty, Uri Lifshin, Deb Lyon, Andy Martens, Molly Maxfield, Simon McCabe, Shannon McCoy, Holly McGregor, Mario Mikulincer, Matt Motyl, Balfour Mount, Randolph Ochsmann, Heather Omahen, Jerry Piven, Markus Quirin, Tomi-Ann Roberts, Abram Rosenblatt, Zach Rosenfeld, Zach Rothschild, Clay Routledge, Bastiaan Rutjens, Mike Salzman, Jeff Schimel, Michelle See, Leila Selimbegovic, Linda Simon, Melissa

Soenke, Eric Strachan, Daniel "Sully" Sullivan, Orit Taubman-Ben-Ari, Ken Vail, Matt Vess, Tyler Volk, Dave Weise, Bob Wicklund, and Todd Williams.

We are also profoundly grateful to Neil Elgee and the Ernest Becker Foundation for keeping Ernest Becker's ideas alive and generative, and for more than two decades of financial, intellectual, and psychosocial support for our terror management theory and research. Thanks to filmmakers Patrick Shen and Greg Bennick for their wonderful award-winning documentary film, *Flight from Death: The Quest for Immortality*, about Ernest Becker and terror management theory (and for their generous permission to use images from their film in our book). Furthermore, we are thankful for permission from Random House to reprint part of W.H. Auden's poem "The Cultural Presupposition"; from Basic Books to reprint passages from Sylvia Anthony's interviews with mothers and their children from *The Discovery of Death in Childhood and After*; and from the Smithsonian Institution Freer Gallery of Art and Arthur M. Sackler Gallery to reprint T'ang Yin's *Dreaming of Immortality in a Thatched Cottage*.

We are additionally obliged to the National Science Foundation (particular thanks to Jean Intermaggio, Steve Breckler, and Brett Pelham), the National Institutes of Health (particular thanks to Lisbeth Nielsen), and the John Templeton Foundation (particular thanks to John Martin Fischer) for financial support for our research. And we are grateful to Skidmore College, the University of Arizona, and the University of Colorado, Colorado Springs, and the many people who make these schools the institutions of higher learning they truly are, for providing academic environments that have afforded us the freedom and resources to pursue our research and writing.

Extraordinary thanks and praise to Jill Kneerim, our fabulous agent, and her staff (especially Hope Denekamp) at the Kneerim, Williams & Bloom Literary Agency. Jill's unwavering good cheer, wise guidance, and enthusiasm for this project from start to finish have been critical to making this book a reality. We are also very grateful to Random House senior editor Will Murphy for sharing Jill's belief that we had important ideas to disseminate to a wide audience, and for resolutely insisting that we keep rewriting the manuscript until we got it right. Thanks to assistant editor Mika Kasuga for providing extremely useful feedback, and to Evan Camfield and the rest of the Random House production team. Also kudos and thanks to Bronwyn Fryer, who helped with background research, contributed some of the stories, provided input on organizational matters, and helped make our prose, especially the descriptions of our studies, more lively and engaging throughout.

Finally we thank our parents, spouses, and children: Blanche and Frank Solomon, Maureen Monaghan, Ruby and Sam Solomon, Murray, Edith, Liz, Jonathan, and Camila Greenberg, Thomas P. Pyszczynski, Mary Anne Petershack, Wendy Matuszewski, and Marya Myszczynski. Their love and support helped us arrive here, where we could produce this book. They have served throughout our lives as reminders of the wisdom of Sherwood Anderson's tombstone epitaph: "Life, not death, is the great adventure."

Notes

INTRODUCTION

vii   **"Back of everything is the great spectre":** William James, *The Varieties of Religious Experience: A Study in Human Nature* (New York: Mentor, 1958; first published 1902), 121.

vii   **"You are catching me *in extremis*":** Sam Keen, "Beyond Psychology: A Conversation with Ernest Becker," in Daniel Liechty, ed., *The Ernest Becker Reader* (Seattle: University of Washington Press, 2005), 219, reprinted from "The Heroics of Everyday Life: A Conversation with Ernest Becker by Sam Keen," *Psychology Today*, April 1974, 71–80.

viii   **"What makes people act the way they do?":** Ernest Becker, *The Birth and Death of Meaning: An Interdisciplinary Perspective on the Problem of Man,* 2nd ed. (New York: Free Press, 1971), vii.

viii   **"We build character and culture":** Keen, "Beyond Psychology," 219.

CHAPTER 1: MANAGING THE TERROR OF DEATH

3   **"The cradle rocks above an abyss":** Vladimir Nabokov, *Speak, Memory: A Memoir* (New York: Putnam, 1966; first published 1951 by Grosset and Dunlap), 1.

3   **On Christmas Eve 1971:** Juliane Koepcke and Piper Verlag, *When I Fell from the Sky* (New York: Titletown Publishing, 2011). Her story was made into a documentary (*Wings of Hope*) by the German filmmaker Werner Herzog, who had unsuccessfully tried to board the same doomed flight.

6   **"temporal representative of the cosmic primal force":** Otto Rank, *Truth and Reality* (New York: Norton, 1978; first published 1936), 4.

7   **"Happy the hare at morning":** W. H. Auden, "The Cultural Presupposition," in *The Collected Poetry of W. H. Auden* (New York: Random House, 1945), 46.

12   **How did Judge Garner and the other judges:** A. Rosenblatt, J. Greenberg, S. Solomon, T. Pyszczynski, and D. Lyon, "Evidence for Terror Management Theory I: The Effects of Mortality Salience on Reactions to Those Who Violate or Uphold

Cultural Values," *Journal of Personality and Social Psychology* 57, no. 4 (1989), 681–90, doi:10.1037/0022-3514.57.4.681.

13   **tripled the monetary reward:** Ibid.

13   **we asked each group to read two interviews:** J. Greenberg, T. Pyszczynski, S. Solomon, and A. Rosenblatt, "Evidence for Terror Management Theory II: The Effects of Mortality Salience on Reactions to Those Who Threaten or Bolster the Cultural Worldview," *Journal of Personality and Social Psychology* 58, no. 2 (1990), 308–18, doi:10.1037/0022-3514.58.2.308.

14   **When confronted with reminders of death:** J. Greenberg, S. Solomon, and J. Arndt, "A Basic but Uniquely Human Motivation: Terror Management," in J. Y. Shah and W. L. Gardner, eds., *Handbook of Motivation Science* (New York: Guilford Press, 2008), 114–34.

14   **Participants have been reminded of death:** J. Greenberg, L. Simon, E. Harmon-Jones, S. Solomon, T. Pyszczynski, and D. Lyon, "Testing Alternative Explanations for Mortality Salience Effects: Terror Management, Value Accessibility, or Worrisome Thoughts?" *European Journal of Social Psychology* 25, no. 4 (1995), 417–33, doi:10.1002/ejsp.2420250406.

CHAPTER 2: THE SCHEME OF THINGS

15   **"The scheme of things is a system of order":** Allen Wheelis, *The Scheme of Things* (New York: Harcourt Brace Jovanovich, 1980), 69, 72, 73.

15   **"From the child of five to myself":** Quoted in Ernest Becker, *The Denial of Death* (New York: Free Press, 1973), 25.

18   **Harry Harlow conducted a set of famous experiments:** Harry F. Harlow, "The Nature of Love," *American Psychologist* 13 (1958), 573–685.

19   **Bowlby proposed that if an infant is to survive:** John Bowlby, *Attachment and Loss,* vol. 1, *Attachment* (New York: Basic Books, 1969).

20   **"Pull out his eyes":** James Joyce, *A Portrait of the Artist as a Young Man* (Wilder Publications, 2011; first published 1916), 4–5.

25   **even very young children are concerned about death:** Sylvia Anthony, *The Discovery of Death in Childhood and After* (New York: Basic Books, 1972; first published 1940), 139.

25   **At bath time:** Ibid., 157, 158.

25   **asking them what they were typically afraid of:** R. Lapouse and M. Monk, "Fears and Worries in a Representative Sample of Children," *American Journal of Orthopsychiatry* 29 (1959), 803–13.

26   **It turns out that children:** Irvin Yalom, *Existential Psychotherapy* (New York: Basic Books, 1980).

26   **children's conceptions of death:** Jean Piaget, *The Language and Thought of the Child,* 3rd ed., translated by M. Gabain (London: Routledge and Kegan Paul, 1959; first published 1926).

26 "going shopping and buying things": Anthony, *Discovery of Death in Childhood and After*, 154, 158.

26 "don't worry, be happy" thoughts: C. DeWall and R. Baumeister, "From Terror to Joy: Automatic Tuning to Positive Affective Information Following Mortality Salience," *Psychological Science* 18, no. 11 (2007), 984–90, doi:10.1111 /j.1467-9280.2007.02013.x.

28 "Nothing was more difficult for me": E. de Selincourt and H. Darbishire, eds., *The Poetical Works of William Wordsworth* (Oxford: Clarendon Press, 1947), 463.

28 Research conducted by our Israeli colleagues: V. Florian and M. Mikulincer, "Terror Management in Childhood: Does Death Conceptualization Moderate the Effects of Mortality Salience on Acceptance of Similar and Different Others?" *Personality and Social Psychology Bulletin* 24, no. 10 (1998), 1104–12, doi:10.1177 /01461672982410007.

29 Similarly, Italians reminded of death: E. Castano, V. Yzerbyt, M. Paladino, and S. Sacchi, "I Belong, Therefore I Exist: Ingroup Identification, Ingroup Entitativity, and Ingroup Bias," *Personality and Social Psychology Bulletin* 28, no. 2 (2002), 135–43, doi:10.1177/0146167202282001.

30 preferred German food, German cars: E. Jonas, I. Fritsche, and J. Greenberg, "Currencies as Cultural Symbols: An Existential Psychological Perspective on Reactions of Germans Toward the Euro," *Journal of Economic Psychology* 26, no. 1 (2005), 129–46, doi:10.1016/j.joep.2004.02.003.

30 Let's imagine Steve: J. Greenberg, L. Simon, J. Porteus, T. Pyszczynski, and S. Solomon, "Evidence of a Terror Management Function of Cultural Icons: The Effects of Mortality Salience on the Inappropriate Use of Cherished Cultural Symbols," *Personality and Social Psychology Bulletin* 21, no. 11 (1995), 1221–28, doi: 10.1177 /01461672952111010.

33 William Carney served: http://en.wikipedia.org/wiki/William__Harvey__Carney.

33 Let's say you're strolling down the street: J. Greenberg, T. Pyszczynski, S. Solomon, L. Simon, and M. Breus, "Role of Consciousness and Accessibility of Death-Related Thoughts in Mortality Salience Effects," *Journal of Personality and Social Psychology* 67, no. 4 (1994), 627–37, retrieved from http://www.ncbi.nlm.nih.gov /pubmed/7965609.

35 To find out: J. Schimel, J. Hayes, T. Williams, and J. Jahrig, "Is Death Really the Worm at the Core? Converging Evidence That Worldview Threat Increases Death-Thought Accessibility," *Journal of Personality and Social Psychology* 92, no. 5 (2007), 789–803, doi:10.1037/0022-3514.92.5.789.

35 Gould cited evidence from the fossil record: Stephen J. Gould, *Dinosaur in a Haystack: Reflections in Natural History* (New York: Three Rivers Press, 1997; first published 1995), 369.

35 This finding is not confined to religious beliefs: Schimel et al., "Is Death Really the Worm at the Core?"

CHAPTER 3: SELF-ESTEEM: THE FOUNDATION OF FORTITUDE

38   "The seemingly trite words 'self-esteem' ": Ernest Becker, *The Birth and Death of Meaning: An Interdisciplinary Perspective on the Problem of Man,* 2nd ed. (New York: Free Press, 1971), 67.

39   **As Lewis Geist, the student body president:** Carol Pogash, "Free Lunch Isn't Cool, So Some Students Go Hungry," *New York Times,* March 1, 2008, retrieved from http://www.nytimes.com/2008/03/01/education/01lunch.html ?pagewanted=all&__r=0.

40   **Sambian boys in Papua New Guinea:** Gilbert Herdt, *Guardians of the Flutes: Idioms of Masculinity* (New York: McGraw-Hill, 1981).

40   **people with durable, high self-esteem:** S. Solomon, J. Greenberg, and T. Pyszczynski, "A Terror Management Theory of Self-esteem," in C. R. Snyder and D. Forsyth, eds., *Handbook of Social and Clinical Psychology: The Health Perspective* (New York: Pergamon Press, 1991), 21–40.

41   **what happens when self-esteem is undermined:** D. H. Bennett and D. S. Holmes, "Influence of Denial (Situation Redefinition) and Projection on Anxiety Associated with Threat to Self-esteem," *Journal of Personality and Social Psychology* 32, no. 5 (1975), 915–21, doi:10.1037/0022-3514.32.5.915; T. G. Burish and B. K. Houston, "Causal Projection, Similarity Projection, and Coping with Threat to Self-esteem," *Journal of Personality* 47, no. 1 (1979), 57–70, doi:10.1111 /j.1467-6494.1979.tb00614.x.

41   **Does raising people's self-esteem shield them:** J. Greenberg, S. Solomon, T. Pyszczynski, A. Rosenblatt, J. Burling, D. Lyon, L. Simon, and E. Pinel, "Why Do People Need Self-Esteem? Converging Evidence that Self-esteem Serves an Anxiety-Buffering Function," *Journal of Personality and Social Psychology* 63, no. 6 (1992), 913–22, doi:10.1037/0022-3514.63.6.913.

42   **"Thanks for coming in today, George":** Ibid.

45   **But when Americans who are naturally high in self-esteem:** E. Harmon-Jones, L. Simon, J. Greenberg, T. Pyszczynski, S. Solomon, and H. McGregor, "Terror Management Theory and Self-Esteem: Evidence That Increased Self-esteem Reduces Mortality Salience Effects," *Journal of Personality and Social Psychology* 72, no. 1 (1997), 24–36, doi:10.1037/0022-3514.72.1.24.

45   **Threats to self-esteem have the same effect:** D. M. Ogilvie, F. Cohen, and S. Solomon, "The Undesired Self: Deadly Connotations," *Journal of Research in Personality* 42, no. 3 (2008), 564–76, doi:10.1016/j.jrp.2007.07.012.

45   **low scores on a supposed IQ test:** J. Hayes, J. Schimel, E. H. Faucher, and T. J. Williams, "Evidence for the DTA Hypothesis II: Threatening Self-esteem Increases Death-Thought Accessibility," *Journal of Experimental Social Psychology* 44, no. 3 (2008), 600–613, doi:10.1016/j.jesp.2008.01.004.

46   **In May 2008, Kennedy was diagnosed:** "Ted Kennedy and Health Care Re-

form," *Newsweek*, July 2009, retrieved from http://www.newsweek.com/ted -kennedy-and-health-care-reform-82011?piano__t=1.

47 **Israeli soldiers whose self-esteem:** O. Ben-Ari, V. Florian, and M. Mikulincer, "The Impact of Mortality Salience on Reckless Driving: A Test of Terror Management Mechanisms," *Journal of Personality and Social Psychology* 76, no. 1 (1999), 35–45, doi:10.1037/0022-3514.76.1.35.

47 **generated a stronger handgrip:** H. J. Peters, J. Greenberg, J. M. Williams, and N. R. Schneider, "Applying Terror Management Theory to Performance: Can Reminding Individuals of Their Mortality Increase Strength Output?" *Journal of Sport and Exercise Physiology* 27, no. 1 (2005), 111–16.

47 **concern about their appearance:** J. L. Goldenberg, S. K. McCoy, T. Pyszczynski, J. Greenberg, and S. Solomon, "The Body as a Source of Self-esteem: The Effect of Mortality Salience on Identification with One's Body, Interest in Sex, and Appearance Monitoring," *Journal of Personality and Social Psychology* 79, no. 1 (2000), 118–30, doi:10.1037/0022-3514.79.1.118.

47 **"If there were any doubt":** Ernest Becker, *The Birth and Death of Meaning: An Interdisciplinary Perspective on the Problem of Man,* 2nd ed. (New York: Free Press, 1971), 75.

48 **the Yup'ik people of Alaska:** M. B. Salzman, "Cultural Trauma and Recovery: Perspectives from Terror Management Theory," *Trauma, Violence, and Abuse* 2, no. 2 (2001), 172–91, doi:10.1177/1524838001002002005.

48 **"We have lost our gods":** R. Fournier and S. Quinton, "How Americans Lost Trust in Our Greatest Institutions," *The Atlantic,* April 20, 2012, retrieved from http://www.theatlantic.com/politics/archive/2012/04/how-americans-lost-trust -in-our-greatest-institutions/256163/.

49 **"People treat animals better than us":** Tom O'Neill, "Untouchable," *National Geographic,* June 2003, retrieved from http://ngm.nationalgeographic.com /features/world/asia/india/untouchables-text.

51 **"Can you imagine that magnificence":** Arthur Miller, *Death of a Salesman,* http:// www.pelister.org/literature/ArthurMiller/Miller__Salesman.pdf, 100.

51 **"They're so beautiful and everything":** M. A. Milkie, "Social Comparisons, Reflected Appraisals, and Mass Media: The Impact of Pervasive Beauty Images on Black and White Girls' Self Concepts," *Social Psychology Quarterly* 62, no. 2 (1999), 190–210, doi:10.2307/2695857, 200.

52 **"A man's Self is the sum total":** William James, *Principles of Psychology* (1890), retrieved from http://www.archive.org/stream/theprinciplesofp01jameuoft /theprinciplesofp01jameuoft__djvu.txt.

53 **The list of problems associated with low self-esteem:** M. Donnellan, K. H. Trzesniewski, R. W. Robins, T. E. Moffitt, and A. Caspi, "Low Self-esteem Is Related to Aggression, Antisocial Behavior, and Delinquency," *Psychological Science* 16, no. 4 (2005), 328–35, doi:10.1111/j.0956-7976.2005.01535.x; T. D'Zurilla, E. C. Chang, and L. J. Sanna, "Self-esteem and Social Problem Solving as Predictors of

Aggression in College Students," *Journal of Social and Clinical Psychology* 22, no. 4 (2003), 424–40, doi:10.1521/jscp.22.4.424.22897; L. Krabbendam, I. Janssen, M. Bak, R. V. Bijl, R. de Graaf, and J. van Os, "Neuroticism and Low Self-esteem as Risk Factors for Psychosis," *Social Psychiatry and Psychiatric Epidemiology* 37, no. 1 (2002), 1–6, doi:10.1007/s127-002-8207-y; A. Laye-Gindhu and K. A. Schonert-Reichl, "Nonsuicidal Self-harm Among Community Adolescents: Understanding the 'Whats' and 'Whys' of Self-harm," *Journal of Youth and Adolescence* 34, no. 5 (2005), 447–57, doi:10.1007/s10964-005-7262-z; P. M. Lewinsohn, P. Rohde, and J. R. Seeley, "Psychosocial Risk Factors for Future Adolescent Suicide Attempts," *Journal of Consulting and Clinical Psychology* 62, no. 2 (1994), 297–305, doi:10.1037/0022-006X.62.2.297; T. E. Lobel and I. Levanon, "Self-esteem, Need for Approval, and Cheating Behavior in Children," *Journal of Educational Psychology* 80, no. 1 (1988), 122–23, doi:10.1037/0022-0663.80.1.122; R. McGee and S. Williams, "Does Low Self-esteem Predict Health Compromising Behaviours Among Adolescents?" *Journal of Adolescence* 23, no. 5 (2000), 569–82, doi:10.1006/jado.2000.0344; R. Rodríguez-Villarino, M. González-Lorenzo, Á. Fernández-González, M. Lameiras-Fernández, and M. L. Foltz, "Individual Factors Associated with Buying Addiction: An Empirical Study," *Addiction Research and Theory* 14, no. 5 (2006), 511–25, doi:10.1080/16066350500527979; M. Rosario, E. W. Schrimshaw, and J. Hunter, "A Model of Sexual Risk Behaviors Among Young Gay and Bisexual Men: Longitudinal Associations of Mental Health, Substance Abuse, Sexual Abuse, and the Coming-Out Process," *AIDS Education and Prevention* 18, no. 5 (2006), 444–60, doi:10.1521/aeap.2006.18.5.444; D. Stinson, C. Logel, M. P. Zanna, J. G. Holmes, J. J. Cameron, J. V. Wood, and S. J. Spencer, "The Cost of Lower Self-esteem: Testing a Self- and Social-Bonds Model of Health," *Journal of Personality and Social Psychology* 94, no. 3 (2008), 412–28, doi:10.1037/0022-3514.94.3.412; K. H. Trzesniewski, M. Donnellan, T. E. Moffitt, R. W. Robins, R. Poulton, and A. Caspi, "Low Self-esteem During Adolescence Predicts Poor Health, Criminal Behavior, and Limited Economic Prospects During Adulthood," *Developmental Psychology* 42, no. 2 (2006), 381–90, doi:10.1037/0012-1649.42.2.381; V. R. Wilburn and D. E. Smith, "Stress, Self-esteem, and Suicidal Ideation in Late Adolescents," *Adolescence* 40, no. 157 (2005), 33–45; L. G. Wild, A. J. Flisher, A. Bhana, and C. Lombard, "Associations Among Adolescent Risk Behaviours and Self-esteem in Six Domains," *Journal of Child Psychology and Psychiatry* 45, no. 8 (2004), 1454–67, doi:10.1111/j.1469-7610.2004.00330.x.

53   **Following such religious conversions:** R. F. Paloutzian, J. T. Richardson, and L. R. Rambo, "Religious Conversion and Personality Change," *Journal of Personality* 67, no. 6 (1999), 1047–79, doi:10.1111/1467-6494.00082.

54   **"Do you know what it feels like":** M. A. Johnson, "Gunman Sent Package to NBC News," 2007, retrieved from http://www.nbcnews.com/id/18195423/page/2/#.VA4N5__PD9Mw.

55   **low self-esteem at age eleven:** M. Donnellan, K. H. Trzesniewski, R. W. Robins, T. E. Moffitt, and A. Caspi, "Low Self-esteem Is Related to Aggression, Antisocial

Behavior, and Delinquency," *Psychological Science* 16, no. 4 (2005), 328–35, doi:10.1111/j.0956-7976.2005.01535.x.

55 **"I'm glad I have a job":** Philip Kennicott, "Yo-Yo Ma, a Virtuoso at More Than the Cello," *Washington Post,* December 2, 2007, retrieved from http://www .washingtonpost.com/lifestyle/style/yo-yo-ma-a-virtuoso-at-more-than-the -cello/2011/11/22/gIQAkvNnKO__story.html.

56 **How do psychologists sort people:** C. H. Jordan, S. J. Spencer, M. P. Zanna, E. Hoshino-Browne, and J. Correll, "Secure and Defensive High Self-esteem," *Journal of Personality and Social Psychology* 85, no. 5 (2003), 969–78, doi:10.1037 /0022-3514.85.5.969.

57 **people high in narcissism:** B. J. Bushman and R. F. Baumeister, "Threatened Ego- tism, Narcissism, Self-esteem, and Direct and Displaced Aggression: Does Self- love or Self-hate Lead to Violence?" *Journal of Personality and Social Psychology* 75, no. 1 (1998), 219–29, doi:10.1037/0022-3514.75.1.219.

57 **narcissistic self-esteem is associated with bullying:** K. A. Fanti and E. R. Kimo- nis, "Bullying and Victimization: The Role of Conduct Problems and Psychopathic Traits," *Journal of Research on Adolescence* 22, no. 4 (2012), 617–31, doi:10.1111 /j.1532-7795.2012.00809.x.

59 **nineteen-year-old Kendall Bailey:** Alan Schwarz, "A Disabled Swimmer's Dream, a Mother's Fight," *New York Times,* June 18, 2008, retrieved from http://www .nytimes.com/2008/06/18/sports/othersports/18swimmer.html?pagewanted =all&__r=0.

59 **highest concentration of centenarians:** Dan Buettner, *The Blue Zones: Lessons for Living Longer from the People Who've Lived the Longest* (Washington, D.C.: National Geographic, 2008).

CHAPTER 4: HOMO MORTALIS: FROM PRIMATE TO HUMAN

63 **"exploded in a different direction":** Julian Jaynes, *The Origin of Consciousness in the Breakdown of the Bicameral Mind* (Boston, Mass.: Houghton Mifflin, 1976), 9.

63 **DNA with chimps:** Jared Diamond, *The Third Chimpanzee: The Evolution and Future of the Human Animal* (New York: HarperCollins, 1992).

64 **evolutionary innovation was bipedalism:** See E. O. Wilson, *The Social Conquest of Earth* (New York: Liveright Publishing Corporation, 2012) for an overview of im- portant mammalian and primate adaptations leading up to bipedalism.

64 **manipulate their surroundings:** Jonathan Kingdon, *Lowly Origin: Where, When, and Why Our Ancestors First Stood Up* (Princeton, N.J.: Princeton University Press, 2003).

64 **social structure ensued:** Steven Mithen, *The Prehistory of the Mind: The Cognitive Or- igins of Art, Religion, and Science* (London: Thames and Hudson, 1996).

65 **better social harmony:** Terrence Deacon, *The Symbolic Species: The Co-evolution of Language and the Brain* (New York: W. W. Norton, 1997).

65 **a primarily social function:** L. Aiello and R. Dunbar, "Neocortex Size, Group Size, and the Evolution of Language," *Current Anthropology* 34, no. 2 (1993), 184–93, re-

trieved from http://www.jstor.org/stable/2743982; R.I.M. Dunbar, "Co-evolution of Neocortical Size, Group Size and Language in Humans," *Behavioral and Brain Sciences* 16, no. 4 (2010), 681–735, doi:10.1017/S0140525X00032325.

65   **a "precise designation" of herself:** Ernest Becker, *The Birth and Death of Meaning: An Interdisciplinary Perspective on the Problem of Man,* 2nd ed. (New York: Free Press, 1971), 19.

66   **those around them:** Nicholas Humphrey, *Consciousness Regained* (Oxford: Oxford University Press, 1976).

66   **"keenly conscious of himself":** Friedrich Nietzsche, *The Gay Science,* translated by Walter Kaufmann (New York: Vintage Books/Random House, 1974; first published 1882), 299.

66   **increasing self-consciousness was born:** Mithen, *The Prehistory of the Mind.*

66   **to tell intricate stories:** R. G. Klein, "Paleoanthropology: Whither the Neanderthals?" *Science* 299, no. 5612 (2003), 1525–27, doi:10.1126/science.1082025.

66   **or is now, able to do:** Jacob Bronowski, "The Reach of Imagination," *American Scholar* 36, no. 2 (1967), 193–201.

66   **"make the unreal real":** Otto Rank, *Will Therapy and Truth and Reality* (New York: Alfred A. Knopf, 1945; first published 1936).

67   **"their brief earthly careers":** Susanne K. Langer, *Mind: An Essay on Human Feeling,* vol. 3 (Baltimore: Johns Hopkins University Press, 1982), 87, 103.

67   **"for survival and reproductive fitness":** Ajit Varki, "Human Uniqueness and the Denial of Death," *Nature* 460, no. 7256 (2009), 684, doi:10.1038/460684c.

68   **intention to living things:** Paul Bloom, "Is God an Accident?" *The Atlantic* 296 (December 2005), 105–12; Pascal Boyer, *Religion Explained: The Evolutionary Origins of Religious Thought* (New York: Basic Books, 2001).

68   **flanked by two mammoth tusks:** V. Formicola, "From the Sunghir Children to the Romito Dwarf: Aspects of the Upper Paleolithic Funerary Landscape," *Current Anthropology* 48, no. 3 (2007), 446–53.

68   **the Creative Explosion:** J. E. Pfeiffer, *The Creative Explosion: An Inquiry into the Origins of Art and Religion* (New York: Harper and Row, 1982).

68   **bone tools became common:** Mithen, *The Prehistory of the Mind.*

69   **features of every known culture:** Ian Tattersall, *Becoming Human: Evolution and Human Uniqueness* (New York: Harcourt Brace, 1998).

69   **"above material decay and death":** Ernest Becker, *Escape from Evil* (New York: Free Press, 1975), 7.

69   **development of art, myth, and religion:** Roy A. Rappaport, *Ritual and Religion in the Making of Humanity* (New York: Cambridge University Press, 1999).

69   **"a thing done":** Jane Ellen Harrison, *Ancient Art and Ritual* (New York: Henry Holt, 1913).

69   **formalized and copied by others:** Ellen Dissanayake, *Homo Aestheticus: Where Art Comes From and Why* (Seattle: University of Washington Press, 1995; first published 1992).

70   **immature infants and their mothers:** Steven Mithen, *The Singing Neanderthals: The*

Origins of Music, Language, Mind, and Body (Cambridge, Mass.: Harvard University Press, 2006).

70   **coordinated activity soothing:** William Hardy McNeill, *Keeping Together in Time: Dance and Drill in Human History* (Cambridge, Mass.: Harvard University Press, 1995).

70   **"high as the spade has gone":** Examples from Harrison, *Ancient Art and Ritual.*

71   **"bridge over which it could pass":** Ernest Becker, *Escape from Evil* (New York: Free Press, 1975), 102–3.

72   **"brought back Life":** Examples from Harrison, *Ancient Art and Ritual.*

72   **primal forces and the living relatives:** I. Chukwukere, "A Coffin for 'The Loved One': The Structure of Fante Death Rituals," *Current Anthropology* 22, no. 1 (1981), 61–68.

72   **continue their daily routines:** P. L. Berger and T. Luckmann, *The Social Construction of Reality: A Treatise in the Sociology of Knowledge* (Garden City, N.Y.: Anchor Books, 1967; first published 1966).

74   **oldest known cave paintings in the world:** Recent studies in Spain with more accurate dating techniques suggest that some cave paintings are at least forty thousand years old. A.W.G. Pike, D. L. Hoffmann, M. García-Diez, P. B. Pettitt, J. Alcolea, R. De Balbín, C. González-Sainz, C. de las Heras, J. A. Lasheras, R. Montes, and J. Zilhão, "U-Series Dating of Paleolithic Art in 11 Caves in Spain," *Science* 336, no. 6087 (2012), 1409–13, doi:10.1126/science.1219957.

74   **great artists were rare:** S. Kraft, "Spelunker's Passion Pays Off: Jean-Marie Chauvet and His Small Team of Cave-Diggers 'Hit the Jackpot,' Finding a Cache of Stone Age Art," *Los Angeles Times,* Culture section, February 14, 1995; J. Thurman, "First Impressions: What Does the World's Oldest Art Say About Us?" *The New Yorker,* June 2008, retrieved from http://www.newyorker.com/magazine /2008/06/23/first-impressions; Werner Herzog's 2010 documentary film *Cave of Forgotten Dreams.*

74   **different states of human consciousness:** David Lewis-Williams, *The Mind in the Cave* (London: Thames and Hudson, 2002).

75   **"in people's thoughts and minds":** Ibid., 209–10.

75   **on the fringes of consciousness:** F. Cohen, D. Sullivan, S. Solomon, J. Greenberg, and D. M. Ogilvie, "Finding Everland: Flight Fantasies and the Desire to Transcend Mortality," *Journal of Experimental Social Psychology* 47, no. 1 (2010), doi:10.1016/j.jesp.2010.08.013.

75   **concrete signs of a supernatural world:** Dissanayake, *Homo Aestheticus.*

75   **"make the world unbearable":** George Bernard Shaw, *Back to Methuselah,* 1921, http://www.gutenberg.org/files/13084/13084-8.txt.

75   **death-transcending conceptions of reality:** J. Lyons, "Paleolithic Aesthetics: The Psychology of Cave Art," *Journal of Aesthetics and Art Criticism* 26, no. 1 (1967), 107–14, doi:10.2307/429249.

77   **"then came the city":** http://www.smithsonianmag.com/history/gobekli-tepe -the-worlds-first-temple-83613665/?no-ist=.

77 **evidence of domestic agriculture:** M. Balter, "Why Settle Down? The Mystery of Communities," *Science* 282, no. 5393 (1998), 1442–45.

77 **the advent of agriculture:** E. O. Wilson, *Consilience: The Unity of Knowledge* (New York: Alfred A. Knopf, 1998).

78 **would suffice to grow food:** Grant Allen, *The Evolution of the Idea of God: An Inquiry into the Origins of Religions* (Escondido, Calif.: Book Tree, 2000; first published 1897).

78 **"how-do-I-milk-this-goat?" questions:** Merlin Donald, *Origins of the Modern Mind: Three Stages in the Evolution of Culture and Cognition* (Cambridge, Mass.: Harvard University Press, 1991).

79 **"of endless cicada singing":** Alfonso Ortiz, *The Tewa World: Space, Time, Being, and Becoming in a Pueblo Society* (Chicago: University of Chicago Press, 1969).

79 **all aspects of social behavior:** Walter Burkert, *Homo Necans: The Anthropology of Ancient Greek Sacrificial Ritual and Myth,* translated by Peter Bing (Berkeley: University of California Press, 1983).

79 **fostered social cohesion and coordination:** David Sloan Wilson, *Darwin's Cathedral: Evolution, Religion, and the Nature of Society* (Chicago: University of Chicago Press, 2002).

79 **"further the survival of human societies":** Nicholas Wade, *The Faith Instinct: How Religion Evolved and Why It Endures* (New York: Penguin Press, 2009).

80 **no adaptive significance or enduring value:** Steven Pinker, *How the Mind Works* (New York: W. W. Norton, 1997).

80 **"concurrent and supporting . . . phantasies":** Susan Isaacs, "The Nature and Function of Phantasy," *International Journal of Psycho-Analysis* 29 (1948), 73–97. Quotation is from p. 94.

81 **their sophisticated mental abilities:** Ajit Varki and Danny Brower, *Denial: Self-deception, False Beliefs, and the Origins of the Human Mind* (New York: Twelve, 2013).

CHAPTER 5: LITERAL IMMORTALITY

82 **"yet everything is completely different":** Aldous Huxley, *The Devils of Loudun* (New York: Harper and Brothers, 1952), 259.

83 **"I am afraid of death":** *The Epic of Gilgamesh,* translated by N. K. Sandars (London: Penguin Books, 1972; first published 1960), 97.

84 **"the blight of involuntary death":** www.imminst.org.

84 **This *symbolic immortality* promises:** Robert Jay Lifton, *The Broken Connection: On Death and the Continuity of Life* (New York: Simon and Schuster, 1979).

85 **buried alive with them when they died:** O. L. Mazzatenta, "A Chinese Emperor's Army for an Eternity," *National Geographic* 182, no. 2 (1992), 114–30.

85 **water birds to soothe him:** Jane Portal, ed., *The First Emperor: China's Terracotta Army* (Cambridge, Mass.: Harvard University Press, 2007).

86 **magical formulas for banishing them:** Erik Hornung and Betsy M. Bryan, eds., *The Quest for Immortality: Treasures of Ancient Egypt,* National Gallery of Art, Washington, and United Exhibits Group (New York: Prestel Publishers, 2002).

86   **"living in this land forever"**: A. R. Williams, "Death on the Nile," *National Geographic* 202, no. 4 (2002), 2–25.

87   **but without intoxication**: R. P. Taylor, *Death and the Afterlife: A Cultural Encyclopedia* (Santa Barbara, Calif.: ABC-CLIO, 2000).

87   **occur today as in ancient times**: "U.S. Religious Landscape Survey: Religious Beliefs and Practices: Diverse and Politically Relevant," Pew Forum on Religion and Public Life, June 2008, http://www.pewforum.org/files/2008/06/report2 -religious-landscape-study-full.pdf.

88   **emotional well-being and low death anxiety**: M. Soenke, M. J. Landau, and J. Greenberg, "Sacred Armor: Religion's Role as a Buffer Against the Anxieties of Life and the Fear of Death," in K. I. Pargament, J. J. Exline, and J. W. Jones, eds., *APA Handbook of Psychology, Religion, and Spirituality,* vol. 1, *Context, Theory, and Research* (Washington, D.C.: American Psychological Association, 2013), 105–22, doi:10.1037/14045-005.

88   **supernatural phenomena in general**: A. Norenzayan and I. G. Hansen, "Belief in Supernatural Agents in the Face of Death," *Personality and Social Psychology Bulletin* 32, no. 2 (2006), 174–87, doi:10.1177/0146167205280251.

88   **"implicit" or unconscious religiosity**: J. Jong, J. Halberstadt, and M. Bluemke, "Foxhole Atheism Revisited: The Effects of Mortality Salience on Explicit and Implicit Religious Belief," *Journal of Experimental Social Psychology* 48, no. 5 (2012), 983–89, doi:10.1016/j.jesp.2012.03.005.

88   **without reacting defensively**: E. Jonas and P. Fischer, "Terror Management and Religion: Evidence That Intrinsic Religiousness Mitigates Worldview Defense Following Mortality Salience," *Journal of Personality and Social Psychology* 91, no. 3 (2006), 553–67, doi:10.1037/0022-3514.91.3.553.

88   **"immutable biological fact of death"**: Otto Rank, *Psychology and the Soul: A Study of the Origin, Conceptual Evolution, and Nature of the Soul,* translated by G. C. Richter and E. James Lieberman (Baltimore: Johns Hopkins University Press, 1998; first published 1930), xi.

89   **reunited with their resurrected bodies**: Ibid.

89   **"Everything comes into being from its own opposite"**: http://www.iep.utm .edu/phaedo/.

90   **"immortality of the soul"**: http://www.philosophy-index.com/descartes /meditations/.

90   **"does not imply the destruction of the mind"**: Maxine Sheets-Johnstone, "Death and Immortality Ideologies in Western Philosophy," *Continental Philosophy Review* 36, no. 3 (2003), 235–62, doi:10.1023/B:MAWO.0000003937.47171.a9; Descartes quote on p. 238.

90   **indestructible soul of some sort**: http://cnsnews.com/news/article/susan-jones /poll-americans-belief-god-strong-declining.

91   **"drugs of no death"**: Y. Yu, "Life and Immortality in the Mind of Han China," *Harvard Journal of Asiatic Studies* 25 (1964), 80–122, doi:10.2307/2718339.

92   **"lengthens his life indefinitely"**: Gerald J. Gruman, "A History of Ideas About

the Prolongation of Life: The Evolution of Prolongevity Hypotheses to 1800," *Transactions of the American Philosophical Society* 56, no. 9 (1966), 1–102, doi:10.2307 /1006096.

92   contemporary "immortalists": Alan Harrington, *The Immortalist* (New York: Random House, 1969).

93   "an earthen machine": René Descartes, *Treatise of Man*, ed. T. S. Hall (Cambridge, Mass.: Harvard University Press, 1972), 4.

93   "all at present known": René Descartes, "Discourse on the Method of Rightly Conducting the Reason, and Seeking Truth in the Sciences," in John Veitch, trans., *A Discourse on Method, etc.* (London, Toronto, and New York: Everyman's Library, 1912), 50.

93   ripe old age of fifty-four: Gruman, "A History of Ideas About the Prolongation of Life."

93   "not excepting even that of old age": J. Sparks, *The Works of Benjamin Franklin*, vol. 8 (Boston: Hilliard, Gray and Company, 1840), 418.

94   "organism could be prolonged indefinitely": A. Carrel, "On the Permanent Life of Tissues Outside of the Organism," *Journal of Experimental Medicine* 15 (1912), 516–28. Quotation is from p. 516.

94   *"contingent et non nécessaire"*: J. A. Witkowski, "Dr. Carrel's Immortal Cells," *Medical History* 24 (1980), 129–42. Quotation is from p. 130.

94   but merely a contingent, phenomenon: David M. Friedman, *The Immortalists: Charles Lindbergh, Dr. Alexis Carrel, and Their Daring Quest to Live Forever* (New York: Harper Perennial, 2008), 13.

94   "nothing good about death; it was terrible": Charles Lindbergh, *Autobiography of Values* (New York: Harcourt Brace Jovanovich, 1978), 5.

94   ONE STEP NEARER TO IMMORTALITY: Friedman, *Immortalists*, 77.

95   slow down metabolism: http://www.drfuhrman.com/library/metabolism _longevity.aspx.

95   "escape the yoke of nature": http://video.google.com/videoplay?docid= 3847943059984264388.

95   "complete repair as it becomes available": B. Best, "Aubrey de Grey, Ph.D.: An Exclusive Interview with the Renowned Biogerontologist," *Life Extension Magazine*, February 2006, retrieved from http://www.lef.org/magazine/mag2006 /feb2006_profile_01.htm.

95   keep an older mouse alive: http://www.mfoundation.org/.

95   "only the relatively wealthy can afford": Aubrey de Grey, "The War on Aging," in *The Scientific Conquest of Death: Essays on Infinite Lifespans* (Libros en Red, 2004), 29–46.

97   "replaced during revival anyway": http://www.alcor.org/FAQs/faq02 .html#neuropreservation.

97   "'It really worked'": Quoted in the 2000 documentary film *I Dismember Mama* by Errol Morris.

97   as Alcor puts it: "Freezing Time: Ted Williams," *New York Times*, July 11, 2002, re-

trieved from http://www.nytimes.com/2002/07/11/opinion/freezing-time-ted
-williams.html.

97   **"we will be a new species":** Quoted in 2000 documentary film *I Dismember
Mama* by Errol Morris.

97   **250 vitamin supplements a day to stay young:** http://forum.bodybuilding.com
/showthread.php?t=141791771&page=1.

98   **replacing bowel functions:** Raymond Kurzweil, "Human Body Version 2.0," in
The Scientific Conquest of Death: Essays on Infinite Lifespans (Libros en Red, 2004), 93–
106.

98   **maintenance or repair of the body:** de Grey, "War on Aging."

98   **keep it in an external storage device:** William Sims Bainbridge, "Progress
Toward Cyberimmortality," in *The Scientific Conquest of Death: Essays on Infinite Lifespans* (Libros en Red, 2004), 107–22.

98   **"throw it out of their systems":** Thomas Robert Malthus, *An Essay on the Principle
of Population, as It Affects the Future Improvement of Society, with Remarks on the Specula-
tions of Mr. Godwin, M. Condorcet, and Other Writers* (London: J. Johnson, 1798),
240–41.

CHAPTER 6: SYMBOLIC IMMORTALITY

100   **"the ultimate futility of life":** Zygmunt Bauman, *Mortality, Immortality, and Other
Life Strategies* (Stanford, Calif.: Stanford University Press, 1992), 7.

101   **"'plasters, pills and ointment boxes'":** Adam Kirsch, "Cloudy Trophies:
John Keats's Obsession with Fame and Death," *The New Yorker*, July 2008,
retrieved from http://www.newyorker.com/magazine/2008/07/07/cloudy
-trophies.

101   **"a kind memorial graven":** http://lit.genius.com/John-keats-sleep-and-poetry
-annotated#note-2742995.

102   **"for this sort of suffering":** Kirsch, "Cloudy Trophies."

103   **"someone who can do this will not die":** Ernest Becker, *The Birth and Death of
Meaning: An Interdisciplinary Perspective on the Problem of Man*, 2nd ed. (New York:
Free Press, 1971), 149–50.

104   **who wrote about being in pain:** I. Fritsche, P. Fischer, N. Koranyi, N. Berger, and
B. Fleischmann, "Mortality Salience and the Desire for Offspring," *Journal of Experimental Social Psychology* 43, no. 5 (2007), 753–62, doi:10.1016/j.jesp.2006
.10.003.

104   **one-child-per-family policy:** "Familial Self as a Potent Source of Affirmation:
Evidence from China," *Social Psychological and Personality Science* 4, no. 5 (2012),
529–37, doi:10.1177/1948550612469039.

104   **name future offspring after themselves:** A. M. Vicary, "Mortality Salience and
Namesaking: Does Thinking About Death Make People Want to Name Their
Children After Themselves?" *Journal of Research in Personality* 45, no. 1 (2011), 138–
41, doi:10.1016/j.jrp.2010.11.016.

104 **progeny was brought to mind:** E. Yaakobi, M. Mikulincer, and P. R. Shaver, "Parenthood as a Terror Management Mechanism: The Moderating Role of Attachment Orientations," *Personality and Social Psychology Bulletin* 40, no. 6 (2014), 762–74, doi:10.1177/0146167214525473.

104 **support for a rival political party:** http://www.malaysia-today.net/political-malay/.

105 **"leave behind me an enduring name":** *The Epic of Gilgamesh,* translated by N. K. Sandars (London: Penguin Books, 1972; first published 1960), 73.

105 **rewarded by "imperishable fame":** Leo Braudy, *The Frenzy of Renown: Fame and Its History* (New York: Oxford University Press, 1986), 30.

106 **"remember [great men] this way":** Matthew V. Wells, "Self as Historical Artifact: Ge Hong and Early Chinese Autobiographical Writing," *Early Medieval China* 9 (2003), 71–103. Quotation is from p. 85.

106 **"everybody will be famous":** Andy Warhol and Bob Colacello, *Andy Warhol's Exposures* (London: Hutchinson, 1979), 48.

106 **garner international renown:** V. Belenkaya and S. Goldsmith, "Nathan's Hot Dog Eating Contest 2009: Joey Chestnut Defends Title, Sets World Record with 68 Dogs," New York *Daily News,* July 5, 2009, retrieved from http://www.nydailynews.com/new-york/nathan-hot-dog-eating-contest-2009-joey-chesnut-defends-title-sets-world-record-68-dogs-article-1.398371.

106 **and guest TV appearances:** https://www.youtube.com/watch?v=8jE0GWIOuy8.

107 **magical sense of your own immortality:** P. Kesebir, C.-Y. Chiu, and Y.-H. Kim, "Existential Functions of Famous People," unpublished manuscript, University of Illinois at Urbana-Champaign, 2014.

108 **Johnny Depp more admirable:** J. Greenberg, S. Kosloff, S. Solomon, F. Cohen, and M. Landau, "Toward Understanding the Fame Game: The Effect of Mortality Salience on the Appeal of Fame," *Self and Identity* 9, no. 1 (2010), 1–18, doi:10.1080/15298860802391546.

108 **spend more money to do so:** Ibid.

108 **notoriety topped their list of motives:** R. A. Fein and B. Vossekuil, *Protective Intelligence and Threat Assessment Investigations: A Guide for State and Local Law Enforcement Officials,* 1998, retrieved from http://www.secretservice.gov/ntac/PI__Guide.pdf.

109 **"some national attention":** Braudy, *The Frenzy of Renown,* 3.

110 **"deciding between stocks and bonds":** Paul Krugman, "Who Was Milton Friedman?" *New York Review of Books,* February 15, 2007.

110 **considering the costs and benefits:** Gary S. Becker, *The Economic Approach to Human Behavior* (Chicago: University of Chicago Press, 1978).

110 **offering to the heroic ancestors:** Robert J. Sardello and Randolph Severson, *Money and the Soul of the World* (Dallas: Pegasus Foundation, 1983).

110 **"basking in reflected glory":** R. B. Cialdini, R. J. Borden, A. Thorne, M. R. Walker, S. Freeman, and L. R. Sloan, "Basking in Reflected Glory: Three (Football) Field Studies," *Journal of Personality and Social Psychology* 34, no. 3 (1976), 366–75.

110   **ancestors depicted on them:** William H. Desmonde, *Magic, Myth, and Money: The Origin of Money in Religious Ritual* (New York: Free Press of Glencoe, 1962).

111   **exchange for money:** G. Roheim, "The Evolution of Culture," *International Journal of Psycho-Analysis* 15 (1934), 387–418.

111   *tambu,* **which means "sacred":** Frederic L. Pryor, "The Origins of Money," *Journal of Money, Credit and Banking* 9, no. 3 (1977), 391–409.

111   **as an immortal person:** Stéphane Breton, "Social Body and Icon of the Person: A Symbolic Analysis of Shell Money Among the Wodani, Western Highlands of Irian Jaya," *American Ethnologist* 26, no. 3 (1999), 558–82.

111   **to those who reach the top:** Joseph Campbell, with Bill Moyers, *The Power of Myth,* edited by B. S. Flowers (New York: Doubleday, 1988).

111   **"to dust you will return":** Genesis 3:19 (New International Version), 1973.

111   **"art, philosophy, and politics":** Adriano Tilgher, *Homo Faber: Work Through the Ages,* translated by D. C. Fisher (New York: Harcourt Brace, 1930), 5.

111   **"that wait upon riches":** Cf. P. L. Payne, "Industrial Entrepreneurship in Great Britain," in *The Cambridge Economic History of Europe,* part 1, edited by P. Mathias and M. M. Postan (Cambridge: Cambridge University Press, 1978), 180–230. Smith quotation is from p. 183.

112   **"an endless supply of wealth":** Sergei Kan, *Symbolic Immortality: The Tlingit Potlatch of the Nineteenth Century* (Washington, D.C.: Smithsonian Institution Press, 1989), 232.

113   **specially constructed on her property:** Richard O'Connor, *The Golden Summers: An Antic History of Newport* (New York: Putnam Publishing Group, 1974).

113   **and giant plasma television screens:** Philip Sherwell, "Gift Ideas for the Haves and Have Yachts," *Sunday Telegraph,* November 25, 2007, retrieved from http:// www.telegraph.co.uk/news/uknews/1570466/Gift-ideas-for-the-haves-and-have -yachts.html.

113   **the lower the number, the higher the price:** Cameron Houston, "How Do You Know You've Really Made It? Step Up to the Plate," *The Age,* January 20, 2007, 6.

113   **bedrooms, a bar, and a gym:** B. Surk and A. Johnson, "Saudi Prince Buying Private Superjumbo 'Flying Palace' Jet, Airbus Says," *Seattle Times,* November 12, 2007, retrieved from http://seattletimes.com/html/businesstechnology /2004009433__websaudiluxury12.html.

113   **soon-to-be-underwater home mortgages:** Jane H. Furse, Jess Wisloski, and Bill Hutchinson, "It's Ka-Chingle All the Way! Shoppers Drop Bundle in Robust Start to Season," New York *Daily News,* November 26, 2007, retrieved from www .lexisnexis.com/hottopics/lnacademic.

114   **"I'm on my way to a six-figure income!":** David Van Biema and Jeff Chu, "Does God Want You to Be Rich?" *Time,* September 10, 2006, retrieved from http:// content.time.com/time/magazine/article/0,9171,1533448,00.html.

115   **self-esteem-boosting Lexus or Rolex:** N. Mandel and S. J. Heine, "Terror Management and Marketing: He Who Dies with the Most Toys Wins," *Advances in Consumer Research* 26 (1999), 527–32.

115   **shaky self-esteem:** A. N. Christopher, K. Drummond, J. R. Jones, P. Marek, and
       K. M. Therriault, "Beliefs About One's Own Death, Personal Insecurity, and Mate-
       rialism," *Personality and Individual Differences* 40, no. 3 (2006), 441–51, doi:10.1016/j
       .paid.2005.09.017.

115   **luxuries like clothing and entertainment:** T. Kasser and K. M. Sheldon, "Of
       Wealth and Death: Materialism, Mortality Salience, and Consumption Behavior,"
       Psychological Science 11, no. 4 (2000), 348–51, doi:10.1111/1467-9280.00269.

115   **plan more extravagant parties:** N. Mandel and D. Smeesters, "The Sweet Escape:
       Effects of Mortality Salience on Consumption Quantities for High and Low Self-
       esteem Consumers," *Journal of Consumer Research* 35, no. 2 (2008), 309–23,
       doi:10.1086/587626.

116   **reported a reduced fear of death:** T. Zaleskiewicz, A. Gasiorowska, P. Kesebir, A.
       Luszczynska, and T. Pyszczynski, "Money and the Fear of Death: The Symbolic
       Power of Money as an Existential Anxiety Buffer," *Journal of Economic Psychology*
       36(C) (2013), 55–67, doi:10.1016/j.joep.2013.02.008.

116   **"purchases will be life everlasting":** Tennessee Williams, *Cat on a Hot Tin Roof*
       (New York: New Directions, 2004; first published 1940), 91.

116   **"without the hope of immortality":** Cicero, *Tusculanarum Disputationum,* I, 15.

116   **"national, religious, and artistic heroes":** Otto Rank, *Art and Artist: Creative Urge
       and Personality Development* (Agathon Press, 1968; first published 1932), 41.

117   **"a certain quality of an individual personality":** Max Weber, *The Theory of Social
       and Economic Organization,* translated by A. M. Henderson and Talcott Parsons
       (Glencoe, Ill.: Free Press, 1947; first published 1922), 358.

118   **"The National Revolution has begun!":** http://www.historyplace.com
       /worldwar2/timeline/putsch2.htm.

118   **"I cannot remember in my entire life":** http://www.sources.com/SSR/Docs
       /SSRW-Beer__Hall__Putsch.htm.

119   **"We want no other God except Germany":** J. W. Baird, *Hitler's War Poets:
       Literature and Politics in the Third Reich* (Cambridge: Cambridge University Press,
       2008), 3.

119   **"These sixteen soldiers have celebrated":** Mark Neocleous, "Long Live Death!
       Fascism, Resurrection, Immortality," *Journal of Political Ideologies* 10, no. 1 (2005),
       31–49, doi:10.1080/1356931052000310272. Quotation is from pp. 39, 43.

120   **Many refused to believe it:** K. Riegel, "Marxism-Leninism as a Political Reli-
       gion," *Totalitarian Movements and Political Religions* 6, no. 1 (2005), 97–126,
       doi:10.1080/14690760500099788.

121   **"eternal and indestructible" . . . "soar lightly":** Robert Jay Lifton, *Revolutionary
       Immortality: Mao Tse-tung and the Chinese Cultural Revolution* (New York: Random
       House, 1968), 40, 48, 51.

121   **for the charismatic candidate:** F. Cohen, S. Solomon, M. Maxfield, T. Pyszczynski,
       and J. Greenberg, "Fatal Attraction: The Effects of Mortality Salience on Evalua-
       tions of Charismatic, Task-Oriented, and Relationship-Oriented Leaders," *Psycho-
       logical Science* 15, no. 12 (2004), 846–51, doi:10.1111/j.0956-7976.2004.00765.x.

121 "succession of immortality ideologies": Ernest Becker, *The Denial of Death* (New York: Free Press, 1973), 190.

122 "we shall never be fulfilled": playwright Eugene Ionesco, from epigraph of Lifton, *Revolutionary Immortality*.

122 "through not dying": http://www.quotationspage.com/quote/52.html.

122 During a battle in the *Iliad*: Achilles' search for immortality is recounted in the *Iliad*, book 12, lines 363–69, http://www.essortment.com/achilles-search -immortality-iliad-61186.html.

CHAPTER 7: THE ANATOMY OF HUMAN DESTRUCTIVENESS

127 "deny the fact of death": James Baldwin, *The Fire Next Time* (New York: Vintage Books, 1993; first published 1962), 91.

128 "lunatics, or madmen as among us": Edwin G. Burrows and Mike Wallace, *Gotham: A History of New York City to 1898* (New York: Oxford University Press, 1999), 11.

128 "beat his head off": Ibid., 39.

129 "I slowly tore off his skin": Daniel D. Luckenbill, *Ancient Records of Assyria and Babylonia II* (Chicago: University of Chicago Press, 1927), 314.

129 dozen countries around the world: http://www.un.org/Depts/dpko/list/list.pdf.

129 "We will fight them": http://www.spiegel.de/international/world /0,1518,553724,00.html.

129 Jewish graffiti artists in Jerusalem: http://en.wikipedia.org/wiki/Anti-Arabism.

129 tolerant treatment of homosexuals: http://en.wikipedia.org/wiki/Fred__Phelps.

130 do not belong to their group: John C. Mitani, David P. Watts, and Sylvia J. Amsler, "Lethal Intergroup Aggression Leads to Territorial Expansion in Wild Chimpanzees," *Current Biology* 20, no. 12 (2010), R507–8, doi:10.1016/j.cub .2010.04.021.

130 food, water, and mates: S. Bowles, "Did Warfare Among Ancestral Hunter-Gatherers Affect the Evolution of Human Social Behaviors?" *Science* 324, no. 5932 (2009), 1293–98, doi:10.1126/science.1168112.

130 "see what he'll do if I poke him": Alan Harrington, *The Immortalist* (Millbrae, Calif.: Celestial Arts, 1969), 138–39.

130 "totally alien to one's own": Ernest Becker, *The Birth and Death of Meaning: An Interdisciplinary Perspective on the Problem of Man,* 2nd ed. (New York: Free Press, 1971), 140.

131 "rumble of panic": Ernest Becker, *The Denial of Death* (New York: Free Press, 1973), 284.

132 means "man" or "human": Ellen Dissanayake, *Homo Aestheticus: Where Art Comes From and Why* (Seattle: University of Washington Press, 1995; first published 1992 by Free Press).

132 "vomit from the sea": R. F. Worth, "A Black Imam Breaks Ground in Mecca," *New York Times,* April 10, 2009, retrieved from https://www.google.com/#q=A+Black +Imam+Breaks+Ground+Leading+the+Faithful+in+Mecca.

132   **likening Iraqis to ants and cockroaches:** Douglas Kellner, *The Persian Gulf TV War* (Boulder, Colo.: Westview Press, 1992).

132   **"I don't brake for Iraqis":** D. Merskin, "The Construction of Arabs as Enemies: Post-September 11 Discourse of George W. Bush," *Mass Communication and Society* 7, no. 2 (2004), 157–75, doi:10.1207/s15327825mcs0702_2.

132   **less human and more animalistic:** J. Goldenberg, N. Heflick, J. Vaes, M. Motyl, and J. Greenberg, "Of Mice and Men, and Objectified Women: A Terror Management Account of Infrahumanization," *Group Processes and Intergroup Relations* 12, no. 6 (2009), 763–76, doi:10.1177/1368430209340569.

132   **disparages "different" others:** J. Arndt, J. Greenberg, S. Solomon, T. Pyszczynski, and L. Simon, "Suppression, Accessibility of Death-Related Thoughts, and Cultural Worldview Defense: Exploring the Psychodynamics of Terror Management," *Journal of Personality and Social Psychology* 73, no. 1 (1997), 5–18, retrieved from http://www.ncbi.nlm.nih.gov/pubmed/9216076.

133   **"His Son from heaven":** T. Hiney, *On the Missionary Trail: A Journey Through Polynesia, Asia, and Africa with the London Missionary Society* (New York: Grove Press, 2001), 5.

133   **centuries before Jesus' birth:** James H. Grayson, *Early Buddhism and Christianity in Korea: A Study in the Emplantation of Religion* (Leiden: Brill Academic Publishers, 1997).

133   **"reason with them in the better way":** Larry Poston, *Islamic Da'wah in the West: Muslim Missionary Activity and the Dynamics of Conversion to Islam* (New York: Oxford University Press, 1992). Quotation is from sura 16:125 of the Qur'an.

134   **don't worry so much about my own death:** S. Kosloff, J. Cesario, and A. Martens, "Mortality Salience Motivates Attempts to Assimilate Differing Others to One's Own Worldview," unpublished manuscript, Michigan State University, 2012.

135   **babysit the neighbor's kids:** J. Schimel, L. Simon, J. Greenberg, T. Pyszczynski, S. Solomon, J. Waxmonsky, and J. Arndt, "Stereotypes and Terror Management: Evidence That Mortality Salience Enhances Stereotypic Thinking and Preferences," *Journal of Personality and Social Psychology* 77, no. 5 (1999), 905–26, doi:10.1037 /0022-3514.77.5.905.

136   **"buttoned-down" African American:** Ibid.

138   **"words of humiliation hurt more than bullets":** Evelin Lindner, *Making Enemies: Humiliation and International Conflict* (Westport, Conn.: Praeger, 2006), xvi.

139   **"avoid a humiliating U.S. defeat":** Blema Steinberg, *Shame and Humiliation: Presidential Decision-Making on Vietnam* (Pittsburgh, Penn.: The University of Pittsburgh Press, 1996).

139   **"sense of frustration and humiliation":** Mark Juergensmeyer, "From Bhindranwale to Bin Laden: The Rise of Religious Violence," *Orfalea Center for Global and International Studies* (University of California, Santa Barbara: Global and International Studies, 2004), retrieved from http://escholarship.org/uc/item /7322q2p5.

139   **Battle of Kosovo in 1389:** Vamik Volkan, *Killing in the Name of Identity: A Study of Bloody Conflicts* (Charlottesville, Va.: Pitchstone Publishing, 2006).

139   **"cycle of mayhem and murder":** Lindner, *Making Enemies*, xv.

140 **"devil's supporters allying with them"**: "Jihad Against Jews and Crusaders," World Islamic Front statement, http://fas.org/irp/world/para/docs/980223 -fatwa.htm.

140 **one-two death-threat punch to Americans**: T. Pyszczynski, S. Solomon, and J. Greenberg, *In the Wake of 9/11: The Psychology of Terror* (Washington, D.C.: APA Books, 2003).

141 **"a very evil and wicked religion"**: http://www.historycommons.org/context .jsp?item=a1001grahamislam.

141 **"guy called Satan"**: "Rumsfeld Praises Army General Who Ridicules Islam as 'Satan,'" *New York Times*, October 17, 2003, retrieved from http://www.nytimes .com/2003/10/17/world/rumsfeld-praises-army-general-who-ridicules-islam-as -satan.html.

141 **"they need to be hit"**: M. E. O'Connell, "The Myth of Preemptive Self-defense," *The American Society of International Law Task Force on Terrorism*, August 2002, re- trieved from https://www.yumpu.com/en/document/view/8336695/the-myth-of -preemptive-self-defense-american-society-of-.

141 **"full wrath of the United States"**: M. E. O'Connell, "Seductive Drones: Learning from a Decade of Lethal Operations," *Journal of Law, Information and Science* 21, no. 2 (2012), retrieved from http://www.austlii.edu.au/au/journals/JlLawInfoSci/2012 /7.html.

141 **President Bush and his policies in Iraq**: M. J. Landau, S. Solomon, J. Greenberg, F. Cohen, T. Pyszczynski, J. Arndt, C. H. Miller, D. M. Ogilvie, and A. Cook, "De- liver Us from Evil: The Effects of Mortality Salience and Reminders of 9/11 on Support for President George W. Bush," *Personality and Social Psychology Bulletin* 30, no. 9 (2004), 1136–50, doi:10.1177/0146167204267988.

142 **more favorably evaluated than Kerry**: Ibid.

142 **by an almost 3-to-1 margin**: F. Cohen, D. M. Ogilvie, S. Solomon, J. Greenberg, and T. Pyszczynski, "American Roulette: The Effect of Reminders of Death on Support for George W. Bush in the 2004 Presidential Election," *Analyses of Social Issues and Public Policy* 5, no. 1 (2005), 177–87, doi:10.1111/j.1530-2415.2005 .00063.x.

142 **"that it is a good deal"**: "Evangelist Admits Warzone Proselytizing Results in Deaths, Saying It's a 'Good Decision,'" *Alexandria: Crossroads of Civilization*, Decem- ber 2008, retrieved from http://www.aleksandreia.com/2008/12/20/evangelist -admits-warzone-proselytizing-results-in-deaths-saying-its-a-good-decision/.

142 **"single sustainable model of national success"**: A. J. Bacevich and E. H. Pro- dromou, "God Is Not Neutral: Religion and U.S. Foreign Policy After 9/11," *Orbis* 48, no. 1 (2004), 43–54, doi:10.1016/j.orbis.2003.10.012.

143 **in Iraq were justified**: "A Year After Iraq War: Mistrust of America in Europe Ever Higher, Muslim Anger Persists: A Nine-Country Survey," Pew Research Center for the People and the Press, 2004, retrieved from http://www.people-press.org/files /legacy-pdf/206.pdf.

143 **"never did anything so grand"**: N. Kristof, "Kids with Bombs," *New York Times*,

April 5, 2002, retrieved from http://www.nytimes.com/2002/04/05/opinion
/kids-with-bombs.html.

143   "blow up America": E. Rubin, "The Most Wanted Palestinian," *New York Times*,
       June 30, 2002, retrieved from http://www.nytimes.com/2002/06/30
       /magazine/the-most-wanted-palestinian.html.

143   fundamentalist version of Islam: I. Blumi, "Competing for the Albanian Soul:
       Are Islamic Missionaries Making Another Lebanon in the Balkans?" September
       2002, retrieved from http://www.wilsoncenter.org/publication/260-competing
       -for-the-albanian-soul-are-islamic-missionaries-making-another-lebanon-the.

144   they were enemies, too: David D. Kirkpatrick, "Morsi's Slurs Against Jews Stir
       Concern," *New York Times,* January 14, 2013, retrieved from http://www.nytimes
       .com/2013/01/15/world/middleeast/egypts-leader-morsi-made-anti-jewish-slurs
       .html?pagewanted=all&_r=0.

144   Barack Obama is a Muslim: "Growing Number of Americans Say Obama Is a
       Muslim," Pew Research Center Religion and Public Life Project, August 2010,
       retrieved from http://www.pewforum.org/2010/08/18/growing-number-of
       -americans-say-obama-is-a-muslim/.

144   following reminders of death: F. Cohen, M. Soenke, S. Solomon, and J. Green-
       berg, "Evidence for a Role of Death Thought in American Attitudes Toward Sym-
       bols of Islam," *Journal of Experimental Social Psychology* 49, no. 2 (2013), 189–94,
       doi:10.1016/j.jesp.2012.09.006.

144   "like hats in a gust of wind": George Bernard Shaw, *Heartbreak House* (Mineola,
       N.Y.: Dover Publications, 1996; first published 1919), 12.

144   two years in jail and a $2,000 fine: http://news.google.com/newspapers?nid=
       110&dat=19950607&id=BilQAAAAIBAJ&sjid=oVUDAAAAIBAJ&pg=
       4112,6102055.

145   drink hot sauce as punishment: H. A. McGregor, J. D. Lieberman, J. Greenberg,
       S. Solomon, J. Arndt, L. Simon, and T. Pyszczynski, "Terror Management and
       Aggression: Evidence That Mortality Salience Motivates Aggression Against
       Worldview-Threatening Others," *Journal of Personality and Social Psychology* 74, no. 3
       (1998), 590–605, retrieved from http://www.ncbi.nlm.nih.gov/pubmed
       /9523407.

146   killed or injured in the process: T. Pyszczynski, A. Abdollahi, S. Solomon, J.
       Greenberg, F. Cohen, and D. Weise, "Mortality Salience, Martyrdom, and Military
       Might: The Great Satan Versus the Axis of Evil," *Personality and Social Psychology
       Bulletin* 32, no. 4 (2006), 525–37, doi:10.1177/0146167205282157.

146   (torture) on foreign suspects: T. J. Luke and M. Hartwig, "The Effects of Mortal-
       ity Salience and Reminders of Terrorism on Perceptions of Interrogation Tech-
       niques," *Psychiatry, Psychology and Law* 21, no. 4 (2013), 1–13, doi:10.1080/13218719
       .2013.842625.

146   nuclear attack on Iran: G. Hirschberger and T. Ein-Dor, "Defenders of a Lost
       Cause: Terror Management and Violent Resistance to the Disengagement Plan,"

Personality and Social Psychology Bulletin 32, no. 6 (2006), 761–69, doi:10.1177 /0146167206286628.

146   **becoming suicide bombers themselves:** Pyszczynski et al., "Mortality Salience, Martyrdom."

147   **reduced their own mortal terror:** J. Hayes, J. Schimel, and T. J. Williams, "Fighting Death with Death: The Buffering Effects of Learning That Worldview Violators Have Died," *Psychological Science* 19, no. 5 (2008), 501–7, doi:10.1111/j.1467-9280 .2008.02115.x.

147   **"natural and inevitable urge":** Ernest Becker, *Escape from Evil* (New York: Free Press, 1975), xvii.

148   **"according to human nature":** Thucydides, *History,* 2 vols., edited by Henry Stuart Jones and J. Enoch Powell (Oxford: Clarendon, 1963); cf. P. J. Ahrensdorf, "The Fear of Death and the Longing for Immortality: Hobbes and Thucydides on Human Nature and the Problem of Anarchy," *American Political Science Review* 94, no. 3 (2000), 579–93.

148   **"suffered [injustice] oneself":** Ibid.

148   **"nobility or piety, or justice":** Ahrensdorf, "Fear of Death," 591.

148   **"not a ladder of predictable progress":** Stephen Jay Gould, *Wonderful Life: The Burgess Shale and the Nature of History* (New York: W. W. Norton, 1989), 35.

CHAPTER 8: BODY AND SOUL: AN UNEASY ALLIANCE

150   **"The body is the closest that we come":** A. Simon, "The Existential Deal: An Interview with David Cronenberg," *Critical Quarterly* 43, no. 3 (2001), 34–56. Quotation is from pp. 45–46.

150   **never needed to defecate:** Ernest Becker, *The Denial of Death* (New York: Free Press, 1973).

150   **is believed to be fatal:** Nici Nelson, " 'Selling Her Kiosk': Kikuyu Notions of Sexuality and Sex for Sale in Mathare Valley, Kenya," in Patricia Caplan, ed., *The Cultural Construction of Sexuality* (London and New York: Tavistock, 1987), 217–39.

151   **humans are very similar to animals:** J. L. Goldenberg, T. Pyszczynski, J. Greenberg, S. Solomon, B. Kluck, and R. Cornwell, "I Am Not an Animal: Mortality Salience, Disgust, and the Denial of Human Creatureliness," *Journal of Experimental Psychology: General* 130, no. 3 (2001), 427–35, doi:10.1037/0096-3445.130.3.427.

152   **less time having a foot massage:** J. L. Goldenberg, J. Hart, T. Pyszczynski, G. M. Warnica, M. Landau, and L. Thomas, "Ambivalence Toward the Body: Death, Neuroticism, and the Flight from Physical Sensation," *Personality and Social Psychology Bulletin* 32, no. 9 (2006), 1264–77, doi:10.1177/0146167206289505.

152   **conduct breast self-exams:** J. L. Goldenberg, J. Arndt, J. Hart, and C. Routledge, "Uncovering an Existential Barrier to Breast Self-exam Behavior," *Journal of Experimental Social Psychology* 44, no. 2 (2008), 260–74. Retrieved from http://dx.doi .org/10.1016/j.jesp.2007.05.002.

152   **product testing, and medical research:** R. M. Beatson and M. J. Halloran, "Humans Rule! The Effects of Creatureliness Reminders, Mortality Salience and Self-esteem on Attitudes Toward Animals," *British Journal of Social Psychology* 46, no. 3 (2007), 619–32, doi:10.1348/014466606X147753.

152   **dolphins may be smarter than humans:** M. Soenke, F. Cohen, J. Greenberg, and U. Lifshin, "Are You Smarter Than a Cetacean? On the Terror Management Function of Belief in Human Superiority," unpublished manuscript, Skidmore College, 2015.

152   **could literally kill them:** P. Rozin and A. E. Fallon, "A Perspective on Disgust," *Psychological Review* 94, no. 1 (1987), 23–41, doi:10.1037/0033-295X.94.1.23.

152   **bodily products like feces:** C. R. Cox, J. L. Goldenberg, T. Pyszczynski, and D. Weise, "Disgust, Creatureliness and the Accessibility of Death-Related Thoughts," *European Journal of Social Psychology* 37, no. 3 (2007), 494–507, doi:10.1002/ejsp .370.

153   **"number two" instead of defecation:** N. L. McCallum and N. S. McGlone, "Death Be Not Profane: Mortality Salience and Euphemism Use," *Western Journal of Communication* 75, no. 5 (2011), 565–84, doi:10.1080/10570314.2011.608405.

153   **"male and female created he them":** Genesis 1:21–27 (King James Version).

154   **"some holy, noble, divine thought":** S. Federici, "The Great Caliban: The Struggle Against the Rebel Body—Part Two," *Capitalism Nature Socialism* 15, no. 3 (2004), 13–28, doi:10.1080/1045575042000247211.

154   **not the world of nature:** Robert Brain, *The Decorated Body* (London: Hutchinson, 1979), 146.

155   **ideal of beauty of their day:** O. Y. Oumeish, "The Cultural and Philosophical Concepts of Cosmetics in Beauty and Art Through the Medical History of Mankind," *Clinics in Dermatology* 19, no. 4 (2001), 375–86, doi:10.1016/S0738 -081X(01)00194-8.

155   **spends for all its agencies and funds:** "Pots of Promise: An Industry Driven by Sexual Instinct Will Always Thrive," *The Economist,* May 2003, retrieved from http://www.economist.com/node/1795852?story__id=E1__TSJVRVN.

156   **sexually promiscuous, or perverted animality:** C. R. Hallpike, "Social Hair," *Man* 4, no. 2 (1969), 256–64.

156   **"be rough with bristling hair":** Quoted in Brain, *Decorated Body,* 147.

156   **Queen Victoria's husband:** Aglaja Stirn, "Body Piercing: Medical Consequences and Psychological Motivations," *Lancet* 361, no. 9364 (2003), 1205–15, doi:10.1016/S0140-6736(03)12955-8.

157   **"testimony of mean descent":** Quoted in Brain, *Decorated Body,* 52.

157   **and assure immortality:** Clinton R. Sanders and D. Angus Vail, *Customizing the Body: The Art and Culture of Tattooing* (Philadelphia: Temple University Press, 1989).

157   **does not have the slightest charm:** *Decorated Body.*

157   **one in four Americans:** Anne E. Laumann and Amy J. Derick, "Tattoos and Body Piercings in the United States: A National Data Set," *Journal of the American Academy of Dermatology* 55, no. 3 (2006), 413–21, doi:10.1016/j.jaad.2006.03.026.

157 **half of those younger than forty:** *A Portrait of "Generation Next": How Young People View Their Lives, Futures and Politics,* Pew Research Center, 2007, retrieved from http://www.people-press.org/files/legacy-pdf/300.pdf.

157 **wrap it tightly in cloth:** http://en.wikipedia.org/wiki/Artificial__cranial __deformation.

157 **ideal measurement of thirteen inches:** E. A. Saltzberg and J. C. Chrisler, "Beauty Is the Beast: Psychological Effects of the Pursuit of the Perfect Female Body," in J. Freeman, ed., *Women: A Feminist Perspective* (Mountain View, Calif.: Mayfield Publishing, 1995), 306–15.

157 **no longer than three inches:** Howard S. Levy, *The Lotus Lovers: The Complete History of the Curious Erotic Custom of Footbinding in China* (New York: Prometheus Books, 1991).

157 **the more attractive they were considered to be:** Saltzberg and Chrisler, "Beauty Is the Beast."

158 **"a survival of fashion's fittest":** P. Fritch, "Cosmetic Toe Amputation Surgery," *Kitsch Magazine,* Spring 2007, retrieved from http://kitschmag.com/index .php?option=com__content&task=view&id=185&Itemid=33.

158 **the vast majority of them on women:** http://www.plasticsurgery.org/news-and -resources.html.

158 **currently the most popular options:** http://www.beautyforlife.com/costs.aspx.

158 **"they'd just die if they had to look old":** Mary Brophy Marcus, "Cosmetic Surgery Gets a Lift from Boomers: Some Say They'd Just Die if They Had to Look Old," *USA Today,* December 11, 2006, retrieved from http://usatoday30.usatoday .com/printedition/life/20061211/bl__cover11.art.htm.

158 **"Sex and Death Are Twins":** Ernest Becker, *The Denial of Death* (New York: Free Press, 1973), 163.

158 **"sometimes you have to hunt around":** http://thinkexist.com/quotation /violence__and__smut__are__of__course__everywhere__on__the/202645.html.

159 **evil spirits and lethal illnesses:** Thomas Gregor, *Anxious Pleasures: The Sexual Lives of an Amazonian People* (Chicago: University of Chicago Press, 1985).

159 **"sex is of the body":** Becker, *Denial of Death,* 162.

160 **less appealing after a death reminder:** J. L. Goldenberg, T. Pyszczynski, S. K. McCoy, J. Greenberg, and S. Solomon, "Death, Sex, Love, and Neuroticism: Why Is Sex Such a Problem?" *Journal of Personality and Social Psychology* 77, no. 6 (1999), 1173–87, retrieved from http://www.ncbi.nlm.nih.gov/pubmed/10626370.

161 **the carnal aspects of sex:** Ibid.

161 **concerns about death and their physicality:** Ibid.

162 **"secretions of the body":** M. C. Nussbaum, "Danger to Human Dignity: The Revival of Disgust and Shame in the Law," *The Chronicle of Higher Education,* August 2004, retrieved from http://chronicle.com/article/Danger-to-Human-Dignity -the/21047.

163 **the creaturely side of being female:** T. A. Roberts, J. L. Goldenberg, C. Power, and T. Pyszczynski, " 'Feminine Protection': The Effects of Menstruation on Attitudes

Towards Women," *Psychology of Women Quarterly* 26, no. 2 (2002), 131–39, doi:10.1111/1471-6402.00051.

163 **photos showed them pregnant:** J. L. Goldenberg, J. Goplen, C. R. Cox, and J. Arndt, " 'Viewing' Pregnancy as an Existential Threat: The Effects of Creatureliness on Reactions to Media Depictions of the Pregnant Body," *Media Psychology* 10, no. 2 (2007), 211–30, doi:10.1080/15213260701375629.

163 **believed was breast-feeding:** C. R. Cox, J. L. Goldenberg, J. Arndt, and T. Pyszczynski, "Mother's Milk: An Existential Perspective on Negative Reactions to Breast-Feeding," *Personality and Social Psychology Bulletin* 33, no. 1 (2007), 110–22, doi:10.1177/0146167206294202.

164 **"Is that a gun in your pocket":** http://womenshistory.about.com/od/quotes/a /mae__west.htm.

164 **modestly attired women:** M. J. Landau, J. L. Goldenberg, J. Greenberg, O. Gillath, S. Solomon, C. Cox, A. Martens, and T. Pyszczynski, "The Siren's Call: Terror Management and the Threat of Men's Sexual Attraction to Women," *Journal of Personality and Social Psychology* 90, no. 1 (2006), 129–46, doi:10.1037/0022-3514.90.1.129.

164 **reported less sexual interest:** Ibid.

165 **light sentences for the abusive boyfriend:** Ibid.

165 **tolerance of violence against women:** http://www.wjla.com/articles/2011/12 /study-shows-rise-in-violence-against-women-70334.html.

CHAPTER 9: DEATH NEAR AND FAR

167 **"Not me, not now":** S. Chaplin, *The Psychology of Time and Death* (Ashland, Ohio: Sonnet Press, 2000), 150.

168 **then raped and killed her:** As reported by the BBC World News, *The New York Times,* and *The Huffington Post.*

168 **violent acts on television alone:** http://www.turnoffyourtv.com/healtheducation /children.html.

168 **5,400 incidents per month:** http://www.lionlamb.org/violence__vid__games __facts.htm.

168 **annually in Pennsylvania alone:** http://www.aami.com.au/Resources/File .aspx?id=139; J. Robbins, "As Cars Hit More Animals on Roads, Toll Rises," *New York Times,* December 22, 2007, retrieved from http://www.nytimes.com /2007/12/22/us/22crash.html?__r=0.

169 **injuries in America each year:** https://www.homeminders.com/Articles /HomemindersArticle/tabid/77/ArticleId/245/Default.aspx.

170 **participants' desire to punish:** R. Ochsmann and K. Reichelt, "Evaluation of Moral and Immoral Behavior: Evidence for Terror Management Theory," Unpublished manuscript, Universität Mainz, Mainz, Germany.

170 **to the anti-American target:** J. Greenberg, T. Pyszczynski, S. Solomon, L. Simon, and M. Breus, "Role of Consciousness and Accessibility of Death-Related

Thoughts in Mortality Salience Effects," *Journal of Personality and Social Psychology* 67, no. 4 (1994), 627–37, doi:10.1037/0022-3514.67.4.627.

171   **exaggerated defensive reactions:** Ibid.

171   **and fortified by additional research:** J. Arndt, J. Greenberg, S. Solomon, T. Pyszczynski, and L. Simon, "Suppression, Accessibility of Death-Related Thoughts, and
Cultural Worldview Defense: Exploring the Psychodynamics of Terror Management," *Journal of Personality and Social Psychology* 73, no. 1 (1997), 5–18,
doi:10.1037/0022-3514.73.1.5; J. Greenberg, J. Arndt, L. Simon, T. Pyszczynski, and
S. Solomon, "Proximal and Distal Defenses in Response to Reminders of One's
Mortality: Evidence of a Temporal Sequence," *Personality and Social Psychology Bulletin* 26, no. 1 (2000), 91–99, doi:10.1177/0146167200261009; T. Pyszczynski, J.
Greenberg, and S. Solomon, "A Dual-Process Model of Defense Against Conscious and Unconscious Death-Related Thoughts: An Extension of Terror Management Theory," *Psychological Review* 106, no. 4 (1999), 835–45, doi:10.1037
/0033-295X.106.4.835.

174   **this (completely spurious) association:** G. A. Quattrone and A. Tversky, "Causal
Versus Diagnostic Contingencies: On Self-Deception and on the Voter's Illusion,"
Journal of Personality and Social Psychology 46, no. 2 (1984), 237–48, doi:10.1037
/0022-3514.46.2.237.

175   **he had fabricated his findings:** http://en.wikipedia.org/wiki/James__Vicary.

175   **less moral, and more anxious:** M. W. Baldwin, S. E. Carrell, and D. F. Lopez,
"Priming Relationship Schemas: My Advisor and the Pope Are Watching Me from
the Back of My Mind," *Journal of Experimental Social Psychology* 26, no. 5 (1990),
435–54, doi:10.1016/0022-1031(90)90068-W.

176   **intensified their disdain for the anti-U.S. student:** J. Arndt, J. Greenberg, T.
Pyszczynski, and S. Solomon, "Subliminal Exposure to Death-Related Stimuli Increases Defense of the Cultural Worldview," *Psychological Science* 8, no. 5 (1997),
379–85, doi:10.1111/j.1467-9280.1997.tb00429.x.

177   **more potent sunblock to use at the beach:** J. Arndt, J. Schimel, and J. L. Goldenberg, "Death Can Be Good for Your Health: Fitness Intentions as a Proximal and
Distal Defense Against Mortality Salience," *Journal of Applied Social Psychology* 33,
no. 8 (2003), 1726–46, doi:10.1111/j.1559-1816.2003.tb01972.x; C. Routledge, J.
Arndt, and J. L. Goldenberg, "A Time to Tan: Proximal and Distal Effects of Mortality Salience on Sun Exposure Intentions," *Personality and Social Psychology Bulletin*
30, no. 10 (2004), 1347–58, doi:10.1177/0146167204264056.

177   **intended to cut back on cigarettes:** J. Arndt, K. Vail, C. R. Cox, J. L. Goldenberg,
T. M. Piasecki, and F. X. Gibbons, "The Interactive Effect of Mortality Reminders
and Tobacco Craving on Smoking Topography," *Health Psychology* 32, no. 5 (2013),
525–32, doi:10.1037/a0029201.

178   **avoid focusing on themselves after thinking about death:** J. Arndt, J. Greenberg, L. Simon, T. Pyszczynski, and S. Solomon, "Terror Management and Self-
Awareness: Evidence That Mortality Salience Provokes Avoidance of the

Self-Focused State," *Personality and Social Psychology Bulletin* 24, no. 11 (1998), 1216–27, doi:10.1177/01461672982411008.

179   **people received the flyers about pain:** T. Ein-Dor, G. Hirschberger, A. Perry, N. Levin, R. Cohen, H. Horesh, and E. Rothschild, "Implicit Death Primes Increase Alcohol Consumption," *Health Psychology* 33, no. 7 (2013), 748–51, doi:10.1037/a0033880.

179   **more likely to seek distractions or deny the threat:** J. L. Goldenberg and J. Arndt, "The Implications of Death for Health: A Terror Management Health Model for Behavioral Health Promotion," *Psychological Review* 115, no. 4 (2008), 1032–53, doi:10.1037/a0013326.

180   **no change in your exercise intentions:** Arndt, Schimel, and Goldenberg, "Death Can Be Good for Your Health."

180   **emulating the rich and famous:** S. McCabe, K. E. Vail, J. Arndt, and J. L. Goldenberg, "Hails from the Crypt: A Terror Management Health Model Investigation of the Effectiveness of Health-Oriented Versus Celebrity-Oriented Endorsements," *Personality and Social Psychology Bulletin* 40, no. 3 (2014), 289–300, doi:10.1177/0146167213510745.

181   ***greater* interest in going to a tanning salon:** Routledge, Arndt, and Goldenberg, "A Time to Tan."

181   **being more open to trying to quit:** J. Hansen, S. Winzeler, and S. Topolinski, "When the Death Makes You Smoke: A Terror Management Perspective on the Effectiveness of Cigarette On-Pack Warnings," *Journal of Experimental Social Psychology* 46, no. 1 (2010), 226–28, doi:10.1016/j.jesp.2009.09.007.

181   **drove more rapidly and recklessly:** O. Taubman-Ben-Ari, V. Florian, and M. Mikulincer, "The Impact of Mortality Salience on Reckless Driving: A Test of Terror Management Mechanisms," *Journal of Personality and Social Psychology* 76, no. 1 (1999), 35–45, retrieved from http://www.ncbi.nlm.nih.gov/pubmed/9972551.

181   **forgo a safety stop to decompress while ascending:** G. Miller and O. Taubman-Ben-Ari, "Scuba Diving Risk Taking: A Terror Management Theory Perspective," *Journal of Sport and Exercise Psychology* 26, no. 2 (2004), 269–82.

181   **more sexual partners in the future:** S. Lam, K. Morrison, and D. Smeesters, "Gender, Intimacy, and Risky Sex: A Terror Management Account," *Personality and Social Psychology Bulletin* 35, no. 8 (2009), 1046–56, doi:10.1177/0146167209336607.

181   **go whitewater rafting:** G. Hirschberger, V. Florian, M. Mikulincer, J. L. Goldenberg, and T. Pyszczynski, "Gender Differences in the Willingness to Engage in Risky Behavior: A Terror Management Perspective," *Death Studies* 26, no. 2 (2002), 117–41, doi:10.1080/074811802753455244.

182   **in a circle to pray as he expired:** S. M. Asser and R. Swan, "Child Fatalities from Religion-Motivated Medical Neglect," *Pediatrics* 101, no. 4 (1998), 625–29.

182   **people surrounded her and prayed:** D. Schoetz, "Parents' Faith Fails to Save Diabetic Girl," ABC News, March 27, 2008, retrieved from http://abcnews.go.com/Health/DiabetesResource/story?id=4536593&page=1.

182   **dissatisfied with their doctors:** http://www.imt.ie/opinion/2009/09/can
       _belief__in__faith__healing__de.html.

182   **microchips slipped into the vaccinations:** http://www.examiner.com/examiner
       /x-10438-Peace-Studies-Examiner percent7Ey2009m8d7-Part-3-H1N1-vaccine
       -for-profit-genocide-and-the-US-martial-law-factor.

183   **recovering from a physical ailment:** M. Vess, J. Arndt, C. R. Cox, C. Routledge,
       and J. L. Goldenberg, "Exploring the Existential Function of Religion: The Effect
       of Religious Fundamentalism and Mortality Salience on Faith-Based Medical Re-
       fusals," *Journal of Personality and Social Psychology* 97, no. 2 (2009), 334–50,
       doi:10.1037/a0015545.

184   **"disease or infirmity":** http://www.who.int/about/definition/en/print.html.

CHAPTER 10: CRACKS IN THE SHIELDS

185   **"We may take for granted":** G. Zilboorg, "Fear of Death," *Psychoanalytic Quarterly*
       12 (1943), 465–75. Quotation is from pp. 465, 466, and 477.

190   **"clumsy modes of dealing with terror":** Irvin Yalom, *Existential Psychotherapy*
       (New York: Basic Books, 1980), 111.

190   **"everyone was out to get me":** From a delusions chat room on www
       .schizophrenic.com from the late 1980s (no longer posted).

191   **times when the symptoms were magnified:** K. Planansky and R. Johnston, "Pre-
       occupation with Death in Schizophrenic Men," *Diseases of the Nervous System* 38,
       no. 3 (1977), 194–97.

191   **terrors grew with every passing month:** http://www.guardian.co.uk
       /lifeandstyle/2010/mar/04/i-have-phobia-of-pregnancy/print.

192   **at the bottom of which lies death:** Sigmund Freud, "Totem and Taboo," in J.
       Strachey, ed. and trans., *The Standard Edition of the Complete Psychological Works of Sig-
       mund Freud,* vol. 13 (London: Hogarth Press, 1955; first published 1913), vii–162.

192   **various phobias and obsessions:** For a fascinating list of phobias, see http://
       phobialist.com/.

193   **reactions to the spiders:** E. Strachan, J. Schimel, J. Arndt, T. Williams, S. Solo-
       mon, T. Pyszczynski, and J. Greenberg, "Terror Mismanagement: Evidence That
       Mortality Salience Exacerbates Phobic and Compulsive Behaviors," *Personality and
       Social Psychology Bulletin* 33, no. 8 (2007), 1137–51, doi:10.1177/0146167207303018.

193   **middle of the night to check it:** From an obsessions-compulsions chat room on
       www.schizophrenia.com from the late 1980s (no longer posted).

194   **especially long time to do this:** Strachan, Schimel, et al., "Terror Mismanage-
       ment."

194   **social event harrowing and exhausting:** http://www.anxietynetwork.com
       /spcase.html.

195   **lingered in their cubicles considerably longer:** Strachan, Schimel, et al., "Terror
       Mismanagement."

195 **animal body destined to decay and die:** Z. Hochdorf, Y. Latzer, L. Canetti, and E. Bachar, "Attachment Styles and Attraction to Death: Diversities Among Eating Disorder Patients," *American Journal of Family Therapy* 33, no. 3 (2005), 237–52, doi:10.1080/01926180590952418.

195 **"You eat—you die":** Aimee Liu, *Solitaire* (New York: Harper and Row, 1979). Cf. C. C. Jackson and G. P. Davidson, "The Anorexic Patient as a Survivor: The Denial of Death and Death Themes in the Literature on Anorexia Nervosa," *International Journal of Eating Disorders* 5, no. 5 (1986), 821–35, doi:10.1002 /1098-108X(198607)5:5<821::AID-EAT2260050504>3.0.CO;2-9, p. 825.

196 **pain-primed counterparts:** J. L. Goldenberg, J. Arndt, J. Hart, and M. Brown, "Dying to Be Thin: The Effects of Mortality Salience and Body Mass Index on Restricted Eating Among Women," *Personality and Social Psychology Bulletin* 31, no. 10 (2005), 1400–12, doi:10.1177/0146167205277207.

197 **see his children only every other weekend:** David Tarrant, "For Iraq Veteran, PTSD Is the Enemy That Stays on the Attack, but He's Fighting Back," *The Dallas Morning News*, August 22, 2010, retrieved from http://www.dallasnews.com/news /state/headlines/20100822-for-iraq-veteran-ptsd-is-the-enemy-that-stays-on -the-attack-but-he__s-fighting-back.ece.

197 **return with some form of PTSD:** *The Veterans Health Administration's Treatment of PTSD and Traumatic Brain Injury Among Recent Combat Veterans* (Washington, D.C.: Congressional Budget Office, 2012), http://www.cbo.gov/sites/default/files /cbofiles/attachments/02-09-PTSD.pdf.

197 **panic, and uncontrollable thoughts:** http://www.nimh.nih.gov/health /publications/the-numbers-count-mental-disorders-in-america/index.shtml.

198 **prone to subsequently develop PTSD:** E. J. Ozer, S. R. Best, T. L. Lipsey, and D. S. Weiss, "Predictors of Posttraumatic Stress Disorder and Symptoms in Adults: A Meta-Analysis," *Psychological Bulletin* 129, no. 1 (2003), 52–73, doi:10.1037 /0033-2909.129.1.52.

198 **dissociate and subsequently develop PTSD:** B. S. Gershuny, M. Cloitre, and M. W. Otto, "Peritraumatic Dissociation and PTSD Severity: Do Event-Related Fears About Death and Control Mediate Their Relation?" *Behaviour Research and Therapy* 41, no. 2 (2003), 157–66, doi:10.1016/S0005-7967(01)00134-6.

198 **more anxieties about the future:** S. Kosloff, S. Solomon, J. Greenberg, F. Cohen, B. Gershuny, C. Routledge, and T. Pyszczynski, "Fatal Distraction: The Impact of Mortality Salience on Dissociative Responses to 9/11 and Subsequent Anxiety Sensitivity," *Basic and Applied Social Psychology* 28, no. 4 (2006), 349–56, doi:10.1207/s15324834basp2804__8.

198 **those who had not dissociated:** A. Abdollahi, T. Pyszczynski, M. Maxfield, and A. Luszczynska, "Posttraumatic Stress Reactions as a Disruption in Anxiety-Buffer Functioning: Dissociation and Responses to Mortality Salience as Predictors of Severity of Post-Traumatic Symptoms," *Psychological Trauma: Theory, Research, Practice, and Policy* 3, no. 4 (2011), 329–41, doi: 10.1037/a0021084.

199 **survivors of a civil war in the Ivory Coast:** A. Chatard, T. Pyszczynski, J. Arndt,

L. Selimbegović, P. N. Konan, and M. Van der Linden, "Extent of Trauma Exposure and PTSD Symptom Severity as Predictors of Anxiety-Buffer Functioning," *Psychological Trauma: Theory, Research, Practice, and Policy* 4, no. 1 (2012), 47–55, doi:10.1037/a0021085.

199 **shields against such mortal terror:** A. D. Mancini, G. Prati, and G. A. Bonanno, "Do Shattered Worldviews Lead to Complicated Grief? Prospective and Longitudinal Analyses," *Journal of Social and Clinical Psychology* 30, no. 2 (2011), 184–215, doi:10.1521/jscp.2011.30.2.184.

199 **population of the United States in a given year:** http://www.nimh.nih.gov /health/publications/the-numbers-count-mental-disorders-in-america/index .shtml.

200 **"instinct and intellect to disconnect":** http://www.vanityfair.com/magazine /archive/1989/12/styron198912.

200 **"torture without end":** John Milton, *Paradise Lost* (1667), book 1, http:// andromeda.rutgers.edu/~jlynch/Texts/pl-beginning.html.

200 **"a form of madness":** William Styron, *Darkness Visible: A Memoir of Madness* (New York: Random House, 1990).

200 **difficulties perceiving purpose and meaning in life:** G. Kleftaras, "Meaning in Life, Psychological Well-Being and Depressive Symptomatology: A Comparative Study," *Psychology* 3, no. 4 (2012), 337–45, doi:10.4236/psych.2012.34048.

200 **downward spiral of anxiety and despair:** A. M. Abdel-Khalek, "Death, Anxiety, and Depression," *Omega: Journal of Death and Dying* 35, no. 2 (1997), 219–29, doi:10.2190/H120-9U9D-C2MH-NYQ5.

201 **more nationalistic than their fellow citizens:** L. Simon, J. Greenberg, E. H. Jones, S. Solomon, and T. Pyszczynski, "Mild Depression, Mortality Salience and Defense of the Worldview: Evidence of Intensified Terror Management in the Mildly Depressed," *Personality and Social Psychology Bulletin* 22, no. 1 (1996), 81–90, doi:10.1177/0146167296221008.

201 **reported that life was more meaningful:** L. Simon, J. Arndt, J. Greenberg, T. Pyszczynski, and S. Solomon, "Terror Management and Meaning: Evidence That the Opportunity to Defend the Worldview in Response to Mortality Salience Increases the Meaningfulness of Life in the Mildly Depressed," *Journal of Personality* 66, no. 3 (1998), 359–82, doi:10.1111/1467-6494.00016.

201 **"not wait for death":** Miguel de Unamuno, *Tragic Sense of Life,* translated by J. E. Crawford Flitch (New York: Dover Publications, 1954), 233.

202 **"I don't want to have the fear of death":** Fyodor Dostoyevsky, *The Possessed,* translated by Andrew R. MacAndrew (New York: Signet Classics, 1962; first published 1872), 357.

202 **long-standing wishes may be fulfilled:** Israel Orbach, Peri Kedem, Orna Gorchover, Alan Apter, and Sam Tyano, "Fears of Death in Suicidal and Nonsuicidal Adolescents," *Journal of Abnormal Psychology* 102, no. 4 (1993), 553–58, doi:10.1037/0021-843X.102.4.553.

202 **"I have immortal longings in me":** William Shakespeare, *Antony and Cleopatra*, V,

ii, 282–83, http://www.enotes.com/shakespeare-quotes/give-me-my-robe-put
-my-crown.

202   **"birthday to immortality"**: Everett Ferguson, "Early Christian Martyrdom
and Civil Disobedience," *Journal of Early Christian Studies* 1, no. 1 (1993), 73–83,
doi:10.1353/earl.0.0161.

202   **"everlasting paradise for the martyrs"**: "Translation of Sept. 11 Hijacker Mohamed Atta's Suicide Note: Part One" (2001), retrieved from http://abcnews.go
.com/International/story?id=79168&page=1.

202   **suicidal martyrs after thinking about dying**: T. Pyszczynski, A. Abdollahi, S. Solomon, J. Greenberg, F. Cohen, and D. Weise, "Mortality Salience, Martyrdom, and
Military Might: The Great Satan Versus the Axis of Evil," *Personality and Social Psychology Bulletin* 32, no. 4 (2006), 525–37, doi:10.1177/0146167205282157.

202   **"this earth, this England"**: C. Routledge and J. Arndt, "Self-Sacrifice as Self-
Defence: Mortality Salience Increases Efforts to Affirm a Symbolic Immortal Self
at the Expense of the Physical Self," *European Journal of Social Psychology* 38, no. 3
(2008), 531–41, doi:10.1002/ejsp.442.

203   **may even have beneficial effects**: Andrew T. Weil, *The Natural Mind: A New Way of
Looking at Drugs and the Higher Consciousness* (New York: Mariner Books, 1998; first
published 1972).

203   **using them in moderation**: R. W. Firestone and J. Catlett, *Beyond Death Anxiety*
(New York: Springer Publishing, 2009).

204   **amount of nicotine they inhaled**: J. Arndt, K. E. Vail, C. R. Cox, J. L. Goldenberg,
T. M. Piasecki, and F. X. Gibbons, "The Interactive Effect of Mortality Reminders
and Tobacco Craving on Smoking Topography," *Health Psychology* 32, no. 5 (2013),
525–32, doi:10.1037/a0029201.

204   **Other activities, such as gambling**: http://www.ncpgambling.org/i4a/pages
/Index.cfm?pageID=3314#widespread.

204   **serious concern in recent years**: D. Gentile, "Pathological Video-Game Use
Among Youth Ages 8 to 18: A National Study," *Psychological Science* 20, no. 5
(2009), 594–602, doi:10.1111/j.1467-9280.2009.02340.x.

207   **death thoughts closer to consciousness**: M. Mikulincer, V. Florian, and G.
Hirschberger, "The Existential Function of Close Relationships: Introducing
Death into the Science of Love," *Personality and Social Psychology Review* 7, no. 1
(2003), 20–40, doi:10.1207/S15327957PSPR0701_2.

208   **"fall strangely and miserably flat"**: Ernest Becker, *The Birth and Death of Meaning:
An Interdisciplinary Perspective on the Problem of Man*, 2nd ed. (New York: Free Press,
1971), 28–29.

209   **"will some day, inescapably, end"**: H. F. Searles, "Schizophrenia and the Inevitability of Death," *Psychiatric Quarterly* 35, no. 4 (1961), 631–65. Quotation is from
p. 632.

209   **less fearful of and defensive about their own mortality**: L. L. Carstensen, D. M.
Isaacowitz, and S. T. Charles, "Taking Time Seriously: A Theory of Socioemotional

Selectivity," *American Psychologist* 54, no. 3 (1999), 165–81, doi:10.1037
/0003-066X.54.3.165; N. Krause, "Meaning in Life and Healthy Aging," in P. P.
Wong, ed., *The Human Quest for Meaning: Theories, Research, and Applications*, 2nd ed.
(New York: Routledge, 2012), 409–32; Z. Klemenc-Ketis, "Life Changes in
Patients After Out-of-Hospital Cardiac Arrest: The Effect of Near-Death
Experiences," *International Journal of Behavioral Medicine* 20, no. 1 (2013), 7–12,
doi:10.1007/s12529-011-9209-y.

CHAPTER 11: LIVING WITH DEATH

210   **and we pass on the same:** Walt Whitman, *Life and Death*, Walt Whitman Archive,
http://www.whitmanarchive.org/manuscripts/transcriptions/loc.00213.html.

212   **"ward off incipient death awareness":** D. P. Judges, "Scared to Death: Capital
Punishment as Authoritarian Terror Management," *U.C. Davis Law Review* 33, no. 1
(1999), 155–248. Quotation is from pp. 163, 186, 187.

212   **decreased in liberal ones:** S.J.H. McCann, "Societal Threat, Authoritarianism,
and U.S. State Death Penalty Sentencing (1977–2004)," *Journal of Personality and
Social Psychology* 94, no. 5 (2008), 913–23, retrieved from http://www.ncbi.nlm.
nih.gov/pubmed/18444747.

212   **"a fairer death penalty system":** J. L. Kirchmeier, "Our Existential Death Penalty:
Judges, Jurors, and Terror Management," *Law and Psychology Review* 32 (Spring
2008), 57–107. Quotation is from p. 102.

213   **to manage their own death anxiety:** study reported in S. Solomon and K. Lawler,
"Death Anxiety: The Challenge and the Promise of Whole Person Care," in T. A.
Hutchinson, ed., *Whole Person Care: A New Paradigm for the 21st Century* (New York:
Springer, 2011), 92–107.

213   **rather than the patient's wishes:** J. Arndt, M. Vess, C. R. Cox, J. L. Goldenberg,
and S. Lagle, "The Psychosocial Effect of Thoughts of Personal Mortality on Cardiac Risk Assessment," *Medical Decision Making* 29, no. 2 (2009), 175–81,
doi:10.1177/0272989X08323300.

216   **"this world and the next":** A. Smith, *Dreamthorp* (London: Oxford University
Press, 1934; first published 1863), 49.

216   **death is necessary for life to go on:** M. C. Nussbaum, "Mortal Immortals: Lucretius on Death and the Voice of Nature," *Philosophy and Phenomenological Research* 50,
no. 2 (1989), 303–51; S. Cave, *Immortality: The Quest to Live Forever and How It Drives
Civilization* (New York: Crown, 2012); T. Volk and D. Sagan, *Death and Sex* (New
York: Chelsea Green, 2009).

217   **"but is everyone's to use":** M. C. Nussbaum, *The Therapy of Desire: Theory and
Practice in Hellenistic Ethics* (Princeton, N.J.: Princeton University Press, 1994), 222.

218   **"anything is possible":** Cf. Herman Melville, *Moby-Dick*, edited with an introduction and commentary by H. Beaver (New York: Penguin Classics, 1986; first published 1851), 799.

219 **"and with how many dangers it threatens it"**: Michel de Montaigne, *The Complete Essays of Michel de Montaigne,* edited by W. C. Hazlitt and C. Cotton, Digireads. com, 2004, p. 52. First published 1580.

220 **"as a sated guest from a feast"**: Ibid.

220 **of necessity a personal undertaking:** Martin Heidegger, *Being and Time* (Albany: State University of New York Press, 2010; first published 1927).

221 **"positive and life enhancing process"**: Jon Underwood, personal communication, October 19, 2014.

221 **on literal and symbolic immortality:** Robert Jay Lifton, *The Broken Connection: On Death and the Continuity of Life* (New York: Simon and Schuster, 1979).

221 **"can we continue living"**: Charles Lindbergh, *Autobiography of Values* (New York: Harcourt Brace Jovanovich, 1978), 6.

222 **"life-enhancing illusion"**: Ernest Becker, *The Denial of Death* (New York: Free Press, 1973), 158.

222 **"the more we see, the less sure we are"**: J. Talbot, *The Wolf Man,* Universal Pictures, 1941.

222 **We call one the rock:** T. Pyszczynski, S. Solomon, and J. Greenberg, *In the Wake of 9/11: The Psychology of Terror* (Washington, D.C.: American Psychological Association, 2003), doi:10.1037/10478-000.

223 **"persecutes those who do not subject themselves to it"**: Paul Tillich, *Theology of Culture* (New York: Oxford University Press, 1964), 9.

223 **"build a strong Germany"**: S. White, *Führer: Seduction of a Nation* (Brook Productions, 1991).

223 **"temples of his Gods"**: Thomas Babington Macaulay, *Lays of Ancient Rome* (London: Longman, 1847), 37ff.

Index